CU00871041

# Just The facts101

## Textbook Key Facts

Doing Business and Investing

in Samoa (American) Guide

by Cram101
Textbook NOT Included

# Table of Contents

# Just The Facts101

Exam Prep for

Doing Business and Investing in Samoa (American) Guide

Just The Facts101 Exam Prep is your link from
the textbook and lecture to your exams.

**Just The Facts101 Exam Preps are unauthorized and comprehensive reviews
of your textbooks.**

All material provided by CTI Publications (c) 2019

Textbook publishers and textbook authors do not participate in or contribute to these reviews.

Just The Facts101 Exam Prep

eAIN 460058

## Foundations of Business

A business, also known as an enterprise, agency or a firm, is an entity
involved in the provision of goods and/or services to consumers. Businesses are
prevalent in capitalist economies, where most of them are privately owned and
provide goods and services to customers in exchange for other goods, services,
or money.

:: Energy and fuel journals ::

In physics, energy is the quantitative property that must be transferred to
an object in order to perform work on, or to heat, the object. Energy is a
conserved quantity; the law of conservation of energy states that energy can be
converted in form, but not created or destroyed. The SI unit of energy is the
joule, which is the energy transferred to an object by the work of moving it a
distance of 1 metre against a force of 1 newton.

Exam Probability: **Low**

1. *Answer choices:*

(see index for correct answer)

- a. Heat and Mass Transfer
- b. Energies
- c. Journal of Renewable and Sustainable Energy
- d. Oil Shale

*Guidance:* level 1

:: Management ::

_____ is the practice of initiating, planning, executing, controlling, and closing the work of a team to achieve specific goals and meet specific success criteria at the specified time.

Exam Probability: **High**

2. *Answer choices:*
(see index for correct answer)

- a. Social business model
- b. Project management
- c. Preventive action
- d. Strategic lenses

*Guidance:* level 1

---

:: Management ::

_____ is the identification, evaluation, and prioritization of risks followed by coordinated and economical application of resources to minimize, monitor, and control the probability or impact of unfortunate events or to maximize the realization of opportunities.

Exam Probability: **Medium**

3. *Answer choices:*
(see index for correct answer)

- a. Corticon
- b. Technology scouting
- c. Risk management
- d. Earned schedule

*Guidance:* level 1

---

:: Actuarial science ::

_____ is the possibility of losing something of value. Values can be gained or lost when taking _____ resulting from a given action or inaction, foreseen or unforeseen . _____ can also be defined as the intentional interaction with uncertainty. Uncertainty is a potential, unpredictable, and uncontrollable outcome; _____ is a consequence of action taken in spite of uncertainty.

Exam Probability: **Low**

4. *Answer choices:*

(see index for correct answer)

- a. Asset allocation
- b. Demography
- c. Actuarial control cycle
- d. Risk

*Guidance:* level 1

---

:: Market research ::

_____ , an acronym for Information through Disguised Experimentation is an annual market research fair conducted by the students of IIM-Lucknow. Students create games and use various other simulated environments to capture consumers' subconscious thoughts. This innovative method of market research removes the sensitization effect that might bias peoples answers to questions. This ensures that the most truthful answers are captured to research questions. The games are designed in such a way that the observers can elicit all the required information just by observing and noting down the behaviour and the responses of the participants.

Exam Probability: **Low**

5. *Answer choices:*

(see index for correct answer)

- a. PreTesting Company
- b. INDEX
- c. Portable People Meter
- d. Shanghai Metals Market

*Guidance:* level 1

An _____ is a contingent motivator. Traditional _____ s are extrinsic motivators which reward actions to yield a desired outcome. The effectiveness of traditional _____ s has changed as the needs of Western society have evolved. While the traditional _____ model is effective when there is a defined procedure and goal for a task, Western society started to require a higher volume of critical thinkers, so the traditional model became less effective. Institutions are now following a trend in implementing strategies that rely on intrinsic motivations rather than the extrinsic motivations that the traditional _____ s foster.

Exam Probability: **High**

6. *Answer choices:*
(see index for correct answer)

- a. hierarchical perspective
- b. empathy
- c. Incentive
- d. levels of analysis

*Guidance:* level 1

---

:: Statistical terminology ::

_____ is the magnitude or dimensions of a thing. _____ can be measured as length, width, height, diameter, perimeter, area, volume, or mass.

Exam Probability: **High**

7. *Answer choices:*
(see index for correct answer)

- a. Raw score
- b. Law of large numbers
- c. Deviation
- d. Size

*Guidance:* level 1

---

:: Competition regulators ::

The _____ is an independent agency of the United States government, established in 1914 by the _____ Act. Its principal mission is the promotion of consumer protection and the elimination and prevention of anticompetitive business practices, such as coercive monopoly. It is headquartered in the _____ Building in Washington, D.C.

Exam Probability: **Medium**

8. *Answer choices:*
(see index for correct answer)

- a. Federal Trade Commission
- b. Office of Fair Trading
- c. Netherlands Competition Authority
- d. Commerce Commission

*Guidance:* level 1

:: Business models ::

_____ es are privately owned corporations, partnerships, or sole proprietorships that have fewer employees and/or less annual revenue than a regular-sized business or corporation. Businesses are defined as "small" in terms of being able to apply for government support and qualify for preferential tax policy varies depending on the country and industry.

_____ es range from fifteen employees under the Australian Fair Work Act 2009, fifty employees according to the definition used by the European Union, and fewer than five hundred employees to qualify for many U.S. _____ Administration programs. While _____ es can also be classified according to other methods, such as annual revenues, shipments, sales, assets, or by annual gross or net revenue or net profits, the number of employees is one of the most widely used measures.

Exam Probability: **Medium**

9. *Answer choices:*
(see index for correct answer)

- a. Co-operative economics
- b. Interactive contract manufacturing
- c. Paid To Click
- d. Small business

*Guidance:* level 1

:: Business law ::

A _____ is a group of people who jointly supervise the activities of an organization, which can be either a for-profit business, nonprofit organization, or a government agency. Such a board's powers, duties, and responsibilities are determined by government regulations and the organization's own constitution and bylaws. These authorities may specify the number of members of the board, how they are to be chosen, and how often they are to meet.

Exam Probability: **High**

10. *Answer choices:*
(see index for correct answer)

- a. Tacit relocation
- b. Companies law
- c. Contract A
- d. Board of directors

*Guidance:* level 1

:: ::

_____ is a marketing communication that employs an openly sponsored, non-personal message to promote or sell a product, service or idea. Sponsors of _____ are typically businesses wishing to promote their products or services. _____ is differentiated from public relations in that an advertiser pays for and has control over the message. It differs from personal selling in that the message is non-personal, i.e., not directed to a particular individual. _____ is communicated through various mass media, including traditional media such as newspapers, magazines, television, radio, outdoor _____ or direct mail; and new media such as search results, blogs, social media, websites or text messages. The actual presentation of the message in a medium is referred to as an advertisement, or "ad" or advert for short.

Exam Probability: **High**

11. *Answer choices:*
(see index for correct answer)

- a. Advertising

- b. similarity-attraction theory
- c. process perspective
- d. Sarbanes-Oxley act of 2002

*Guidance:* level 1

---

:: Information technology ::

_____ is the use of computers to store, retrieve, transmit, and manipulate data, or information, often in the context of a business or other enterprise. IT is considered to be a subset of information and communications technology . An _____ system is generally an information system, a communications system or, more specifically speaking, a computer system – including all hardware, software and peripheral equipment – operated by a limited group of users.

Exam Probability: **High**

12. *Answer choices:*
(see index for correct answer)

- a. Infolink
- b. Consumerization
- c. Information Technology Architecture
- d. PC Supporters

*Guidance:* level 1

---

:: Organizational theory ::

_____ is the process of groups of organisms working or acting together for common, mutual, or some underlying benefit, as opposed to working in competition for selfish benefit. Many animal and plant species cooperate both with other members of their own species and with members of other species .

Exam Probability: **Medium**

13. *Answer choices:*
(see index for correct answer)

- a. Battlefield promotion
- b. Organisational semiotics
- c. High reliability organization
- d. Strategic Choice Theory

:: Television commercials ::

_____ is a characteristic that distinguishes physical entities that have biological processes, such as signaling and self-sustaining processes, from those that do not, either because such functions have ceased , or because they never had such functions and are classified as inanimate. Various forms of _____ exist, such as plants, animals, fungi, protists, archaea, and bacteria. The criteria can at times be ambiguous and may or may not define viruses, viroids, or potential synthetic _____ as "living". Biology is the science concerned with the study of _____ .

Exam Probability: **Low**

14. *Answer choices:*
(see index for correct answer)

- a. Creativity
- b. Life
- c. Lemmings
- d. World History. Bank Imperial

:: Project management ::

Some scenarios associate "this kind of planning" with learning "life skills". _____ s are necessary, or at least useful, in situations where individuals need to know what time they must be at a specific location to receive a specific service, and where people need to accomplish a set of goals within a set time period.

Exam Probability: **High**

15. *Answer choices:*
(see index for correct answer)

- a. ISO 10006
- b. Project Initiation Documentation
- c. Risk register
- d. Dependency

_____ Corporation is a Japanese multinational conglomerate corporation headquartered in Konan, Minato, Tokyo. Its diversified business includes consumer and professional electronics, gaming, entertainment and financial services. The company owns the largest music entertainment business in the world, the largest video game console business and one of the largest video game publishing businesses, and is one of the leading manufacturers of electronic products for the consumer and professional markets, and a leading player in the film and television entertainment industry. _____ was ranked 97th on the 2018 Fortune Global 500 list.

Exam Probability: **Medium**

16. *Answer choices:*
(see index for correct answer)

- a. Fairchild Semiconductor
- b. Sony
- c. Sharp Corporation
- d. Arteris

*Guidance:* level 1

:: Business ::

_____ is the activity of making one's living or making money by producing or buying and selling products . Simply put, it is "any activity or enterprise entered into for profit. It does not mean it is a company, a corporation, partnership, or have any such formal organization, but it can range from a street peddler to General Motors."

Exam Probability: **High**

17. *Answer choices:*
(see index for correct answer)

- a. Business
- b. Sustainopreneurship
- c. Planned obsolescence
- d. Corporate services

*Guidance:* level 1

:: Private equity ::

_____ is a type of private equity, a form of financing that is provided by firms or funds to small, early-stage, emerging firms that are deemed to have high growth potential, or which have demonstrated high growth . _____ firms or funds invest in these early-stage companies in exchange for equity, or an ownership stake, in the companies they invest in. _____ ists take on the risk of financing risky start-ups in the hopes that some of the firms they support will become successful. Because startups face high uncertainty, VC investments do have high rates of failure. The start-ups are usually based on an innovative technology or business model and they are usually from the high technology industries, such as information technology , clean technology or biotechnology.

Exam Probability: **Medium**

18. *Answer choices:*
(see index for correct answer)

- a. Venture capital
- b. Firstpex
- c. Public Market Equivalent
- d. Equity co-investment

*Guidance:* level 1

---

:: Financial statements ::

In financial accounting, a _____ or statement of financial position or statement of financial condition is a summary of the financial balances of an individual or organization, whether it be a sole proprietorship, a business partnership, a corporation, private limited company or other organization such as Government or not-for-profit entity. Assets, liabilities and ownership equity are listed as of a specific date, such as the end of its financial year. A _____ is often described as a "snapshot of a company's financial condition". Of the four basic financial statements, the _____ is the only statement which applies to a single point in time of a business' calendar year.

Exam Probability: **Low**

19. *Answer choices:*

- a. Consolidated financial statement
- b. Emphasis of matter
- c. PnL Explained
- d. Quarterly finance report

*Guidance:* level 1

---

:: International trade ::

The law or principle of _____ holds that under free trade, an agent will produce more of and consume less of a good for which they have a _____ . _____ is the economic reality describing the work gains from trade for individuals, firms, or nations, which arise from differences in their factor endowments or technological progress. In an economic model, agents have a _____ over others in producing a particular good if they can produce that good at a lower relative opportunity cost or autarky price, i.e. at a lower relative marginal cost prior to trade. One shouldn't compare the monetary costs of production or even the resource costs of production. Instead, one must compare the opportunity costs of producing goods across countries.

Exam Probability: **Low**

20. *Answer choices:*

- a. Franz Oppenheimer
- b. Import sensitive product
- c. Comparative advantage
- d. Trade commissioner

*Guidance:* level 1

---

:: Statistical terminology ::

_____ es can be learned implicitly within cultural contexts. People may develop _____ es toward or against an individual, an ethnic group, a sexual or gender identity, a nation, a religion, a social class, a political party, theoretical paradigms and ideologies within academic domains, or a species. _____ ed means one-sided, lacking a neutral viewpoint, or not having an open mind. _____ can come in many forms and is related to prejudice and intuition.

21. *Answer choices:*
(see index for correct answer)

- a. Ridge regression
- b. Law of large numbers
- c. Bias
- d. Standard normal deviate

*Guidance:* level 1

---

:: Financial markets ::

A _____ is a financial market in which long-term debt or equity-backed securities are bought and sold. _____ s channel the wealth of savers to those who can put it to long-term productive use, such as companies or governments making long-term investments. Financial regulators like the Bank of England and the U.S. Securities and Exchange Commission oversee _____ s to protect investors against fraud, among other duties.

Exam Probability: **Medium**

22. *Answer choices:*
(see index for correct answer)

- a. Lit pool
- b. GEOS
- c. Market maker
- d. Capital market

*Guidance:* level 1

---

:: Telecommunication theory ::

In reliability theory and reliability engineering, the term _____ has the following meanings.

Exam Probability: **High**

23. *Answer choices:*
(see index for correct answer)

- a. Availability
- b. Bandwidth compression
- c. Electrical length

- d. Channel

*Guidance:* level 1

---

:: Money ::

In economics, _____ is money in the physical form of currency, such as banknotes and coins. In bookkeeping and finance, _____ is current assets comprising currency or currency equivalents that can be accessed immediately or near-immediately . _____ is seen either as a reserve for payments, in case of a structural or incidental negative _____ flow or as a way to avoid a downturn on financial markets.

Exam Probability: **High**

24. *Answer choices:*
(see index for correct answer)

- a. Money multiplier
- b. Cash
- c. Real de alerce
- d. European Monetary System

*Guidance:* level 1

---

:: Decision theory ::

Within economics the concept of _____ is used to model worth or value, but its usage has evolved significantly over time. The term was introduced initially as a measure of pleasure or satisfaction within the theory of utilitarianism by moral philosophers such as Jeremy Bentham and John Stuart Mill. But the term has been adapted and reapplied within neoclassical economics, which dominates modern economic theory, as a _____ function that represents a consumer's preference ordering over a choice set. As such, it is devoid of its original interpretation as a measurement of the pleasure or satisfaction obtained by the consumer from that choice.

Exam Probability: **High**

25. *Answer choices:*
(see index for correct answer)

- a. Regret

- b. Utility
- c. Decision fatigue
- d. Policy

*Guidance:* level 1

---

:: Materials ::

A _____ , also known as a feedstock, unprocessed material, or primary commodity, is a basic material that is used to produce goods, finished products, energy, or intermediate materials which are feedstock for future finished products. As feedstock, the term connotes these materials are bottleneck assets and are highly important with regard to producing other products. An example of this is crude oil, which is a _____ and a feedstock used in the production of industrial chemicals, fuels, plastics, and pharmaceutical goods; lumber is a _____ used to produce a variety of products including all types of furniture. The term " _____ " denotes materials in minimally processed or unprocessed in states; e.g., raw latex, crude oil, cotton, coal, raw biomass, iron ore, air, logs, or water i.e. "...any product of agriculture, forestry, fishing and any other mineral that is in its natural form or which has undergone the transformation required to prepare it for internationally marketing in substantial volumes."

Exam Probability: **Medium**

26. *Answer choices:*
<sub>(see index for correct answer)</sub>

- a. Space blanket
- b. Raw material
- c. Slag
- d. Agricultural lime

*Guidance:* level 1

---

:: Statistical terminology ::

_____ is the ability to avoid wasting materials, energy, efforts, money, and time in doing something or in producing a desired result. In a more general sense, it is the ability to do things well, successfully, and without waste. In more mathematical or scientific terms, it is a measure of the extent to which input is well used for an intended task or function . It often specifically comprises the capability of a specific application of effort to produce a specific outcome with a minimum amount or quantity of waste, expense, or unnecessary effort. _____ refers to very different inputs and outputs in different fields and industries.

Exam Probability: **Low**

27. *Answer choices:*
(see index for correct answer)

- a. Iterated conditional modes
- b. Efficiency
- c. Permutation test
- d. Observed information

*Guidance:* level 1

---

:: Commerce ::

_____ relates to "the exchange of goods and services, especially on a large scale". It includes legal, economic, political, social, cultural and technological systems that operate in a country or in international trade.

Exam Probability: **Medium**

28. *Answer choices:*
(see index for correct answer)

- a. Retail loss prevention
- b. RFM
- c. Economic entity
- d. Commerce

*Guidance:* level 1

---

:: Strategic management ::

_____ is a strategic planning technique used to help a person or organization identify strengths, weaknesses, opportunities, and threats related to business competition or project planning. It is intended to specify the objectives of the business venture or project and identify the internal and external factors that are favorable and unfavorable to achieving those objectives. Users of a _____ often ask and answer questions to generate meaningful information for each category to make the tool useful and identify their competitive advantage. SWOT has been described as the tried-and-true tool of strategic analysis.

Exam Probability: **Medium**

29. *Answer choices:*

(see index for correct answer)

- a. First-mover
- b. Operating model
- c. SWOT analysis
- d. Operational objective

*Guidance:* level 1

---

:: Critical thinking ::

In psychology, _____ is regarded as the cognitive process resulting in the selection of a belief or a course of action among several alternative possibilities. Every _____ process produces a final choice, which may or may not prompt action.

Exam Probability: **Medium**

30. *Answer choices:*

(see index for correct answer)

- a. Decidophobia
- b. Precising definition
- c. Moral reasoning
- d. Precision questioning

*Guidance:* level 1

---

:: Manufacturing ::

A _____ is an object used to extend the ability of an individual to modify features of the surrounding environment. Although many animals use simple _____ s, only human beings, whose use of stone _____ s dates back hundreds of millennia, use _____ s to make other _____ s. The set of _____ s needed to perform different tasks that are part of the same activity is called gear or equipment.

Exam Probability: **High**

31. *Answer choices:*
(see index for correct answer)

- a. Blowmolding machine
- b. Batch production
- c. Inventory management software
- d. Flow chemistry

*Guidance:* level 1

---

:: Survey methodology ::

An _____ is a conversation where questions are asked and answers are given. In common parlance, the word "_____" refers to a one-on-one conversation between an _____ er and an _____ ee. The _____ er asks questions to which the _____ ee responds, usually so information may be transferred from _____ ee to _____ er . Sometimes, information can be transferred in both directions. It is a communication, unlike a speech, which produces a one-way flow of information.

Exam Probability: **Medium**

32. *Answer choices:*
(see index for correct answer)

- a. Computer-assisted survey information collection
- b. American Association for Public Opinion Research
- c. Scale analysis
- d. Interview

*Guidance:* level 1

---

:: Goods ::

In most contexts, the concept of _____ denotes the conduct that should be preferred when posed with a choice between possible actions. _____ is generally considered to be the opposite of evil, and is of interest in the study of morality, ethics, religion and philosophy. The specific meaning and etymology of the term and its associated translations among ancient and contemporary languages show substantial variation in its inflection and meaning depending on circumstances of place, history, religious, or philosophical context.

Exam Probability: **High**

33. *Answer choices:*
(see index for correct answer)

- a. Intermediate good
- b. Good
- c. Yellow goods
- d. Speciality goods

*Guidance:* level 1

---

:: Elementary arithmetic ::

In mathematics, a _____ is a number or ratio expressed as a fraction of 100. It is often denoted using the percent sign, "%", or the abbreviations "pct.", "pct"; sometimes the abbreviation "pc" is also used. A _____ is a dimensionless number .

Exam Probability: **High**

34. *Answer choices:*
(see index for correct answer)

- a. Mediant
- b. Number bond
- c. Percentage
- d. 0

*Guidance:* level 1

---

:: Organizational behavior ::

_____ is the state or fact of exclusive rights and control over property, which may be an object, land/real estate or intellectual property. _____ involves multiple rights, collectively referred to as title, which may be separated and held by different parties.

Exam Probability: **High**

35. *Answer choices:*
(see index for correct answer)

- a. Ownership
- b. Conformity
- c. Nut Island effect
- d. Micro-initiative

*Guidance:* level 1

:: Income ::

_____ is a ratio between the net profit and cost of investment resulting from an investment of some resources. A high ROI means the investment's gains favorably to its cost. As a performance measure, ROI is used to evaluate the efficiency of an investment or to compare the efficiencies of several different investments. In purely economic terms, it is one way of relating profits to capital invested. _____ is a performance measure used by businesses to identify the efficiency of an investment or number of different investments.

Exam Probability: **Low**

36. *Answer choices:*
(see index for correct answer)

- a. Net national income
- b. Aggregate expenditure
- c. Return on investment
- d. Creative real estate investing

*Guidance:* level 1

:: Shareholders ::

A _____ is a payment made by a corporation to its shareholders, usually as a distribution of profits. When a corporation earns a profit or surplus, the corporation is able to re-invest the profit in the business and pay a proportion of the profit as a _____ to shareholders. Distribution to shareholders may be in cash or, if the corporation has a _____ reinvestment plan, the amount can be paid by the issue of further shares or share repurchase. When _____ s are paid, shareholders typically must pay income taxes, and the corporation does not receive a corporate income tax deduction for the _____ payments.

Exam Probability: **Medium**

37. *Answer choices:*
(see index for correct answer)

- a. Shareholder yield
- b. Stock dilution
- c. UK Individual Shareholders Society
- d. Dividend

*Guidance:* level 1

---

:: Business law ::

_____ is where a person's financial liability is limited to a fixed sum, most commonly the value of a person's investment in a company or partnership. If a company with _____ is sued, then the claimants are suing the company, not its owners or investors. A shareholder in a limited company is not personally liable for any of the debts of the company, other than for the amount already invested in the company and for any unpaid amount on the shares in the company, if any. The same is true for the members of a _____ partnership and the limited partners in a limited partnership. By contrast, sole proprietors and partners in general partnerships are each liable for all the debts of the business .

Exam Probability: **High**

38. *Answer choices:*
(see index for correct answer)

- a. Statutory authority
- b. Limited liability
- c. Retroactive overtime

- d. Limited liability company

*Guidance:* level 1

---

:: International trade ::

_____ involves the transfer of goods or services from one person or entity to another, often in exchange for money. A system or network that allows _____ is called a market.

Exam Probability: **Low**

39. *Answer choices:*
(see index for correct answer)

- a. Low-cost country sourcing
- b. Debt moratorium
- c. Internationalization
- d. Trade

*Guidance:* level 1

---

:: Globalization-related theories ::

_____ is an economic system based on the private ownership of the means of production and their operation for profit. Characteristics central to _____ include private property, capital accumulation, wage labor, voluntary exchange, a price system, and competitive markets. In a capitalist market economy, decision-making and investment are determined by every owner of wealth, property or production ability in financial and capital markets, whereas prices and the distribution of goods and services are mainly determined by competition in goods and services markets.

Exam Probability: **Low**

40. *Answer choices:*
(see index for correct answer)

- a. postmodernism
- b. post-industrial
- c. Economic Development

*Guidance:* level 1

---

The _____ of a corporation is all of the shares into which ownership of the corporation is divided. In American English, the shares are commonly known as "_____ s". A single share of the _____ represents fractional ownership of the corporation in proportion to the total number of shares. This typically entitles the _____ holder to that fraction of the company's earnings, proceeds from liquidation of assets , or voting power, often dividing these up in proportion to the amount of money each _____ holder has invested. Not all _____ is necessarily equal, as certain classes of _____ may be issued for example without voting rights, with enhanced voting rights, or with a certain priority to receive profits or liquidation proceeds before or after other classes of shareholders.

Exam Probability: **Medium**

41. *Answer choices:*
(see index for correct answer)

- a. Stock
- b. Wealth management
- c. Buy side
- d. Burgundy

*Guidance:* level 1

A _____ , equity market or share market is the aggregation of buyers and sellers of stocks , which represent ownership claims on businesses; these may include securities listed on a public stock exchange, as well as stock that is only traded privately. Examples of the latter include shares of private companies which are sold to investors through equity crowdfunding platforms. Stock exchanges list shares of common equity as well as other security types, e.g. corporate bonds and convertible bonds.

Exam Probability: **Low**

42. *Answer choices:*
(see index for correct answer)

- a. Hybrid market
- b. Lock-up period

- c. Stock market
- d. Untraded shares

*Guidance:* level 1

---

:: Project management ::

In political science, an _____ is a means by which a petition signed by a certain minimum number of registered voters can force a government to choose to either enact a law or hold a public vote in parliament in what is called indirect _____ , or under direct _____ , the proposition is immediately put to a plebiscite or referendum, in what is called a Popular initiated Referendum or citizen-initiated referendum).

Exam Probability: **Low**

43. *Answer choices:*
(see index for correct answer)

- a. Australian Institute of Project Management
- b. Initiative
- c. Project planning
- d. Alexander Laufer

*Guidance:* level 1

---

:: Television commercials ::

_____ is a phenomenon whereby something new and somehow valuable is formed. The created item may be intangible or a physical object .

Exam Probability: **Low**

44. *Answer choices:*
(see index for correct answer)

- a. Terry Tate: Office Linebacker
- b. Revolving Door
- c. Cheer Up!
- d. An American Revolution

*Guidance:* level 1

---

:: Identity management ::

_____ is the ability of an individual or group to seclude themselves, or information about themselves, and thereby express themselves selectively. The boundaries and content of what is considered private differ among cultures and individuals, but share common themes. When something is private to a person, it usually means that something is inherently special or sensitive to them. The domain of _____ partially overlaps with security , which can include the concepts of appropriate use, as well as protection of information. _____ may also take the form of bodily integrity.

Exam Probability: **Low**

45. *Answer choices:*
(see index for correct answer)

- a. DigiD
- b. Service Provisioning Markup Language
- c. Identity verification service
- d. Privacy

*Guidance:* level 1

---

:: Macroeconomics ::

A foreign _____ is an investment in the form of a controlling ownership in a business in one country by an entity based in another country. It is thus distinguished from a foreign portfolio investment by a notion of direct control.

Exam Probability: **Low**

46. *Answer choices:*
(see index for correct answer)

- a. Self-fulfilling crisis
- b. Turnpike theory
- c. Direct investment
- d. Modern Monetary Theory

*Guidance:* level 1

---

:: Business ::

The seller, or the provider of the goods or services, completes a sale in response to an acquisition, appropriation, requisition or a direct interaction with the buyer at the point of sale. There is a passing of title of the item, and the settlement of a price, in which agreement is reached on a price for which transfer of ownership of the item will occur. The seller, not the purchaser typically executes the sale and it may be completed prior to the obligation of payment. In the case of indirect interaction, a person who sells goods or service on behalf of the owner is known as a salesman or saleswoman or salesperson, but this often refers to someone _____ goods in a store/shop, in which case other terms are also common, including salesclerk, shop assistant, and retail clerk.

Exam Probability: **Low**

47. *Answer choices:*
(see index for correct answer)

- a. Selling
- b. Absentee business owner
- c. Distribution
- d. Kingdomality

*Guidance:* level 1

---

:: E-commerce ::

_____ is the activity of buying or selling of products on online services or over the Internet. Electronic commerce draws on technologies such as mobile commerce, electronic funds transfer, supply chain management, Internet marketing, online transaction processing, electronic data interchange , inventory management systems, and automated data collection systems.

Exam Probability: **Low**

48. *Answer choices:*
(see index for correct answer)

- a. ROPO
- b. Onbuy
- c. Mobile payment
- d. E-commerce

*Guidance:* level 1

:: International trade ::

_____ or globalisation is the process of interaction and integration among people, companies, and governments worldwide. As a complex and multifaceted phenomenon, _____ is considered by some as a form of capitalist expansion which entails the integration of local and national economies into a global, unregulated market economy. _____ has grown due to advances in transportation and communication technology. With the increased global interactions comes the growth of international trade, ideas, and culture. _____ is primarily an economic process of interaction and integration that's associated with social and cultural aspects. However, conflicts and diplomacy are also large parts of the history of _____ , and modern _____ .

Exam Probability: **Medium**

49. *Answer choices:*
(see index for correct answer)

- a. DataArt
- b. Consular invoice
- c. Globalization
- d. Gains from trade

*Guidance:* level 1

:: Management ::

The _____ is a strategy performance management tool – a semi-standard structured report, that can be used by managers to keep track of the execution of activities by the staff within their control and to monitor the consequences arising from these actions.

Exam Probability: **Medium**

50. *Answer choices:*
(see index for correct answer)

- a. Marketing plan
- b. Customer Benefit Package
- c. Balanced scorecard
- d. Relational view

*Guidance:* level 1

:: Casting (manufacturing) ::

A _____ is a regularity in the world, man-made design, or abstract ideas. As such, the elements of a _____ repeat in a predictable manner. A geometric _____ is a kind of _____ formed of geometric shapes and typically repeated like a wallpaper design.

Exam Probability: **High**

51. *Answer choices:*
(see index for correct answer)

- a. Plano-convex ingot
- b. Vacuum casting
- c. Evaporative-pattern casting
- d. Full-mold casting

*Guidance:* level 1

:: Debt ::

_____ , in finance and economics, is payment from a borrower or deposit-taking financial institution to a lender or depositor of an amount above repayment of the principal sum , at a particular rate. It is distinct from a fee which the borrower may pay the lender or some third party. It is also distinct from dividend which is paid by a company to its shareholders from its profit or reserve, but not at a particular rate decided beforehand, rather on a pro rata basis as a share in the reward gained by risk taking entrepreneurs when the revenue earned exceeds the total costs.

Exam Probability: **Low**

52. *Answer choices:*
(see index for correct answer)

- a. Consumer debt
- b. Borrowing base
- c. Interest
- d. Rule of 72

*Guidance:* level 1

:: Environmental economics ::

_____ is the process of people maintaining change in a balanced environment, in which the exploitation of resources, the direction of investments, the orientation of technological development and institutional change are all in harmony and enhance both current and future potential to meet human needs and aspirations. For many in the field, _____ is defined through the following interconnected domains or pillars: environment, economic and social, which according to Fritjof Capra is based on the principles of Systems Thinking. Sub-domains of sustainable development have been considered also: cultural, technological and political. While sustainable development may be the organizing principle for _____ for some, for others, the two terms are paradoxical . Sustainable development is the development that meets the needs of the present without compromising the ability of future generations to meet their own needs. Brundtland Report for the World Commission on Environment and Development  introduced the term of sustainable development.

Exam Probability: **Low**

53. *Answer choices:*
(see index for correct answer)

- a. Environmental and Resource Economics
- b. Sustainability
- c. Eco-Management and Audit Scheme
- d. Sustainable tourism

*Guidance:* level 1

:: Stochastic processes ::

_____ is a system of rules that are created and enforced through social or governmental institutions to regulate behavior. It has been defined both as "the Science of Justice" and "the Art of Justice". _____ is a system that regulates and ensures that individuals or a community adhere to the will of the state. State-enforced _____ s can be made by a collective legislature or by a single legislator, resulting in statutes, by the executive through decrees and regulations, or established by judges through precedent, normally in common _____ jurisdictions. Private individuals can create legally binding contracts, including arbitration agreements that may elect to accept alternative arbitration to the normal court process. The formation of _____ s themselves may be influenced by a constitution, written or tacit, and the rights encoded therein. The _____ shapes politics, economics, history and society in various ways and serves as a mediator of relations between people.

Exam Probability: **High**

54. *Answer choices:*
(see index for correct answer)

- a. Law
- b. Voter model
- c. Doob decomposition theorem
- d. D/M/1 queue

*Guidance:* level 1

---

:: Human resource management ::

_____ are the people who make up the workforce of an organization, business sector, or economy. "Human capital" is sometimes used synonymously with " _____ ", although human capital typically refers to a narrower effect . Likewise, other terms sometimes used include manpower, talent, labor, personnel, or simply people.

Exam Probability: **Medium**

55. *Answer choices:*
(see index for correct answer)

- a. Human resources
- b. Diversity Icebreaker
- c. Mechanical aptitude

- d. Organizational ethics

*Guidance:* level 1

---

:: Meetings ::

An _____ is a group of people who participate in a show or encounter a work of art, literature , theatre, music , video games , or academics in any medium. _____ members participate in different ways in different kinds of art; some events invite overt _____ participation and others allowing only modest clapping and criticism and reception.

Exam Probability: **Medium**

56. *Answer choices:*
(see index for correct answer)

- a. Chatham House Rule
- b. AEI World Forum
- c. Audience
- d. Function hall

*Guidance:* level 1

---

:: Management ::

The term _____ refers to measures designed to increase the degree of autonomy and self-determination in people and in communities in order to enable them to represent their interests in a responsible and self-determined way, acting on their own authority. It is the process of becoming stronger and more confident, especially in controlling one's life and claiming one's rights. _____ as action refers both to the process of self-_____ and to professional support of people, which enables them to overcome their sense of powerlessness and lack of influence, and to recognize and use their resources. To do work with power.

Exam Probability: **Medium**

57. *Answer choices:*
(see index for correct answer)

- a. Empowerment
- b. Director
- c. Industrial forensics

- d. Downstream

*Guidance:* level 1

---

:: Public relations ::

_____ is the public visibility or awareness for any product, service or company. It may also refer to the movement of information from its source to the general public, often but not always via the media. The subjects of _____ include people , goods and services, organizations, and works of art or entertainment.

Exam Probability: **Medium**

58. *Answer choices:*
(see index for correct answer)

- a. Upstate California
- b. Contingency theory of accommodation
- c. Public Relations Institute of Australia
- d. Publicity

*Guidance:* level 1

---

:: Accounting software ::

_____ is any item or verifiable record that is generally accepted as payment for goods and services and repayment of debts, such as taxes, in a particular country or socio-economic context. The main functions of _____ are distinguished as: a medium of exchange, a unit of account, a store of value and sometimes, a standard of deferred payment. Any item or verifiable record that fulfils these functions can be considered as _____ .

Exam Probability: **High**

59. *Answer choices:*
(see index for correct answer)

- a. Money
- b. Microsoft Money
- c. MAS 90
- d. TRAVERSE

*Guidance:* level 1

## Management

Management is the administration of an organization, whether it is a business, a not-for-profit organization, or government body. Management includes the activities of setting the strategy of an organization and coordinating the efforts of its employees (or of volunteers) to accomplish its objectives through the application of available resources, such as financial, natural, technological, and human resources.

:: ::

_____ consists of using generic or ad hoc methods in an orderly manner to find solutions to problems. Some of the problem-solving techniques developed and used in philosophy, artificial intelligence, computer science, engineering, mathematics, or medicine are related to mental problem-solving techniques studied in psychology.

Exam Probability: **High**

1. *Answer choices:*

(see index for correct answer)

- a. information systems assessment
- b. open system
- c. hierarchical
- d. co-culture

*Guidance:* level 1

:: Game theory ::

_____ is the idea that rationality is limited when individuals make decisions: by the tractability of the decision problem, the cognitive limitations of the mind, and the time available to make the decision. Decision-makers, in this view, act as satisficers, seeking a satisfactory solution rather than an optimal one.

Exam Probability: **High**

2. *Answer choices:*
(see index for correct answer)

- a. Chess opening
- b. Shapley value
- c. Bounded rationality
- d. Divide and choose

*Guidance:* level 1

---

:: Organizational behavior ::

_____ is the term now used more commonly in business management, particularly human resource management. _____ refers to the number of subordinates a supervisor has.

Exam Probability: **Low**

3. *Answer choices:*
(see index for correct answer)

- a. Span of control
- b. Group behaviour
- c. Positive organizational behavior
- d. Organizational commitment

*Guidance:* level 1

---

:: Systems thinking ::

In business management, a _____ is a company that facilitates the learning of its members and continuously transforms itself. The concept was coined through the work and research of Peter Senge and his colleagues.

**4.** *Answer choices:*
(see index for correct answer)

- a. Learning organization
- b. Ray Hammond
- c. Delphi method
- d. Bioterrorism

*Guidance:* level 1

---

:: Market research ::

_____ is an organized effort to gather information about target markets or customers. It is a very important component of business strategy. The term is commonly interchanged with marketing research; however, expert practitioners may wish to draw a distinction, in that marketing research is concerned specifically about marketing processes, while _____ is concerned specifically with markets.

Exam Probability: **Medium**

**5.** *Answer choices:*
(see index for correct answer)

- a. Multivariate landing page optimization
- b. Offshore 2020
- c. News ratings in Australia
- d. Market research

*Guidance:* level 1

---

:: ::

_____ is a means of protection from financial loss. It is a form of risk management, primarily used to hedge against the risk of a contingent or uncertain loss

Exam Probability: **Medium**

**6.** *Answer choices:*
(see index for correct answer)

- a. interpersonal communication
- b. similarity-attraction theory

- c. Insurance
- d. Sarbanes-Oxley act of 2002

*Guidance:* level 1

---

:: Budgets ::

A _____ is a financial plan for a defined period, often one year. It may also include planned sales volumes and revenues, resource quantities, costs and expenses, assets, liabilities and cash flows. Companies, governments, families and other organizations use it to express strategic plans of activities or events in measurable terms.

Exam Probability: **Medium**

7. *Answer choices:*
(see index for correct answer)

- a. Budget set
- b. Railway Budget
- c. Energy budget
- d. Budget

*Guidance:* level 1

---

:: Cognitive biases ::

The _____ is a type of immediate judgement discrepancy, or cognitive bias, where a person making an initial assessment of another person, place, or thing will assume ambiguous information based upon concrete information. A simplified example of the _____ is when an individual noticing that the person in the photograph is attractive, well groomed, and properly attired, assumes, using a mental heuristic, that the person in the photograph is a good person based upon the rules of that individual's social concept. This constant error in judgment is reflective of the individual's preferences, prejudices, ideology, aspirations, and social perception. The _____ is an evaluation by an individual and can affect the perception of a decision, action, idea, business, person, group, entity, or other whenever concrete data is generalized or influences ambiguous information.

Exam Probability: **Medium**

8. *Answer choices:*

- a. Publication bias
- b. Duration neglect
- c. Fundamental attribution error
- d. Attentional bias

*Guidance:* level 1

---

:: Goods ::

In most contexts, the concept of _____ denotes the conduct that should be preferred when posed with a choice between possible actions. _____ is generally considered to be the opposite of evil, and is of interest in the study of morality, ethics, religion and philosophy. The specific meaning and etymology of the term and its associated translations among ancient and contemporary languages show substantial variation in its inflection and meaning depending on circumstances of place, history, religious, or philosophical context.

Exam Probability: **Medium**

9. *Answer choices:*

- a. Good
- b. Speciality goods
- c. Global commons
- d. Substitute good

*Guidance:* level 1

---

:: Leadership ::

_____ Theory, or the _____ Model, is a model created by Paul Hersey and Ken Blanchard, developed while working on Management of Organizational Behavior. The theory was first introduced in 1969 as "life cycle theory of leadership". During the mid-1970s, life cycle theory of leadership was renamed " _____ Theory."

Exam Probability: **High**

10. *Answer choices:*

- a. The Leadership Council
- b. Situational leadership
- c. Authentic leadership
- d. Situational leadership theory

---

:: Human resource management ::

_____ is the strategic approach to the effective management of people in an organization so that they help the business to gain a competitive advantage. It is designed to maximize employee performance in service of an employer's strategic objectives. HR is primarily concerned with the management of people within organizations, focusing on policies and on systems. HR departments are responsible for overseeing employee-benefits design, employee recruitment, training and development, performance appraisal, and Reward management . HR also concerns itself with organizational change and industrial relations, that is, the balancing of organizational practices with requirements arising from collective bargaining and from governmental laws.

Exam Probability: **Low**

11. *Answer choices:*
(see index for correct answer)

- a. Human resource management
- b. Dr. Marri Channa Reddy Human Resource Development Institute of Andhra Pradesh
- c. Emotional labor
- d. Income bracket

---

:: Employment compensation ::

_____ refers to various incentive plans introduced by businesses that provide direct or indirect payments to employees that depend on company's profitability in addition to employees' regular salary and bonuses. In publicly traded companies these plans typically amount to allocation of shares to employees. One of the earliest pioneers of _____ was Englishman Theodore Cooke Taylor, who is known to have introduced the practice in his woollen mills during the late 1800s .

Exam Probability: **Medium**

12. *Answer choices:*

- a. Profit sharing
- b. Annual enrollment
- c. Performance-related pay
- d. Take-home vehicle

*Guidance:* level 1

---

:: Power (social and political) ::

_____ is a form of reverence gained by a leader who has strong interpersonal relationship skills. _____ , as an aspect of personal power, becomes particularly important as organizational leadership becomes increasingly about collaboration and influence, rather than command and control.

Exam Probability: **Low**

13. *Answer choices:*

- a. Referent power
- b. need for power
- c. Hard power

*Guidance:* level 1

---

:: Project management ::

Contemporary business and science treat as a _____ any undertaking, carried out individually or collaboratively and possibly involving research or design, that is carefully planned to achieve a particular aim.

Exam Probability: **Low**

14. *Answer choices:*

- a. Project plan
- b. Project
- c. Project workforce management
- d. Stages of project finance

*Guidance:* level 1

_____ is a category of property that includes intangible creations of the human intellect. _____ encompasses two types of rights: industrial property rights and copyright. It was not until the 19th century that the term " _____ " began to be used, and not until the late 20th century that it became commonplace in the majority of the world.

Exam Probability: **Medium**

15. *Answer choices:*
(see index for correct answer)

- a. Intellectual property
- b. Electricity liberalization
- c. Price-cap regulation
- d. Network effect

*Guidance:* level 1

:: Business terms ::

Centralisation or _____ is the process by which the activities of an organization, particularly those regarding planning and decision-making, framing strategy and policies become concentrated within a particular geographical location group. This moves the important decision-making and planning powers within the center of the organisation.

Exam Probability: **High**

16. *Answer choices:*
(see index for correct answer)

- a. back office
- b. customer base
- c. front office
- d. Centralization

*Guidance:* level 1

:: Information systems ::

_____ is the process of creating, sharing, using and managing the knowledge and information of an organisation. It refers to a multidisciplinary approach to achieving organisational objectives by making the best use of knowledge.

Exam Probability: **High**

17. *Answer choices:*
(see index for correct answer)

- a. IARP
- b. Information Processes and Technology
- c. Knowledge management
- d. Xcon

*Guidance:* level 1

:: ::

_____ is a kind of action that occur as two or more objects have an effect upon one another. The idea of a two-way effect is essential in the concept of _____ , as opposed to a one-way causal effect. A closely related term is interconnectivity, which deals with the _____ s of _____ s within systems: combinations of many simple _____ s can lead to surprising emergent phenomena. _____ has different tailored meanings in various sciences. Changes can also involve _____ .

Exam Probability: **High**

18. *Answer choices:*
(see index for correct answer)

- a. hierarchical perspective
- b. functional perspective
- c. imperative
- d. Interaction

*Guidance:* level 1

:: ::

A _____ is a leader's method of providing direction, implementing plans, and motivating people. Various authors have proposed identifying many different _____ s as exhibited by leaders in the political, business or other fields. Studies on _____ are conducted in the military field, expressing an approach that stresses a holistic view of leadership, including how a leader's physical presence determines how others perceive that leader. The factors of physical presence in this context include military bearing, physical fitness, confidence, and resilience. The leader's intellectual capacity helps to conceptualize solutions and to acquire knowledge to do the job. A leader's conceptual abilities apply agility, judgment, innovation, interpersonal tact, and domain knowledge. Domain knowledge encompasses tactical and technical knowledge as well as cultural and geopolitical awareness. Daniel Goleman in his article "Leadership that Gets Results" talks about six styles of leadership.

Exam Probability: **Medium**

19. *Answer choices:*
(see index for correct answer)

- a. surface-level diversity
- b. information systems assessment
- c. co-culture
- d. Leadership style

*Guidance:* level 1

---

:: Business ::

_____ is a trade policy that does not restrict imports or exports; it can also be understood as the free market idea applied to international trade. In government, _____ is predominantly advocated by political parties that hold liberal economic positions while economically left-wing and nationalist political parties generally support protectionism, the opposite of _____ .

Exam Probability: **Low**

20. *Answer choices:*
(see index for correct answer)

- a. OrderUp
- b. Business interoperability interface
- c. Demand chain

- d. Free trade

---

:: Production economics ::

_____ is the joint use of a resource or space. It is also the process of dividing and distributing. In its narrow sense, it refers to joint or alternating use of inherently finite goods, such as a common pasture or a shared residence. Still more loosely, " _____ " can actually mean giving something as an outright gift: for example, to "share" one's food really means to give some of it as a gift. _____ is a basic component of human interaction, and is responsible for strengthening social ties and ensuring a person's well-being.

Exam Probability: **Low**

21. *Answer choices:*
(see index for correct answer)

- a. Post-Fordism
- b. Sharing
- c. Isocost
- d. Total factor productivity

---

:: Management ::

The _____ is a strategy performance management tool – a semi-standard structured report, that can be used by managers to keep track of the execution of activities by the staff within their control and to monitor the consequences arising from these actions.

Exam Probability: **High**

22. *Answer choices:*
(see index for correct answer)

- a. Balanced scorecard
- b. Managerial Psychology
- c. Identity formation
- d. Pareto analysis

A _____ is a professional who provides expert advice in a particular area such as security , management, education, accountancy, law, human resources, marketing , finance, engineering, science or any of many other specialized fields.

Exam Probability: **High**

23. *Answer choices:*
(see index for correct answer)

- a. surface-level diversity
- b. empathy
- c. interpersonal communication
- d. co-culture

*Guidance:* level 1

:: Management ::

_____ is a process by which entities review the quality of all factors involved in production. ISO 9000 defines _____ as "A part of quality management focused on fulfilling quality requirements".

Exam Probability: **Medium**

24. *Answer choices:*
(see index for correct answer)

- a. Quality control
- b. Duality
- c. Best practice
- d. Project management simulation

*Guidance:* level 1

:: Workplace ::

A _____ is a process through which feedback from an employee's subordinates, colleagues, and supervisor, as well as a self-evaluation by the employee themselves is gathered. Such feedback can also include, when relevant, feedback from external sources who interact with the employee, such as customers and suppliers or other interested stakeholders. _____ is so named because it solicits feedback regarding an employee's behavior from a variety of points of view . It therefore may be contrasted with "downward feedback" , or "upward feedback" delivered to supervisory or management employees by subordinates only.

Exam Probability: **Medium**

25. *Answer choices:*
(see index for correct answer)

- a. Workplace harassment
- b. Toxic workplace
- c. Feminisation of the workplace
- d. 360-degree feedback

*Guidance:* level 1

:: ::

_____ is the consumption and saving opportunity gained by an entity within a specified timeframe, which is generally expressed in monetary terms. For households and individuals, " _____ is the sum of all the wages, salaries, profits, interest payments, rents, and other forms of earnings received in a given period of time."

Exam Probability: **High**

26. *Answer choices:*
(see index for correct answer)

- a. Income
- b. hierarchical perspective
- c. corporate values
- d. similarity-attraction theory

*Guidance:* level 1

:: ::

The _____ or labour force is the labour pool in employment. It is generally used to describe those working for a single company or industry, but can also apply to a geographic region like a city, state, or country. Within a company, its value can be labelled as its " _____ in Place". The _____ of a country includes both the employed and the unemployed. The labour force participation rate, LFPR , is the ratio between the labour force and the overall size of their cohort . The term generally excludes the employers or management, and can imply those involved in manual labour. It may also mean all those who are available for work.

Exam Probability: **Low**

27. *Answer choices:*
(see index for correct answer)

- a. deep-level diversity
- b. hierarchical
- c. Workforce
- d. personal values

*Guidance:* level 1

---

:: Product design ::

_____ as a verb is to create a new product to be sold by a business to its customers. A very broad coefficient and effective generation and development of ideas through a process that leads to new products. Thus, it is a major aspect of new product development.

Exam Probability: **Medium**

28. *Answer choices:*
(see index for correct answer)

- a. Studio Job
- b. Product design
- c. Andrea Fogli
- d. Rodney Fitch

*Guidance:* level 1

---

:: Information technology management ::

_____ is a collective term for all approaches to prepare , support and help individuals, teams, and organizations in making organizational change. The most common change drivers include: technological evolution, process reviews, crisis, and consumer habit changes; pressure from new business entrants, acquisitions, mergers, and organizational restructuring. It includes methods that redirect or redefine the use of resources, business process, budget allocations, or other modes of operation that significantly change a company or organization. Organizational _____ considers the full organization and what needs to change, while _____ may be used solely to refer to how people and teams are affected by such organizational transition. It deals with many different disciplines, from behavioral and social sciences to information technology and business solutions.

Exam Probability: **Medium**

29. *Answer choices:*
(see index for correct answer)

- a. Telematics
- b. Many-to-many
- c. Prolifics
- d. Change management

*Guidance:* level 1

---

:: Industrial relations ::

_____ or employee satisfaction is a measure of workers' contentedness with their job, whether or not they like the job or individual aspects or facets of jobs, such as nature of work or supervision. _____ can be measured in cognitive , affective , and behavioral components. Researchers have also noted that _____ measures vary in the extent to which they measure feelings about the job . or cognitions about the job .

Exam Probability: **High**

30. *Answer choices:*
(see index for correct answer)

- a. Injury prevention
- b. Job satisfaction
- c. European Journal of Industrial Relations
- d. Industrial violence

---

:: Free trade agreements ::

A _____ is a wide-ranging taxes, tariff and trade treaty that often includes investment guarantees. It exists when two or more countries agree on terms that helps them trade with each other. The most common _____ s are of the preferential and free trade types are concluded in order to reduce tariffs, quotas and other trade restrictions on items traded between the signatories.

Exam Probability: **High**

31. *Answer choices:*
(see index for correct answer)

- a. Investor-state dispute settlement
- b. Central Asian Union
- c. Trade, Development and Cooperation Agreement
- d. Trade agreement

---

:: ::

The _____ officer or just _____ , is the most senior corporate, executive, or administrative officer in charge of managing an organization especially an independent legal entity such as a company or nonprofit institution. CEOs lead a range of organizations, including public and private corporations, non-profit organizations and even some government organizations . The CEO of a corporation or company typically reports to the board of directors and is charged with maximizing the value of the entity, which may include maximizing the share price, market share, revenues or another element. In the non-profit and government sector, CEOs typically aim at achieving outcomes related to the organization's mission, such as reducing poverty, increasing literacy, etc.

Exam Probability: **Low**

32. *Answer choices:*
(see index for correct answer)

- a. empathy

- b. levels of analysis
- c. Chief executive
- d. open system

:: Production and manufacturing ::

An _____ is a manufacturing process in which parts are added as the semi-finished assembly moves from workstation to workstation where the parts are added in sequence until the final assembly is produced. By mechanically moving the parts to the assembly work and moving the semi-finished assembly from work station to work station, a finished product can be assembled faster and with less labor than by having workers carry parts to a stationary piece for assembly.

Exam Probability: **High**

33. *Answer choices:*
(see index for correct answer)

- a. Contract manufacturer
- b. Hydrosila
- c. Assembly line
- d. Simatic S5 PLC

:: ::

_____ is the moral stance, political philosophy, ideology, or social outlook that emphasizes the moral worth of the individual. Individualists promote the exercise of one's goals and desires and so value independence and self-reliance and advocate that interests of the individual should achieve precedence over the state or a social group, while opposing external interference upon one's own interests by society or institutions such as the government. _____ is often defined in contrast to totalitarianism, collectivism, and more corporate social forms.

Exam Probability: **Low**

34. *Answer choices:*
(see index for correct answer)

- a. surface-level diversity
- b. hierarchical
- c. functional perspective
- d. Individualism

*Guidance:* level 1

---

:: International relations ::

A _____ is any event that is going to lead to an unstable and dangerous situation affecting an individual, group, community, or whole society. Crises are deemed to be negative changes in the security, economic, political, societal, or environmental affairs, especially when they occur abruptly, with little or no warning. More loosely, it is a term meaning "a testing time" or an "emergency event".

Exam Probability: **Medium**

35. *Answer choices:*
(see index for correct answer)

- a. Hollings Center
- b. Foreign policy interest group
- c. Coordinator for International Relations
- d. Crisis

*Guidance:* level 1

---

:: Strategic alliances ::

A _____ is an agreement between two or more parties to pursue a set of agreed upon objectives needed while remaining independent organizations. A _____ will usually fall short of a legal partnership entity, agency, or corporate affiliate relationship. Typically, two companies form a _____ when each possesses one or more business assets or have expertise that will help the other by enhancing their businesses. _____ s can develop in outsourcing relationships where the parties desire to achieve long-term win-win benefits and innovation based on mutually desired outcomes.

Exam Probability: **Medium**

36. *Answer choices:*
(see index for correct answer)

- a. Strategic alliance
- b. Cross-licensing
- c. International joint venture
- d. Bridge Alliance

*Guidance:* level 1

:: ::

_____ , in its broadest context, includes both the attainment of that which is just and the philosophical discussion of that which is just. The concept of _____ is based on numerous fields, and many differing viewpoints and perspectives including the concepts of moral correctness based on ethics, rationality, law, religion, equity and fairness. Often, the general discussion of _____ is divided into the realm of social _____ as found in philosophy, theology and religion, and, procedural _____ as found in the study and application of the law.

Exam Probability: **High**

37. *Answer choices:*
(see index for correct answer)

- a. Sarbanes-Oxley act of 2002
- b. Justice
- c. corporate values
- d. Character

*Guidance:* level 1

:: Social networks ::

_____ broadly refers to those factors of effectively functioning social groups that include such things as interpersonal relationships, a shared sense of identity, a shared understanding, shared norms, shared values, trust, cooperation, and reciprocity. However, the many views of this complex subject make a single definition difficult.

Exam Probability: **High**

38. *Answer choices:*
(see index for correct answer)

- a. Geosocial networking

- b. Social capital
- c. Social Networks
- d. Social network automation

*Guidance:* level 1

---

:: Outsourcing ::

_____ is the relocation of a business process from one country to another—typically an operational process, such as manufacturing, or supporting processes, such as accounting. Typically this refers to a company business, although state governments may also employ _____ . More recently, technical and administrative services have been offshored.

Exam Probability: **Medium**

39. *Answer choices:*
(see index for correct answer)

- a. Offshoring
- b. Global sourcing
- c. Divestiture
- d. Farmshoring

*Guidance:* level 1

---

:: Mereology ::

_____ , in the abstract, is what belongs to or with something, whether as an attribute or as a component of said thing. In the context of this article, it is one or more components , whether physical or incorporeal, of a person's estate; or so belonging to, as in being owned by, a person or jointly a group of people or a legal entity like a corporation or even a society. Depending on the nature of the _____ , an owner of _____ has the right to consume, alter, share, redefine, rent, mortgage, pawn, sell, exchange, transfer, give away or destroy it, or to exclude others from doing these things, as well as to perhaps abandon it; whereas regardless of the nature of the _____ , the owner thereof has the right to properly use it , or at the very least exclusively keep it.

Exam Probability: **High**

40. *Answer choices:*

- a. Gunk
- b. Property
- c. Mereological essentialism
- d. Mereology

---

:: ::

A _____ is a problem offering two possibilities, neither of which is unambiguously acceptable or preferable. The possibilities are termed the horns of the _____ , a clichéd usage, but distinguishing the _____ from other kinds of predicament as a matter of usage.

Exam Probability: **Low**

41. *Answer choices:*

- a. information systems assessment
- b. Character
- c. Dilemma
- d. similarity-attraction theory

---

:: Employment ::

_____ is a relationship between two parties, usually based on a contract where work is paid for, where one party, which may be a corporation, for profit, not-for-profit organization, co-operative or other entity is the employer and the other is the employee. Employees work in return for payment, which may be in the form of an hourly wage, by piecework or an annual salary, depending on the type of work an employee does or which sector she or he is working in. Employees in some fields or sectors may receive gratuities, bonus payment or stock options. In some types of _____ , employees may receive benefits in addition to payment. Benefits can include health insurance, housing, disability insurance or use of a gym. _____ is typically governed by _____ laws, regulations or legal contracts.

Exam Probability: **High**

42. *Answer choices:*
(see index for correct answer)

- a. EuroMayDay
- b. Employment
- c. Extreme careerism
- d. Local hiring

*Guidance:* level 1

:: ::

The business environment is a marketing term and refers to factors and forces that affect a firm's ability to build and maintain successful customer relationships. The business environment has been defined as "the totality of physical and social factors that are taken directly into consideration in the decision-making behaviour of individuals in the organisation."

Exam Probability: **High**

43. *Answer choices:*
(see index for correct answer)

- a. Environmental scanning
- b. process perspective
- c. information systems assessment
- d. cultural

*Guidance:* level 1

:: ::

_____ is the process of making predictions of the future based on past and present data and most commonly by analysis of trends. A commonplace example might be estimation of some variable of interest at some specified future date. Prediction is a similar, but more general term. Both might refer to formal statistical methods employing time series, cross-sectional or longitudinal data, or alternatively to less formal judgmental methods. Usage can differ between areas of application: for example, in hydrology the terms "forecast" and "_____" are sometimes reserved for estimates of values at certain specific future times, while the term "prediction" is used for more general estimates, such as the number of times floods will occur over a long period.

Exam Probability: **High**

- a. personal values
- b. Character
- c. surface-level diversity
- d. Forecasting

*Guidance:* level 1

---

:: ::

_____ is the reason for people's actions, willingness and goals. _____ is derived from the word motive in the English language which is defined as a need that requires satisfaction. These needs could also be wants or desires that are acquired through influence of culture, society, lifestyle, etc. or generally innate. _____ is one's direction to behaviour, or what causes a person to want to repeat a behaviour, a set of force that acts behind the motives. An individual's _____ may be inspired by others or events or it may come from within the individual . _____ has been considered as one of the most important reasons that inspires a person to move forward in life. _____ results from the interaction of both conscious and unconscious factors. Mastering _____ to allow sustained and deliberate practice is central to high levels of achievement e.g. in the worlds of elite sport, medicine or music.

Exam Probability: **High**

- a. hierarchical
- b. Motivation
- c. interpersonal communication
- d. hierarchical perspective

*Guidance:* level 1

---

:: Systems theory ::

A _____ is a set of policies, processes and procedures used by an organization to ensure that it can fulfill the tasks required to achieve its objectives. These objectives cover many aspects of the organization's operations . For instance, an environmental _____ enables organizations to improve their environmental performance and an occupational health and safety _____ enables an organization to control its occupational health and safety risks, etc.

Exam Probability: **Medium**

46. *Answer choices:*
(see index for correct answer)

- a. Black box
- b. co-design
- c. subsystem
- d. Management system

*Guidance:* level 1

---

:: Economic globalization ::

_____ is an agreement in which one company hires another company to be responsible for a planned or existing activity that is or could be done internally,and sometimes involves transferring employees and assets from one firm to another.

Exam Probability: **Medium**

47. *Answer choices:*
(see index for correct answer)

- a. Outsourcing
- b. global financial

*Guidance:* level 1

---

:: ::

An _____ is a contingent motivator. Traditional _____ s are extrinsic motivators which reward actions to yield a desired outcome. The effectiveness of traditional _____ s has changed as the needs of Western society have evolved. While the traditional _____ model is effective when there is a defined procedure and goal for a task, Western society started to require a higher volume of critical thinkers, so the traditional model became less effective. Institutions are now following a trend in implementing strategies that rely on intrinsic motivations rather than the extrinsic motivations that the traditional _____ s foster.

Exam Probability: **High**

48. *Answer choices:*
(see index for correct answer)

- a. hierarchical
- b. Incentive
- c. corporate values
- d. similarity-attraction theory

*Guidance:* level 1

:: ::

A _____ is a research instrument consisting of a series of questions for the purpose of gathering information from respondents. The _____ was invented by the Statistical Society of London in 1838.

Exam Probability: **High**

49. *Answer choices:*
(see index for correct answer)

- a. hierarchical perspective
- b. deep-level diversity
- c. Questionnaire
- d. co-culture

*Guidance:* level 1

:: Legal terms ::

_____ , a form of alternative dispute resolution , is a way to resolve disputes outside the courts. The dispute will be decided by one or more persons , which renders the " _____ award". An _____ award is legally binding on both sides and enforceable in the courts.

Exam Probability: **Low**

50. *Answer choices:*
(see index for correct answer)

- a. Dumb laws
- b. Door tenant
- c. Arbitration
- d. Constructive fraud

*Guidance:* level 1

:: Project management ::

A _____ is a team whose members usually belong to different groups, functions and are assigned to activities for the same project. A team can be divided into sub-teams according to need. Usually _____ s are only used for a defined period of time. They are disbanded after the project is deemed complete. Due to the nature of the specific formation and disbandment, _____ s are usually in organizations.

Exam Probability: **Low**

51. *Answer choices:*
(see index for correct answer)

- a. Project team
- b. Hammock activity
- c. The Practice Standard for Scheduling
- d. Bottleneck

*Guidance:* level 1

:: Psychometrics ::

_____ is a dynamic, structured, interactive process where a neutral third party assists disputing parties in resolving conflict through the use of specialized communication and negotiation techniques. All participants in _____ are encouraged to actively participate in the process. _____ is a "party-centered" process in that it is focused primarily upon the needs, rights, and interests of the parties. The mediator uses a wide variety of techniques to guide the process in a constructive direction and to help the parties find their optimal solution. A mediator is facilitative in that she/he manages the interaction between parties and facilitates open communication _____ is also evaluative in that the mediator analyzes issues and relevant norms , while refraining from providing prescriptive advice to the parties .

Exam Probability: **Medium**

52. *Answer choices:*
(see index for correct answer)

- a. Choice set
- b. Standard-setting study
- c. Mediation
- d. Normal curve equivalent

*Guidance:* level 1

---

:: Unemployment ::

In economics, a _____ is a business cycle contraction when there is a general decline in economic activity. Macroeconomic indicators such as GDP , investment spending, capacity utilization, household income, business profits, and inflation fall, while bankruptcies and the unemployment rate rise. In the United Kingdom, it is defined as a negative economic growth for two consecutive quarters.

Exam Probability: **Low**

53. *Answer choices:*
(see index for correct answer)

- a. Recession
- b. Waithood
- c. Phillips curve
- d. Reserve army of labour

*Guidance:* level 1

_____ is the ability to avoid wasting materials, energy, efforts, money, and time in doing something or in producing a desired result. In a more general sense, it is the ability to do things well, successfully, and without waste. In more mathematical or scientific terms, it is a measure of the extent to which input is well used for an intended task or function . It often specifically comprises the capability of a specific application of effort to produce a specific outcome with a minimum amount or quantity of waste, expense, or unnecessary effort. _____ refers to very different inputs and outputs in different fields and industries.

Exam Probability: **Medium**

54. *Answer choices:*
(see index for correct answer)

- a. Completeness
- b. Shape parameter
- c. Efficiency
- d. Formation matrix

*Guidance:* level 1

_____ is the right to exercise power, which can be formalized by a state and exercised by way of judges, appointed executives of government, or the ecclesiastical or priestly appointed representatives of a God or other deities.

Exam Probability: **High**

55. *Answer choices:*
(see index for correct answer)

- a. Project Management Professional
- b. Authority
- c. Scrumedge
- d. Disciplined Agile Delivery

*Guidance:* level 1

An _____ is someone who has a prolonged or intense experience through practice and education in a particular field. Informally, an _____ is someone widely recognized as a reliable source of technique or skill whose faculty for judging or deciding rightly, justly, or wisely is accorded authority and status by peers or the public in a specific well-distinguished domain. An _____ , more generally, is a person with extensive knowledge or ability based on research, experience, or occupation and in a particular area of study. _____ s are called in for advice on their respective subject, but they do not always agree on the particulars of a field of study. An _____ can be believed, by virtue of credential, training, education, profession, publication or experience, to have special knowledge of a subject beyond that of the average person, sufficient that others may officially rely upon the individual's opinion. Historically, an _____ was referred to as a sage . The individual was usually a profound thinker distinguished for wisdom and sound judgment.

Exam Probability: **Medium**

56. *Answer choices:*

(see index for correct answer)

- a. Expert
- b. Emotional reasoning
- c. Merseyside Skeptics Society
- d. Rigour

*Guidance:* level 1

---

:: Human resource management ::

_____ encompasses values and behaviors that contribute to the unique social and psychological environment of a business. The _____ influences the way people interact, the context within which knowledge is created, the resistance they will have towards certain changes, and ultimately the way they share knowledge. _____ represents the collective values, beliefs and principles of organizational members and is a product of factors such as history, product, market, technology, strategy, type of employees, management style, and national culture; culture includes the organization's vision, values, norms, systems, symbols, language, assumptions, environment, location, beliefs and habits.

Exam Probability: **Medium**

57. *Answer choices:*
(see index for correct answer)

- a. Behavioral Competencies
- b. Occupational Information Network
- c. Internal communications
- d. Diversity Icebreaker

*Guidance:* level 1

:: Evaluation ::

A _____ is an evaluation of a publication, service, or company such as a movie , video game , musical composition , book ; a piece of hardware like a car, home appliance, or computer; or an event or performance, such as a live music concert, play, musical theater show, dance show, or art exhibition. In addition to a critical evaluation, the _____ 's author may assign the work a rating to indicate its relative merit. More loosely, an author may _____ current events, trends, or items in the news. A compilation of _____ s may itself be called a _____ . The New York _____ of Books, for instance, is a collection of essays on literature, culture, and current affairs. National _____ , founded by William F. Buckley, Jr., is an influential conservative magazine, and Monthly _____ is a long-running socialist periodical.

Exam Probability: **Low**

58. *Answer choices:*
(see index for correct answer)

- a. Formative assessment
- b. Review
- c. Teaching and Learning International Survey
- d. Continuous assessment

:: ::

_____ is the means to see, hear, or become aware of something or someone through our fundamental senses. The term _____ derives from the Latin word perceptio, and is the organization, identification, and interpretation of sensory information in order to represent and understand the presented information, or the environment.

Exam Probability: **Low**

59. *Answer choices:*
(see index for correct answer)

- a. hierarchical
- b. process perspective
- c. interpersonal communication
- d. corporate values

## Business law

Corporate law (also known as business law) is the body of law governing the
rights, relations, and conduct of persons, companies, organizations and
businesses. It refers to the legal practice relating to, or the theory of
corporations. Corporate law often describes the law relating to matters which
derive directly from the life-cycle of a corporation. It thus encompasses the
formation, funding, governance, and death of a corporation.

:: Legal doctrines and principles ::

In the United States, the _____ is a legal rule, based on
constitutional law, that prevents evidence collected or analyzed in violation
of the defendant's constitutional rights from being used in a court of law.
This may be considered an example of a prophylactic rule formulated by the
judiciary in order to protect a constitutional right. The _____ may also,
in some circumstances at least, be considered to follow directly from the
constitutional language, such as the Fifth Amendment's command that no person
"shall be compelled in any criminal case to be a witness against himself" and
that no person "shall be deprived of life, liberty or property without due
process of law".

Exam Probability: **Medium**

1. *Answer choices:*
(see index for correct answer)

- a. Abstention doctrine
- b. Assumption of risk
- c. Exclusionary rule
- d. Attractive nuisance

*Guidance:* level 1

:: Insurance terms ::

A _____ in the broadest sense is a natural person or other legal entity who receives money or other benefits from a benefactor. For example, the _____ of a life insurance policy is the person who receives the payment of the amount of insurance after the death of the insured.

Exam Probability: **Low**

2. *Answer choices:*
(see index for correct answer)

- a. Cash surrender value
- b. Total loss
- c. Loss reserving
- d. Pro rata

*Guidance:* level 1

---

:: ::

In general, _____ is a form of dishonesty or criminal activity undertaken by a person or organization entrusted with a position of authority, often to acquire illicit benefit. _____ may include many activities including bribery and embezzlement, though it may also involve practices that are legal in many countries. Political _____ occurs when an office-holder or other governmental employee acts in an official capacity for personal gain. _____ is most commonplace in kleptocracies, oligarchies, narco-states and mafia states.

Exam Probability: **Medium**

3. *Answer choices:*
(see index for correct answer)

- a. hierarchical
- b. hierarchical perspective
- c. levels of analysis
- d. similarity-attraction theory

*Guidance:* level 1

---

:: Equity (law) ::

An assignment is a legal term used in the context of the law of contract and of property. In both instances, assignment is the process whereby a person, the assignor, transfers rights or benefits to another, the _____ . An assignment may not transfer a duty, burden or detriment without the express agreement of the _____ . The right or benefit being assigned may be a gift or it may be paid for with a contractual consideration such as money.

Exam Probability: **High**

4. *Answer choices:*

- a. Assignee
- b. assignor

*Guidance:* level 1

:: ::

A _____ is a request to do something, most commonly addressed to a government official or public entity. _____ s to a deity are a form of prayer called supplication.

Exam Probability: **Low**

5. *Answer choices:*

- a. imperative
- b. Sarbanes-Oxley act of 2002
- c. deep-level diversity
- d. similarity-attraction theory

*Guidance:* level 1

:: Business ethics ::

_____ is a type of harassment technique that relates to a sexual nature and the unwelcome or inappropriate promise of rewards in exchange for sexual favors. _____ includes a range of actions from mild transgressions to sexual abuse or assault. Harassment can occur in many different social settings such as the workplace, the home, school, churches, etc. Harassers or victims may be of any gender.

Exam Probability: **Medium**

6. *Answer choices:*
(see index for correct answer)

- a. Ethical consumerism
- b. Sexual harassment
- c. CUC International
- d. Interfaith Center on Corporate Responsibility

*Guidance:* level 1

:: Psychometrics ::

_____ is a dynamic, structured, interactive process where a neutral third party assists disputing parties in resolving conflict through the use of specialized communication and negotiation techniques. All participants in _____ are encouraged to actively participate in the process. _____ is a "party-centered" process in that it is focused primarily upon the needs, rights, and interests of the parties. The mediator uses a wide variety of techniques to guide the process in a constructive direction and to help the parties find their optimal solution. A mediator is facilitative in that she/he manages the interaction between parties and facilitates open communication. _____ is also evaluative in that the mediator analyzes issues and relevant norms , while refraining from providing prescriptive advice to the parties .

Exam Probability: **Low**

7. *Answer choices:*
(see index for correct answer)

- a. Psychological statistics
- b. Choice set
- c. Reliability
- d. Person-fit analysis

*Guidance:* level 1

_____ is the body of law that relates to crime. It proscribes conduct perceived as threatening, harmful, or otherwise endangering to the property, health, safety, and moral welfare of people inclusive of one's self. Most _____ is established by statute, which is to say that the laws are enacted by a legislature. _____ includes the punishment and rehabilitation of people who violate such laws. _____ varies according to jurisdiction, and differs from civil law, where emphasis is more on dispute resolution and victim compensation, rather than on punishment or rehabilitation. Criminal procedure is a formalized official activity that authenticates the fact of commission of a crime and authorizes punitive or rehabilitative treatment of the offender.

Exam Probability: **Medium**

8. *Answer choices:*

(see index for correct answer)

- a. Mala in se
- b. mitigating factor
- c. Self-incrimination
- d. Mala prohibita

*Guidance:* level 1

---

In regulatory jurisdictions that provide for it , _____ is a group of laws and organizations designed to ensure the rights of consumers as well as fair trade, competition and accurate information in the marketplace. The laws are designed to prevent the businesses that engage in fraud or specified unfair practices from gaining an advantage over competitors. They may also provides additional protection for those most vulnerable in society. _____ laws are a form of government regulation that aim to protect the rights of consumers. For example, a government may require businesses to disclose detailed information about products—particularly in areas where safety or public health is an issue, such as food.

Exam Probability: **Medium**

9. *Answer choices:*

(see index for correct answer)

- a. Consumer protection
- b. deep-level diversity
- c. hierarchical perspective
- d. functional perspective

*Guidance:* level 1

---

:: Contract law ::

An _____ , or simply option, is defined as "a promise which meets the requirements for the formation of a contract and limits the promisor's power to revoke an offer."

Exam Probability: **Low**

10. *Answer choices:*

(see index for correct answer)

- a. Exceptio non adimpleti contractus
- b. Contra proferentem
- c. Option contract
- d. Verbal contract

*Guidance:* level 1

---

:: ::

Competition arises whenever at least two parties strive for a goal which cannot be shared: where one's gain is the other's loss .

Exam Probability: **High**

11. *Answer choices:*

(see index for correct answer)

- a. open system
- b. cultural
- c. Competitor
- d. deep-level diversity

*Guidance:* level 1

---

:: Legal terms ::

_____ , or exemplary damages, are damages assessed in order to punish the defendant for outrageous conduct and/or to reform or deter the defendant and others from engaging in conduct similar to that which formed the basis of the lawsuit. Although the purpose of _____ is not to compensate the plaintiff, the plaintiff will receive all or some of the _____ award.

Exam Probability: **High**

12. *Answer choices:*
(see index for correct answer)

- a. Indirect liability
- b. Punitive damages
- c. Arguido
- d. Medical advice

*Guidance:* level 1

:: ::

Competition law is a law that promotes or seeks to maintain market competition by regulating anti-competitive conduct by companies. Competition law is implemented through public and private enforcement. Competition law is known as " _____ law" in the United States for historical reasons, and as "anti-monopoly law" in China and Russia. In previous years it has been known as trade practices law in the United Kingdom and Australia. In the European Union, it is referred to as both _____ and competition law.

Exam Probability: **Low**

13. *Answer choices:*
(see index for correct answer)

- a. open system
- b. imperative
- c. Antitrust
- d. co-culture

*Guidance:* level 1

:: ::

An _____ is a criminal accusation that a person has committed a crime. In jurisdictions that use the concept of felonies, the most serious criminal offence is a felony; jurisdictions that do not use the felonies concept often use that of an indictable offence, an offence that requires an _____ .

Exam Probability: **High**

14. *Answer choices:*
(see index for correct answer)

- a. information systems assessment
- b. hierarchical
- c. Indictment
- d. deep-level diversity

*Guidance:* level 1

---

:: Trade secrets ::

The _____ of 1996 was a 6 title Act of Congress dealing with a wide range of issues, including not only industrial espionage , but the insanity defense, matters regarding the Boys & Girls Clubs of America, requirements for presentence investigation reports, and the United States Sentencing Commission reports regarding encryption or scrambling technology, and other technical and minor amendments.

Exam Probability: **Medium**

15. *Answer choices:*
(see index for correct answer)

- a. Xenu
- b. Kayfabe
- c. DuPont v. Kolon Industries
- d. Economic Espionage Act

*Guidance:* level 1

---

:: ::

A _____ , or trial by jury, is a lawful proceeding in which a jury makes a decision or findings of fact. It is distinguished from a bench trial in which a judge or panel of judges makes all decisions.

Exam Probability: **Low**

16. *Answer choices:*
(see index for correct answer)

- a. cultural
- b. imperative
- c. hierarchical perspective
- d. Jury Trial

*Guidance:* level 1

:: Debt ::

_____ is the trust which allows one party to provide money or resources to another party wherein the second party does not reimburse the first party immediately , but promises either to repay or return those resources at a later date. In other words, _____ is a method of making reciprocity formal, legally enforceable, and extensible to a large group of unrelated people.

Exam Probability: **High**

17. *Answer choices:*
(see index for correct answer)

- a. Credit
- b. Debtors Anonymous
- c. Financial assistance
- d. Money disorders

*Guidance:* level 1

:: ::

A _____ can mean the holder of a license, or in U.S. tort law, a _____ is a person who is on the property of another, despite the fact that the property is not open to the general public, because the owner of the property has allowed the _____ to enter. The status of a visitor as a _____ defines the legal rights of the visitor if they are injured due to the negligence of the property possessor .

Exam Probability: **Medium**

18. *Answer choices:*
(see index for correct answer)

- a. cultural
- b. open system
- c. hierarchical
- d. co-culture

*Guidance:* level 1

:: ::

A lawsuit is a proceeding by a party or parties against another in the civil court of law. The archaic term "suit in law" is found in only a small number of laws still in effect today. The term "lawsuit" is used in reference to a civil action brought in a court of law in which a plaintiff, a party who claims to have incurred loss as a result of a defendant's actions, demands a legal or equitable remedy. The defendant is required to respond to the plaintiff's complaint. If the plaintiff is successful, judgment is in the plaintiff's favor, and a variety of court orders may be issued to enforce a right, award damages, or impose a temporary or permanent injunction to prevent an act or compel an act. A declaratory judgment may be issued to prevent future legal disputes.

Exam Probability: **Medium**

19. *Answer choices:*
(see index for correct answer)

- a. Litigation
- b. deep-level diversity
- c. hierarchical perspective
- d. co-culture

*Guidance:* level 1

Labour law is the area of law most commonly relating to the relationship between trade unions, employers and the government.

Exam Probability: **High**

20. *Answer choices:*
(see index for correct answer)

- a. Medical resident work hours
- b. Employment law
- c. Holden v. Hardy
- d. Clyde Engineering Co Ltd v Cowburn

*Guidance:* level 1

:: Contract law ::

In contract law, a _____ is a promise which is not a condition of the contract or an innominate term: it is a term "not going to the root of the contract", and which only entitles the innocent party to damages if it is breached: i.e. the _____ is not true or the defaulting party does not perform the contract in accordance with the terms of the _____. A _____ is not guarantee. It is a mere promise. It may be enforced if it is breached by an award for the legal remedy of damages.

Exam Probability: **Medium**

21. *Answer choices:*
(see index for correct answer)

- a. Subcontractor
- b. Implied authority
- c. Undue influence
- d. Lease purchase contract

*Guidance:* level 1

:: ::

The _____ of 1977 is a United States federal law known primarily for two of its main provisions: one that addresses accounting transparency requirements under the Securities Exchange Act of 1934 and another concerning bribery of foreign officials. The Act was amended in 1988 and in 1998, and has been subject to continued congressional concerns, namely whether its enforcement discourages U.S. companies from investing abroad.

Exam Probability: **High**

22. *Answer choices:*
(see index for correct answer)

- a. hierarchical perspective
- b. Foreign Corrupt Practices Act
- c. Character
- d. information systems assessment

*Guidance:* level 1

---

:: Insurance law ::

_____ exists when an insured person derives a financial or other kind of benefit from the continuous existence, without repairment or damage, of the insured object . A person has an _____ in something when loss of or damage to that thing would cause the person to suffer a financial or other kind of loss.Normally, _____ is established by ownership, possession, or direct relationship. For example, people have _____ s in their own homes and vehicles, but not in their neighbors' homes and vehicles, and almost certainly not those of strangers.

Exam Probability: **High**

23. *Answer choices:*
(see index for correct answer)

- a. Hangarter v. Provident
- b. National Flood Insurance Program
- c. Motor vehicle insurance law in India
- d. Peracomo Inc. v. TELUS Communications Co.

*Guidance:* level 1

---

:: ::

A _____ is an organization, usually a group of people or a company, authorized to act as a single entity and recognized as such in law. Early incorporated entities were established by charter . Most jurisdictions now allow the creation of new _____ s through registration.

Exam Probability: **Medium**

24. *Answer choices:*
(see index for correct answer)

- a. Corporation
- b. functional perspective
- c. levels of analysis
- d. information systems assessment

*Guidance:* level 1

:: White-collar criminals ::

_____ refers to financially motivated, nonviolent crime committed by businesses and government professionals. It was first defined by the sociologist Edwin Sutherland in 1939 as "a crime committed by a person of respectability and high social status in the course of their occupation". Typical _____ s could include wage theft, fraud, bribery, Ponzi schemes, insider trading, labor racketeering, embezzlement, cybercrime, copyright infringement, money laundering, identity theft, and forgery. Lawyers can specialize in _____ .

Exam Probability: **High**

25. *Answer choices:*
(see index for correct answer)

- a. Tongsun Park
- b. Du Jun

*Guidance:* level 1

:: ::

A _____ , in law, is a set of facts sufficient to justify a right to sue to obtain money, property, or the enforcement of a right against another party. The term also refers to the legal theory upon which a plaintiff brings suit . The legal document which carries a claim is often called a `statement of claim` in English law, or a `complaint` in U.S. federal practice and in many U.S. states. It can be any communication notifying the party to whom it is addressed of an alleged fault which resulted in damages, often expressed in amount of money the receiving party should pay/reimburse.

Exam Probability: **High**

26. *Answer choices:*

(see index for correct answer)

- a. Sarbanes-Oxley act of 2002
- b. corporate values
- c. information systems assessment
- d. Cause of action

*Guidance:* level 1

:: Financial regulatory authorities of the United States ::

The _____ is the revenue service of the United States federal government. The government agency is a bureau of the Department of the Treasury, and is under the immediate direction of the Commissioner of Internal Revenue, who is appointed to a five-year term by the President of the United States. The IRS is responsible for collecting taxes and administering the Internal Revenue Code, the main body of federal statutory tax law of the United States. The duties of the IRS include providing tax assistance to taxpayers and pursuing and resolving instances of erroneous or fraudulent tax filings. The IRS has also overseen various benefits programs, and enforces portions of the Affordable Care Act.

Exam Probability: **Low**

27. *Answer choices:*

(see index for correct answer)

- a. Federal Deposit Insurance Corporation
- b. Office of the Comptroller of the Currency
- c. Federal Reserve Board
- d. Commodity Futures Trading Commission

:: ::

In contract law, rescission is an equitable remedy which allows a contractual party to cancel the contract. Parties may _____ if they are the victims of a vitiating factor, such as misrepresentation, mistake, duress, or undue influence. Rescission is the unwinding of a transaction. This is done to bring the parties, as far as possible, back to the position in which they were before they entered into a contract .

Exam Probability: **Low**

28. *Answer choices:*
(see index for correct answer)

- a. levels of analysis
- b. Rescind
- c. information systems assessment
- d. co-culture

:: ::

An _____ is the production of goods or related services within an economy. The major source of revenue of a group or company is the indicator of its relevant _____ . When a large group has multiple sources of revenue generation, it is considered to be working in different industries.
Manufacturing _____ became a key sector of production and labour in European and North American countries during the Industrial Revolution, upsetting previous mercantile and feudal economies. This came through many successive rapid advances in technology, such as the production of steel and coal.

Exam Probability: **Medium**

29. *Answer choices:*
(see index for correct answer)

- a. information systems assessment
- b. Industry
- c. deep-level diversity

- d. cultural

*Guidance:* level 1

---

:: Decision theory ::

A _____ is a deliberate system of principles to guide decisions and achieve rational outcomes. A _____ is a statement of intent, and is implemented as a procedure or protocol. Policies are generally adopted by a governance body within an organization. Policies can assist in both subjective and objective decision making. Policies to assist in subjective decision making usually assist senior management with decisions that must be based on the relative merits of a number of factors, and as a result are often hard to test objectively, e.g. work-life balance _____. In contrast policies to assist in objective decision making are usually operational in nature and can be objectively tested, e.g. password _____ .

Exam Probability: **Medium**

30. *Answer choices:*
(see index for correct answer)

- a. ELECTRE
- b. Taleb distribution
- c. Statistical murder
- d. Policy

*Guidance:* level 1

---

:: Decision theory ::

Within economics the concept of _____ is used to model worth or value, but its usage has evolved significantly over time. The term was introduced initially as a measure of pleasure or satisfaction within the theory of utilitarianism by moral philosophers such as Jeremy Bentham and John Stuart Mill. But the term has been adapted and reapplied within neoclassical economics, which dominates modern economic theory, as a _____ function that represents a consumer's preference ordering over a choice set. As such, it is devoid of its original interpretation as a measurement of the pleasure or satisfaction obtained by the consumer from that choice.

Exam Probability: **Low**

31. *Answer choices:*
(see index for correct answer)

- a. Recognition primed decision
- b. Strategic assumptions
- c. Decision matrix
- d. Utility

*Guidance:* level 1

---

:: ::

In logic and philosophy, an _____ is a series of statements , called the premises or premisses , intended to determine the degree of truth of another statement, the conclusion. The logical form of an _____ in a natural language can be represented in a symbolic formal language, and independently of natural language formally defined " _____ s" can be made in math and computer science.

Exam Probability: **Medium**

32. *Answer choices:*
(see index for correct answer)

- a. imperative
- b. hierarchical
- c. co-culture
- d. hierarchical perspective

*Guidance:* level 1

---

:: Forgery ::

_____ is a white-collar crime that generally refers to the false making or material alteration of a legal instrument with the specific intent to defraud anyone . Tampering with a certain legal instrument may be forbidden by law in some jurisdictions but such an offense is not related to _____ unless the tampered legal instrument was actually used in the course of the crime to defraud another person or entity. Copies, studio replicas, and reproductions are not considered forgeries, though they may later become forgeries through knowing and willful misrepresentations.

Exam Probability: **Medium**

33. *Answer choices:*

(see index for correct answer)

- a. Forgery
- b. Unapproved aircraft part
- c. Forgery Act 1830
- d. Forgery and Counterfeiting Act 1981

*Guidance:* level 1

---

:: Business law ::

The _____ , first published in 1952, is one of a number of Uniform Acts that have been established as law with the goal of harmonizing the laws of sales and other commercial transactions across the United States of America through UCC adoption by all 50 states, the District of Columbia, and the Territories of the United States.

Exam Probability: **High**

34. *Answer choices:*

(see index for correct answer)

- a. Uniform Commercial Code
- b. Operating lease
- c. Leave of absence
- d. Extraordinary resolution

*Guidance:* level 1

---

:: Business ::

_____ is a trade policy that does not restrict imports or exports; it can also be understood as the free market idea applied to international trade. In government, _____ is predominantly advocated by political parties that hold liberal economic positions while economically left-wing and nationalist political parties generally support protectionism, the opposite of _____ .

Exam Probability: **Low**

35. *Answer choices:*

(see index for correct answer)

- a. Planned obsolescence
- b. Growth platform

- c. Free trade
- d. GoCardless

Guidance: level 1

---

:: Legal doctrines and principles ::

_____ is a doctrine that a party is responsible for acts of their agents. For example, in the United States, there are circumstances when an employer is liable for acts of employees performed within the course of their employment. This rule is also called the master-servant rule, recognized in both common law and civil law jurisdictions.

Exam Probability: **Medium**

36. *Answer choices:*
(see index for correct answer)

- a. Caveat emptor
- b. Attractive nuisance
- c. Act of state
- d. Respondeat superior

Guidance: level 1

---

:: Legal terms ::

_____ s may be governments, corporations or investment trusts. _____ s are legally responsible for the obligations of the issue and for reporting financial conditions, material developments and any other operational activities as required by the regulations of their jurisdictions.

Exam Probability: **High**

37. *Answer choices:*
(see index for correct answer)

- a. Divesting abandonment
- b. Officer of the court
- c. Plain meaning rule
- d. Issuer

Guidance: level 1

---

:: Legal terms ::

_____ , or non-absolute contributory negligence outside the United States, is a partial legal defense that reduces the amount of damages that a plaintiff can recover in a negligence-based claim, based upon the degree to which the plaintiff's own negligence contributed to cause the injury. When the defense is asserted, the factfinder, usually a jury, must decide the degree to which the plaintiff's negligence and the combined negligence of all other relevant actors all contributed to cause the plaintiff's damages. It is a modification of the doctrine of contributory negligence that disallows any recovery by a plaintiff whose negligence contributed even minimally to causing the damages.

Exam Probability: **Low**

38. *Answer choices:*
(see index for correct answer)

- a. Additur
- b. Comparative negligence
- c. Parole
- d. Forfeiture

*Guidance:* level 1

:: Fraud ::

In law, _____ is intentional deception to secure unfair or unlawful gain, or to deprive a victim of a legal right. _____ can violate civil law , a criminal law , or it may cause no loss of money, property or legal right but still be an element of another civil or criminal wrong. The purpose of _____ may be monetary gain or other benefits, for example by obtaining a passport, travel document, or driver's license, or mortgage _____ , where the perpetrator may attempt to qualify for a mortgage by way of false statements.

Exam Probability: **Medium**

39. *Answer choices:*
(see index for correct answer)

- a. Cheat sheet
- b. Telephone numbers in the Dominican Republic
- c. Mussolini diaries
- d. Fraud

:: ::

_____ is a concept of English common law and is a necessity for simple contracts but not for special contracts . The concept has been adopted by other common law jurisdictions, including the US.

Exam Probability: **High**

40. *Answer choices:*
(see index for correct answer)

- a. Consideration
- b. hierarchical
- c. cultural
- d. personal values

:: ::

In English law, a _____ or _____ absolute is an estate in land, a form of freehold ownership. It is a way that real estate and land may be owned in common law countries, and is the highest possible ownership interest that can be held in real property. Allodial title is reserved to governments under a civil law structure. The rights of the _____ owner are limited by government powers of taxation, compulsory purchase, police power, and escheat, and it could also be limited further by certain encumbrances or conditions in the deed, such as, for example, a condition that required the land to be used as a public park, with a reversion interest in the grantor if the condition fails; this is a _____ conditional.

Exam Probability: **Low**

41. *Answer choices:*
(see index for correct answer)

- a. Sarbanes-Oxley act of 2002
- b. surface-level diversity
- c. Fee simple
- d. cultural

_____ is that part of a civil law legal system which is part of the jus commune that involves relationships between individuals, such as the law of contracts or torts , and the law of obligations . It is to be distinguished from public law, which deals with relationships between both natural and artificial persons and the state, including regulatory statutes, penal law and other law that affects the public order. In general terms, _____ involves interactions between private citizens, whereas public law involves interrelations between the state and the general population.

Exam Probability: **Low**

42. *Answer choices:*
(see index for correct answer)

- a. Private law
- b. interpersonal communication
- c. co-culture
- d. imperative

*Guidance:* level 1

:: Anti-competitive behaviour ::

Restraints of trade is a common law doctrine relating to the enforceability of contractual restrictions on freedom to conduct business. It is a precursor of modern competition law. In an old leading case of Mitchel v Reynolds Lord Smith LC said,

Exam Probability: **High**

43. *Answer choices:*
(see index for correct answer)

- a. Angelgate
- b. Lang Law
- c. Horizontal territorial allocation
- d. Restraint of trade

*Guidance:* level 1

:: International relations ::

_____ is double mindedness or double heartedness in duplicity, fraud, or deception. It may involve intentional deceit of others, or self-deception.

Exam Probability: **Medium**

44. *Answer choices:*
(see index for correct answer)

- a. United Nations Independent Expert on the Promotion of a Democratic and Equitable International Order
- b. Equal Treatment Directive
- c. Cornelius Ryan Award
- d. Bad faith

*Guidance:* level 1

:: Mereology ::

_____ , in the abstract, is what belongs to or with something, whether as an attribute or as a component of said thing. In the context of this article, it is one or more components , whether physical or incorporeal, of a person's estate; or so belonging to, as in being owned by, a person or jointly a group of people or a legal entity like a corporation or even a society. Depending on the nature of the _____ , an owner of _____ has the right to consume, alter, share, redefine, rent, mortgage, pawn, sell, exchange, transfer, give away or destroy it, or to exclude others from doing these things, as well as to perhaps abandon it; whereas regardless of the nature of the _____ , the owner thereof has the right to properly use it , or at the very least exclusively keep it.

Exam Probability: **Medium**

45. *Answer choices:*
(see index for correct answer)

- a. Mereology
- b. Meronomy
- c. Mereological nihilism
- d. Property

*Guidance:* level 1

:: ::

_____ is a process whereby a person assumes the parenting of another, usually a child, from that person's biological or legal parent or parents. Legal _____ s permanently transfers all rights and responsibilities, along with filiation, from the biological parent or parents.

Exam Probability: **Medium**

46. *Answer choices:*
(see index for correct answer)

- a. empathy
- b. Adoption
- c. surface-level diversity
- d. information systems assessment

*Guidance:* level 1

:: ::

A _____ is a formal presentation of a matter such as a complaint, indictment or bill of exchange. In early-medieval England, juries of _____ would hear inquests in order to establish whether someone should be presented for a crime.

Exam Probability: **High**

47. *Answer choices:*
(see index for correct answer)

- a. functional perspective
- b. deep-level diversity
- c. hierarchical
- d. personal values

*Guidance:* level 1

:: Business law ::

A _____ is a business entity created by two or more parties, generally characterized by shared ownership, shared returns and risks, and shared governance. Companies typically pursue _____ s for one of four reasons: to access a new market, particularly emerging markets; to gain scale efficiencies by combining assets and operations; to share risk for major investments or projects; or to access skills and capabilities.

Exam Probability: **Medium**

48. *Answer choices:*
(see index for correct answer)

- a. Joint venture
- b. Administration
- c. WIPO Copyright Treaty
- d. Double ticketing

*Guidance:* level 1

:: Information technology audit ::

_____ is the act of using a computer to take or alter electronic data, or to gain unlawful use of a computer or system. In the United States, _____ is specifically proscribed by the _____ and Abuse Act, which criminalizes computer-related acts under federal jurisdiction. Types of _____ include.

Exam Probability: **Low**

49. *Answer choices:*
(see index for correct answer)

- a. Host protected area
- b. Code audit
- c. David Coderre
- d. Computer fraud

*Guidance:* level 1

:: Contract law ::

_____ is a legal cause of action and a type of civil wrong, in which a binding agreement or bargained-for exchange is not honored by one or more of the parties to the contract by non-performance or interference with the other party's performance. Breach occurs when a party to a contract fails to fulfill its obligation as described in the contract, or communicates an intent to fail the obligation or otherwise appears not to be able to perform its obligation under the contract. Where there is _____ , the resulting damages will have to be paid by the party breaching the contract to the aggrieved party.

Exam Probability: **Medium**

50. *Answer choices:*
(see index for correct answer)

- a. Perfect tender
- b. Parent company guarantee
- c. Tertius
- d. Breach of contract

*Guidance:* level 1

:: ::

At common law, _____ are a remedy in the form of a monetary award to be paid to a claimant as compensation for loss or injury. To warrant the award, the claimant must show that a breach of duty has caused foreseeable loss. To be recognised at law, the loss must involve damage to property, or mental or physical injury; pure economic loss is rarely recognised for the award of

_____ .

Exam Probability: **Low**

51. *Answer choices:*
(see index for correct answer)

- a. corporate values
- b. hierarchical
- c. cultural
- d. surface-level diversity

*Guidance:* level 1

:: ::

A _____ , in common law jurisdictions, is a civil wrong that causes a claimant to suffer loss or harm resulting in legal liability for the person who commits the _____ ious act. It can include the intentional infliction of emotional distress, negligence, financial losses, injuries, invasion of privacy, and many other things.

Exam Probability: **Medium**

52. *Answer choices:*
(see index for correct answer)

- a. interpersonal communication
- b. levels of analysis
- c. surface-level diversity
- d. Tort

*Guidance:* level 1

:: Legal reasoning ::

_____ is a Latin expression meaning on its first encounter or at first sight. The literal translation would be "at first face" or "at first appearance", from the feminine forms of primus and facies , both in the ablative case. In modern, colloquial and conversational English, a common translation would be "on the face of it". The term _____ is used in modern legal English to signify that upon initial examination, sufficient corroborating evidence appears to exist to support a case. In common law jurisdictions, _____ denotes evidence that, unless rebutted, would be sufficient to prove a particular proposition or fact. The term is used similarly in academic philosophy. Most legal proceedings, in most jurisdictions, require a _____ case to exist, following which proceedings may then commence to test it, and create a ruling.

Exam Probability: **Medium**

53. *Answer choices:*
(see index for correct answer)

- a. Reasonable man
- b. Prima facie
- c. Probable cause

*Guidance:* level 1

Credit is the trust which allows one party to provide money or resources to another party wherein the second party does not reimburse the first party immediately , but promises either to repay or return those resources at a later date. In other words, credit is a method of making reciprocity formal, legally enforceable, and extensible to a large group of unrelated people.

Exam Probability: **Medium**

54. *Answer choices:*
(see index for correct answer)

- a. co-culture
- b. personal values
- c. deep-level diversity
- d. Consumer credit

*Guidance:* level 1

---

:: Real estate ::

_____ , real estate, realty, or immovable property  In English common law refers to landed properties belonging to  some person. It include all structures, crops, buildings, machinery, wells, dams, ponds, mines, canals, and roads, among other things. The term is historic, arising from the now-discontinued form of action, which distinguish between _____ disputes and personal property disputes. Personal property was, and continues to refer to all properties that are not real properties.

Exam Probability: **Low**

55. *Answer choices:*
(see index for correct answer)

- a. Landed nobility
- b. Corporate Real Estate
- c. Pad site
- d. Real property

*Guidance:* level 1

---

:: Business law ::

A _____ is a contractual arrangement calling for the lessee to pay the lessor for use of an asset. Property, buildings and vehicles are common assets that are _____ d. Industrial or business equipment is also _____ d.

Exam Probability: **Medium**

56. *Answer choices:*
(see index for correct answer)

- a. Statutory liability
- b. Lien
- c. Country of origin
- d. Business license

*Guidance:* level 1

:: Legal terms ::

_____ , a form of alternative dispute resolution , is a way to resolve disputes outside the courts. The dispute will be decided by one or more persons , which renders the " _____ award". An _____ award is legally binding on both sides and enforceable in the courts.

Exam Probability: **Medium**

57. *Answer choices:*
(see index for correct answer)

- a. Fair competition
- b. Incorporation of international law
- c. vacant possession
- d. Arbitration

*Guidance:* level 1

:: Business models ::

A _____ is "an autonomous association of persons united voluntarily to meet their common economic, social, and cultural needs and aspirations through a jointly-owned and democratically-controlled enterprise". _____ s may include.

58. *Answer choices:*

(see index for correct answer)

- a. Copy to China
- b. Lawyers on Demand
- c. Open Music Model
- d. Cooperative

*Guidance:* level 1

---

:: Contract law ::

In the United States, the _____ rule refers to the legal right for a buyer of goods to insist upon " _____ " by the seller. In a contract for the sale of goods, if the goods fail to conform exactly to the description in the contract  the buyer may nonetheless accept the goods, or reject the goods, or reject the nonconforming part of the tender and accept the conforming part. The buyer does not have an unfettered ability to reject tender.

Exam Probability: **Medium**

59. *Answer choices:*

(see index for correct answer)

- a. Contractual term
- b. Ticket cases
- c. Perfect tender
- d. Recording contract

*Guidance:* level 1

## Finance

Finance is a field that is concerned with the allocation (investment) of assets and liabilities over space and time, often under conditions of risk or uncertainty. Finance can also be defined as the science of money management. Participants in the market aim to price assets based on their risk level, fundamental value, and their expected rate of return. Finance can be split into three sub-categories: public finance, corporate finance and personal finance.

---

:: Accounting in the United States ::

_____ is the title of qualified accountants in numerous countries in the English-speaking world. In the United States, the CPA is a license to provide accounting services to the public. It is awarded by each of the 50 states for practice in that state. Additionally, almost every state has passed mobility laws to allow CPAs from other states to practice in their state. State licensing requirements vary, but the minimum standard requirements include passing the Uniform _____ Examination, 150 semester units of college education, and one year of accounting related experience.

Exam Probability: **High**

1. *Answer choices:*
(see index for correct answer)

- a. Association of Certified Fraud Examiners
- b. Certified Public Accountant
- c. Federal Accounting Standards Advisory Board
- d. Norwalk Agreement

*Guidance:* level 1

---

:: Accounting terminology ::

_____ of something is, in finance, the adding together of interest or different investments over a period of time. It holds specific meanings in accounting, where it can refer to accounts on a balance sheet that represent liabilities and non-cash-based assets used in _____ -based accounting. These types of accounts include, among others, accounts payable, accounts receivable, goodwill, deferred tax liability and future interest expense.

Exam Probability. **High**

2. *Answer choices:*

(see index for correct answer)

- a. Fair value accounting
- b. Checkoff
- c. revenue recognition principle
- d. Record to report

*Guidance:* level 1

---

:: Financial ratios ::

A _____ or accounting ratio is a relative magnitude of two selected numerical values taken from an enterprise's financial statements. Often used in accounting, there are many standard ratios used to try to evaluate the overall financial condition of a corporation or other organization. _____ s may be used by managers within a firm, by current and potential shareholders of a firm, and by a firm's creditors. Financial analysts use _____ s to compare the strengths and weaknesses in various companies. If shares in a company are traded in a financial market, the market price of the shares is used in certain _____ s.

Exam Probability: **Medium**

3. *Answer choices:*

(see index for correct answer)

- a. Financial ratio
- b. Dividend yield
- c. DuPont analysis
- d. Debt-to-equity ratio

*Guidance:* level 1

---

_____ is the field of accounting concerned with the summary, analysis and reporting of financial transactions related to a business. This involves the preparation of financial statements available for public use. Stockholders, suppliers, banks, employees, government agencies, business owners, and other stakeholders are examples of people interested in receiving such information for decision making purposes.

Exam Probability: **High**

4. *Answer choices:*

(see index for correct answer)

- a. Financial accounting
- b. process perspective
- c. levels of analysis
- d. cultural

*Guidance:* level 1

:: Money ::

Cash and _____ s are the most liquid current assets found on a business's balance sheet. _____ s are short-term commitments "with temporarily idle cash and easily convertible into a known cash amount". An investment normally counts to be a _____ when it has a short maturity period of 90 days or less, and can be included in the cash and _____ s balance from the date of acquisition when it carries an insignificant risk of changes in the asset value; with more than 90 days maturity, the asset is not considered as cash and _____ s. Equity investments mostly are excluded from _____ s, unless they are essentially _____ s, for instance, if the preferred shares acquired within a short maturity period and with specified recovery date.

Exam Probability: **Low**

5. *Answer choices:*

(see index for correct answer)

- a. Cash equivalent
- b. Coin of account
- c. Dam
- d. Slang terms for money

:: ::

_____ involves decision making. It can include judging the merits of multiple options and selecting one or more of them. One can make a _____ between imagined options or between real options followed by the corresponding action. For example, a traveler might choose a route for a journey based on the preference of arriving at a given destination as soon as possible. The preferred route can then follow from information such as the length of each of the possible routes, traffic conditions, etc. The arrival at a _____ can include more complex motivators such as cognition, instinct, and feeling.

Exam Probability: **Medium**

6. *Answer choices:*

- a. Choice
- b. cultural
- c. functional perspective
- d. surface-level diversity

:: Financial accounting ::

_____ refers to any one of several methods by which a company, for `financial accounting` or tax purposes, depreciates a fixed asset in such a way that the amount of depreciation taken each year is higher during the earlier years of an asset's life. For financial accounting purposes, _____ is expected to be much more productive during its early years, so that depreciation expense will more accurately represent how much of an asset's usefulness is being used up each year. For tax purposes, _____ provides a way of deferring corporate income taxes by reducing taxable income in current years, in exchange for increased taxable income in future years. This is a valuable tax incentive that encourages businesses to purchase new assets.

Exam Probability: **High**

7. *Answer choices:*

- a. Deferred financing cost
- b. Accelerated depreciation
- c. Commuted cash value
- d. Net worth

*Guidance:* level 1

---

:: ::

_____ is the process whereby a business sets the price at which it will sell its products and services, and may be part of the business's marketing plan. In setting prices, the business will take into account the price at which it could acquire the goods, the manufacturing cost, the market place, competition, market condition, brand, and quality of product.

Exam Probability: **Medium**

8. *Answer choices:*
(see index for correct answer)

- a. Character
- b. Pricing
- c. process perspective
- d. levels of analysis

*Guidance:* level 1

---

:: Inventory ::

_____ is the amount of inventory a company has in stock at the end of its fiscal year. It is closely related with _____ cost, which is the amount of money spent to get these goods in stock. It should be calculated at the lower of cost or market.

Exam Probability: **Low**

9. *Answer choices:*
(see index for correct answer)

- a. LIFO
- b. Stock keeping unit
- c. Reorder point
- d. Inventory bounce

*Guidance:* level 1

---

:: Mutualism (movement) ::

A _____ is a professionally managed investment fund that pools money from many investors to purchase securities. These investors may be retail or institutional in nature.

Exam Probability: **High**

10. *Answer choices.*
(see index for correct answer)

- a. Sovereigns of Industry
- b. Mutual organization
- c. Benefit society
- d. Mutual fund

*Guidance:* level 1

---

:: Generally Accepted Accounting Principles ::

In business and accounting, _____ is an entity's income minus cost of goods sold, expenses and taxes for an accounting period. It is computed as the residual of all revenues and gains over all expenses and losses for the period, and has also been defined as the net increase in shareholders' equity that results from a company's operations. In the context of the presentation of financial statements, the IFRS Foundation defines _____ as synonymous with profit and loss. The difference between revenue and the cost of making a product or providing a service, before deducting overheads, payroll, taxation, and interest payments. This is different from operating income .

Exam Probability: **Medium**

11. *Answer choices:*
(see index for correct answer)

- a. Net profit
- b. Net income
- c. Gross income
- d. Earnings before interest and taxes

*Guidance:* level 1

---

:: Retirement ::

An _____ is a series of payments made at equal intervals. Examples of annuities are regular deposits to a savings account, monthly home mortgage payments, monthly insurance payments and pension payments. Annuities can be classified by the frequency of payment dates. The payments may be made weekly, monthly, quarterly, yearly, or at any other regular interval of time.

Exam Probability: **Low**

12. *Answer choices:*
<sub>(see index for correct answer)</sub>

- a. Retirement Estimator
- b. Retirement Funds Administrators
- c. Beadsman
- d. Annuity

*Guidance:* level 1

:: ::

Business is the activity of making one's living or making money by producing or buying and selling products . Simply put, it is "any activity or enterprise entered into for profit. It does not mean it is a company, a corporation, partnership, or have any such formal organization, but it can range from a street peddler to General Motors."

Exam Probability: **Low**

13. *Answer choices:*
<sub>(see index for correct answer)</sub>

- a. interpersonal communication
- b. corporate values
- c. Firm
- d. deep-level diversity

*Guidance:* level 1

:: ::

_____ is the consumption and saving opportunity gained by an entity within a specified timeframe, which is generally expressed in monetary terms. For households and individuals, " _____ is the sum of all the wages, salaries, profits, interest payments, rents, and other forms of earnings received in a given period of time."

Exam Probability: **Medium**

14. *Answer choices:*

- a. personal values
- b. levels of analysis
- c. Income
- d. information systems assessment

*Guidance:* level 1

---

:: Commerce ::

A _____ , is a document acknowledging that a person has received money or property in payment following a sale or other transfer of goods or provision of a service. All _____ s must have the date of purchase on them. If the recipient of the payment is legally required to collect sales tax or VAT from the customer, the amount would be added to the _____ and the collection would be deemed to have been on behalf of the relevant tax authority. In many countries, a retailer is required to include the sales tax or VAT in the displayed price of goods sold, from which the tax amount would be calculated at point of sale and remitted to the tax authorities in due course. Similarly, amounts may be deducted from amounts payable, as in the case of wage withholding taxes. On the other hand, tips or other gratuities given by a customer, for example in a restaurant, would not form part of the payment amount or appear on the _____ .

Exam Probability: **Low**

15. *Answer choices:*

- a. Council of the Americas
- b. Receipt
- c. Card association
- d. GT Nexus

:: Asset ::

In accounting, a _____ is any asset which can reasonably be expected to be sold, consumed, or exhausted through the normal operations of a business within the current fiscal year or operating cycle . Typical _____ s include cash, cash equivalents, short-term investments , accounts receivable, stock inventory, supplies, and the portion of prepaid liabilities which will be paid within a year.In simple words, assets which are held for a short period are known as _____ s. Such assets are expected to be realised in cash or consumed during the normal operating cycle of the business.

Exam Probability: **High**

16. *Answer choices:*
(see index for correct answer)

- a. Fixed asset
- b. Current asset

:: Business ::

The seller, or the provider of the goods or services, completes a sale in response to an acquisition, appropriation, requisition or a direct interaction with the buyer at the point of sale. There is a passing of title of the item, and the settlement of a price, in which agreement is reached on a price for which transfer of ownership of the item will occur. The seller, not the purchaser typically executes the sale and it may be completed prior to the obligation of payment. In the case of indirect interaction, a person who sells goods or service on behalf of the owner is known as a salesman or saleswoman or salesperson, but this often refers to someone _____ goods in a store/shop, in which case other terms are also common, including salesclerk, shop assistant, and retail clerk.

Exam Probability: **Medium**

17. *Answer choices:*
(see index for correct answer)

- a. Door-to-door
- b. Business interaction networks
- c. Selling
- d. NEWSCYCLE Solutions

*Guidance:* level 1

---

:: ::

A _____ is an individual or institution that legally owns one or more shares of stock in a public or private corporation. _____ s may be referred to as members of a corporation. Legally, a person is not a _____ in a corporation until their name and other details are entered in the corporation's register of _____ s or members.

Exam Probability: **High**

18. *Answer choices:*
(see index for correct answer)

- a. Shareholder
- b. Sarbanes-Oxley act of 2002
- c. Character
- d. hierarchical perspective

*Guidance:* level 1

---

:: Generally Accepted Accounting Principles ::

_____ , also referred to as the bottom line, net income, or net earnings is a measure of the profitability of a venture after accounting for all costs and taxes. It is the actual profit, and includes the operating expenses that are excluded from gross profit.

Exam Probability: **High**

19. *Answer choices:*
(see index for correct answer)

- a. Gross sales
- b. Net profit
- c. Deferred income
- d. Deferral

*Guidance:* level 1

---

Total _____ is a method of Accounting cost which entails the full cost of manufacturing or providing a service. TAC includes not just the costs of materials and labour, but also of all manufacturing overheads . The cost of each cost center can be direct or indirect. The direct cost can be easily identified with individual cost centers. Whereas indirect cost cannot be easily identified with the cost center. The distribution of overhead among the departments is called apportionment.

Exam Probability: **High**

20. *Answer choices:*
(see index for correct answer)

- a. Absorption costing
- b. Fund accounting
- c. Share premium
- d. Chart of accounts

*Guidance:* level 1

---

:: ::

_____ is the withdrawal from one`s position or occupation or from one`s active working life. A person may also semi-retire by reducing work hours.

Exam Probability: **Low**

21. *Answer choices:*
(see index for correct answer)

- a. Retirement
- b. open system
- c. interpersonal communication
- d. process perspective

*Guidance:* level 1

---

:: ::

An _____ is an asset that lacks physical substance. It is defined in opposition to physical assets such as machinery and buildings. An _____ is usually very hard to evaluate. Patents, copyrights, franchises, goodwill, trademarks, and trade names. The general interpretation also includes software and other intangible computer based assets are all examples of _____ s. _____ s generally—though not necessarily—suffer from typical market failures of non-rivalry and non-excludability.

Exam Probability: **Medium**

22. *Answer choices:*
(see index for correct answer)

- a. interpersonal communication
- b. corporate values
- c. Intangible asset
- d. surface-level diversity

*Guidance:* level 1

:: ::

_____ is a political and social philosophy promoting traditional social institutions in the context of culture and civilization. The central tenets of _____ include tradition, human imperfection, organic society, hierarchy, authority, and property rights. Conservatives seek to preserve a range of institutions such as religion, parliamentary government, and property rights, with the aim of emphasizing social stability and continuity. The more traditional elements—reactionaries—oppose modernism and seek a return to "the way things were".

Exam Probability: **Medium**

23. *Answer choices:*
(see index for correct answer)

- a. Conservatism
- b. corporate values
- c. Character
- d. functional perspective

*Guidance:* level 1

:: Financial ratios ::

_____ or asset turns is a financial ratio that measures the efficiency of a company's use of its assets in generating sales revenue or sales income to the company.

Exam Probability: **Low**

24. *Answer choices:*
(see index for correct answer)

- a. Return on equity
- b. Financial result
- c. Asset turnover
- d. Net interest income

*Guidance:* level 1

:: Business law ::

A _____ is a group of people who jointly supervise the activities of an organization, which can be either a for-profit business, nonprofit organization, or a government agency. Such a board's powers, duties, and responsibilities are determined by government regulations and the organization's own constitution and bylaws. These authorities may specify the number of members of the board, how they are to be chosen, and how often they are to meet.

Exam Probability: **High**

25. *Answer choices:*
(see index for correct answer)

- a. Subordination
- b. Forward-looking statement
- c. United Kingdom commercial law
- d. Board of directors

*Guidance:* level 1

:: Planning ::

_____ is a high level plan to achieve one or more goals under conditions of uncertainty. In the sense of the "art of the general," which included several subsets of skills including tactics, siegecraft, logistics etc., the term came into use in the 6th century C.E. in East Roman terminology, and was translated into Western vernacular languages only in the 18th century. From then until the 20th century, the word "_____" came to denote "a comprehensive way to try to pursue political ends, including the threat or actual use of force, in a dialectic of wills" in a military conflict, in which both adversaries interact.

Exam Probability: **High**

26. *Answer choices:*
(see index for correct answer)

- a. BLUF
- b. Strategy
- c. School timetable
- d. Enterprise architecture planning

*Guidance:* level 1

---

:: ::

From an accounting perspective, _____ is crucial because _____ and _____ taxes considerably affect the net income of most companies and because they are subject to laws and regulations .

Exam Probability: **Medium**

27. *Answer choices:*
(see index for correct answer)

- a. corporate values
- b. Character
- c. deep-level diversity
- d. Payroll

*Guidance:* level 1

---

:: Income ::

_____ is a ratio between the net profit and cost of investment resulting from an investment of some resources. A high ROI means the investment's gains favorably to its cost. As a performance measure, ROI is used to evaluate the efficiency of an investment or to compare the efficiencies of several different investments. In purely economic terms, it is one way of relating profits to capital invested. _____ is a performance measure used by businesses to identify the efficiency of an investment or number of different investments.

Exam Probability: **Medium**

28. *Answer choices:*
(see index for correct answer)

- a. Independent income
- b. Stipend
- c. Return on investment
- d. Real estate investing

*Guidance:* level 1

:: Marketing ::

_____ is a financial mechanism in which a debtor obtains the right to delay payments to a creditor, for a defined period of time, in exchange for a charge or fee. Essentially, the party that owes money in the present purchases the right to delay the payment until some future date. The discount, or charge, is the difference between the original amount owed in the present and the amount that has to be paid in the future to settle the debt.

Exam Probability: **Medium**

29. *Answer choices:*
(see index for correct answer)

- a. Osborne effect
- b. Electronic money
- c. Double-loop marketing
- d. Marketing operations

*Guidance:* level 1

:: ::

_____ , often abbreviated as B/E in finance, is the point of balance making neither a profit nor a loss. The term originates in finance but the concept has been applied in other fields.

Exam Probability: **High**

30. *Answer choices:*
(see index for correct answer)

- a. Character
- b. personal values
- c. imperative
- d. Break-even

*Guidance:* level 1

:: ::

In accounting, the _____ is a measure of the number of times inventory is sold or used in a time period such as a year. It is calculated to see if a business has an excessive inventory in comparison to its sales level. The equation for _____ equals the cost of goods sold divided by the average inventory. _____ is also known as inventory turns, merchandise turnover, stockturn, stock turns, turns, and stock turnover.

Exam Probability: **Medium**

31. *Answer choices:*
(see index for correct answer)

- a. open system
- b. cultural
- c. similarity-attraction theory
- d. Inventory turnover

*Guidance:* level 1

:: Generally Accepted Accounting Principles ::

The first published description of the process is found in Luca Pacioli's 1494 work Summa de arithmetica, in the section titled Particularis de Computis et Scripturis. Although he did not use the term, he essentially prescribed a technique similar to a post-closing _____ .

Exam Probability: **Low**

32. *Answer choices:*
(see index for correct answer)

- a. Treasury stock
- b. Matching principle
- c. Construction in progress
- d. Trial balance

*Guidance:* level 1

---

:: Investment ::

_____ , and investment appraisal, is the planning process used to determine whether an organization's long term investments such as new machinery, replacement of machinery, new plants, new products, and research development projects are worth the funding of cash through the firm's capitalization structure . It is the process of allocating resources for major capital, or investment, expenditures. One of the primary goals of _____ investments is to increase the value of the firm to the shareholders.

Exam Probability: **High**

33. *Answer choices:*
(see index for correct answer)

- a. Lehman scale
- b. Marginal product of capital
- c. Multi-manager investment
- d. Strategic block investing

*Guidance:* level 1

---

:: Financial ratios ::

The _____ is a financial ratio indicating the relative proportion of shareholders' equity and debt used to finance a company's assets. Closely related to leveraging, the ratio is also known as risk, gearing or leverage. The two components are often taken from the firm's balance sheet or statement of financial position , but the ratio may also be calculated using market values for both, if the company's debt and equity are publicly traded, or using a combination of book value for debt and market value for equity financially.

Exam Probability: **Medium**

34. *Answer choices:*
(see index for correct answer)

- a. Put/call ratio
- b. Interest coverage ratio
- c. Debt ratio
- d. Debt-to-equity ratio

*Guidance:* level 1

:: ::

A _____ is any person who contracts to acquire an asset in return for some form of consideration.

Exam Probability: **Low**

35. *Answer choices:*
(see index for correct answer)

- a. functional perspective
- b. surface-level diversity
- c. corporate values
- d. Buyer

*Guidance:* level 1

:: Expense ::

An _____ , operating expenditure, operational expense, operational expenditure or opex is an ongoing cost for running a product, business, or system. Its counterpart, a capital expenditure , is the cost of developing or providing non-consumable parts for the product or system. For example, the purchase of a photocopier involves capex, and the annual paper, toner, power and maintenance costs represents opex. For larger systems like businesses, opex may also include the cost of workers and facility expenses such as rent and utilities.

Exam Probability: **High**

36. *Answer choices:*
(see index for correct answer)

- a. Corporate travel
- b. Business overhead expense disability insurance
- c. Momentem
- d. Freight expense

*Guidance:* level 1

:: Business law ::

The expression " _____ " is somewhat confusing as it has a different meaning based on the context that is under consideration.From a product characteristic stand point, this type of a lease, as distinguished from a finance lease, is one where the lessor takes residual risk. As such, the lease is non full payout. From an accounting stand point, this type of lease results in off balance sheet financing.

Exam Probability: **Low**

37. *Answer choices:*
(see index for correct answer)

- a. Operating lease
- b. Ordinary course of business
- c. Rules of origin
- d. Retained interest

*Guidance:* level 1

:: Business economics ::

A _____ is a term used primarily in cost accounting to describe something to which costs are assigned. Common examples of _____ s are: product lines, geographic territories, customers, departments or anything else for which management would like to quantify cost.

Exam Probability: **High**

38. *Answer choices:*
(see index for correct answer)

- a. Willingness to accept
- b. Average daily rate
- c. Model audit
- d. Cost object

*Guidance:* level 1

---

:: Marketing ::

_____ or stock is the goods and materials that a business holds for the ultimate goal of resale .

Exam Probability: **Medium**

39. *Answer choices:*
(see index for correct answer)

- a. Inventory
- b. Marketing Week
- c. Customer lifetime value
- d. Intent scale translation

*Guidance:* level 1

---

:: Bonds (finance) ::

In finance, a _____ or convertible note or convertible debt is a type of bond that the holder can convert into a specified number of shares of common stock in the issuing company or cash of equal value. It is a hybrid security with debt- and equity-like features. It originated in the mid-19th century, and was used by early speculators such as Jacob Little and Daniel Drew to counter market cornering.

40. *Answer choices:*
(see index for correct answer)

- a. Amortizing loan
- b. Reinsurance sidecar
- c. Convertible bond
- d. Nominal yield

*Guidance:* level 1

---

:: Generally Accepted Accounting Principles ::

In accounting, an economic item's _____ is the original nominal monetary value of that item. _____ accounting involves reporting assets and liabilities at their _____ s, which are not updated for changes in the items' values. Consequently, the amounts reported for these balance sheet items often differ from their current economic or market values.

Exam Probability: **High**

41. *Answer choices:*
(see index for correct answer)

- a. Generally Accepted Accounting Practice
- b. Revenue recognition
- c. Pro forma
- d. Historical cost

*Guidance:* level 1

---

:: International trade ::

_____ involves the transfer of goods or services from one person or entity to another, often in exchange for money. A system or network that allows _____ is called a market.

Exam Probability: **Low**

42. *Answer choices:*
(see index for correct answer)

- a. Trade
- b. Trade in services
- c. Linder hypothesis

- d. OPEC

---

:: Financial ratios ::

_____ is a measure of how revenue growth translates into growth in operating income. It is a measure of leverage, and of how risky, or volatile, a company's operating income is.

Exam Probability: **Medium**

43. *Answer choices:*

(see index for correct answer)

- a. Gross margin
- b. Profit margin
- c. Sharpe ratio
- d. Market-to-book

---

:: Financial statements ::

In financial accounting, a _____ or statement of financial position or statement of financial condition is a summary of the financial balances of an individual or organization, whether it be a sole proprietorship, a business partnership, a corporation, private limited company or other organization such as Government or not-for-profit entity. Assets, liabilities and ownership equity are listed as of a specific date, such as the end of its financial year. A _____ is often described as a "snapshot of a company's financial condition". Of the four basic financial statements, the _____ is the only statement which applies to a single point in time of a business' calendar year.

Exam Probability: **Low**

44. *Answer choices:*

(see index for correct answer)

- a. Government financial statements
- b. Consolidated financial statement
- c. Statements on auditing standards
- d. Quarterly finance report

---

:: Leasing ::

A finance lease is a type of lease in which a finance company is typically the legal owner of the asset for the duration of the lease, while the lessee not only has operating control over the asset, but also has a some share of the economic risks and returns from the change in the valuation of the underlying asset.

Exam Probability: **High**

45. *Answer choices:*
(see index for correct answer)

- a. Capital lease
- b. Synthetic lease

---

:: ::

_____ is the administration of an organization, whether it is a business, a not-for-profit organization, or government body. _____ includes the activities of setting the strategy of an organization and coordinating the efforts of its employees to accomplish its objectives through the application of available resources, such as financial, natural, technological, and human resources. The term " _____ " may also refer to those people who manage an organization.

Exam Probability: **Low**

46. *Answer choices:*
(see index for correct answer)

- a. personal values
- b. information systems assessment
- c. Sarbanes-Oxley act of 2002
- d. Management

---

:: Management accounting ::

_____ is a managerial accounting cost concept. Under this method, manufacturing overhead is incurred in the period that a product is produced. This addresses the issue of absorption costing that allows income to rise as production rises. Under an absorption cost method, management can push forward costs to the next period when products are sold. This artificially inflates profits in the period of production by incurring less cost than would be incurred under a _____ system. _____ is generally not used for external reporting purposes. Under the Tax Reform Act of 1986, income statements must use absorption costing to comply with GAAP.

Exam Probability: **Medium**

47. *Answer choices:*

(see index for correct answer)

- a. Direct material total variance
- b. Overhead
- c. Environmental full-cost accounting
- d. Target income sales

*Guidance:* level 1

---

:: Markets (customer bases) ::

In economics, _____ is the economic price for which a good or service is offered in the marketplace. It is of interest mainly in the study of microeconomics. Market value and _____ are equal only under conditions of market efficiency, equilibrium, and rational expectations.

Exam Probability: **High**

48. *Answer choices:*

(see index for correct answer)

- a. Perfect market
- b. Market price
- c. Nonmarket forces
- d. nonmarket

*Guidance:* level 1

---

:: Financial markets ::

The _____ is the part of the capital market that deals with the issuance and sale of equity-backed securities to investors directly by the issuer. Investor buy securities that were never traded before. _____ s create long term instruments through which corporate entities raise funds from the capital market. It is also known as the New Issue Market .

Exam Probability: **Low**

49. *Answer choices:*
(see index for correct answer)

- a. Primary market
- b. Pfandbrief
- c. Composite
- d. Market clearing

*Guidance:* level 1

---

:: Mathematical finance ::

_____ is the value of an asset at a specific date. It measures the nominal future sum of money that a given sum of money is "worth" at a specified time in the future assuming a certain interest rate, or more generally, rate of return; it is the present value multiplied by the accumulation function. The value does not include corrections for inflation or other factors that affect the true value of money in the future. This is used in time value of money calculations.

Exam Probability: **High**

50. *Answer choices:*
(see index for correct answer)

- a. Quantitative behavioral finance
- b. Modified Dietz method
- c. Convexity
- d. Binomial options pricing model

*Guidance:* level 1

---

:: ::

The _____ is a private, non-profit organization standard-setting body whose primary purpose is to establish and improve Generally Accepted Accounting Principles within the United States in the public's interest. The Securities and Exchange Commission designated the FASB as the organization responsible for setting accounting standards for public companies in the US. The FASB replaced the American Institute of Certified Public Accountants' Accounting Principles Board on July 1, 1973.

Exam Probability: **High**

51. *Answer choices:*
(see index for correct answer)

- a. Sarbanes-Oxley act of 2002
- b. cultural
- c. similarity-attraction theory
- d. co-culture

*Guidance:* level 1

---

:: Auditing ::

_____ , as defined by accounting and auditing, is a process for assuring of an organization's objectives in operational effectiveness and efficiency, reliable financial reporting, and compliance with laws, regulations and policies. A broad concept, _____ involves everything that controls risks to an organization.

Exam Probability: **Low**

52. *Answer choices:*
(see index for correct answer)

- a. Internal control
- b. Auditing Standards Board
- c. Detection risk
- d. Risk-based auditing

*Guidance:* level 1

---

:: ::

In marketing, a _____ is a ticket or document that can be redeemed for a financial discount or rebate when purchasing a product.

53. *Answer choices:*
(see index for correct answer)

- a. similarity-attraction theory
- b. hierarchical
- c. empathy
- d. Sarbanes-Oxley act of 2002

*Guidance:* level 1

:: Project management ::

Some scenarios associate "this kind of planning" with learning "life skills". _____ s are necessary, or at least useful, in situations where individuals need to know what time they must be at a specific location to receive a specific service, and where people need to accomplish a set of goals within a set time period.

54. *Answer choices:*
(see index for correct answer)

- a. Changes clause
- b. Schedule
- c. Burn down chart
- d. Libyan Project Management Association

*Guidance:* level 1

:: Currency ::

A _____ , in the most specific sense is money in any form when in use or circulation as a medium of exchange, especially circulating banknotes and coins. A more general definition is that a _____ is a system of money in common use, especially for people in a nation. Under this definition, US dollars, pounds sterling, Australian dollars, European euros, Russian rubles and Indian Rupees are examples of currencies. These various currencies are recognized as stores of value and are traded between nations in foreign exchange markets, which determine the relative values of the different currencies. Currencies in this sense are defined by governments, and each type has limited boundaries of acceptance.

Exam Probability: **Low**

55. *Answer choices:*
(see index for correct answer)

- a. Currency
- b. Monetae cudendae ratio
- c. Remonetisation
- d. Representative money

*Guidance:* level 1

---

:: Legal terms ::

_____ s may be governments, corporations or investment trusts. _____ s are legally responsible for the obligations of the issue and for reporting financial conditions, material developments and any other operational activities as required by the regulations of their jurisdictions.

Exam Probability: **Medium**

56. *Answer choices:*
(see index for correct answer)

- a. Error
- b. Guarantor
- c. Door tenant
- d. Quasi-legislative capacity

*Guidance:* level 1

---

:: Separation of investment and commercial banking ::

A _____ is a type of bank that provides services such as accepting deposits, making business loans, and offering basic investment products that is operated as a business for profit.

Exam Probability: **Medium**

57. *Answer choices:*
(see index for correct answer)

- a. Independent Commission on Banking
- b. Depository institution
- c. Commercial bank
- d. Bank holding company

*Guidance:* level 1

:: Inventory ::

In business and accounting/accountancy, _____ or continuous inventory describes systems of inventory where information on inventory quantity and availability is updated on a continuous basis as a function of doing business. Generally this is accomplished by connecting the inventory system with order entry and in retail the point of sale system. In this case, book inventory would be exactly the same as, or almost the same, as the real inventory.

Exam Probability: **Low**

58. *Answer choices:*
(see index for correct answer)

- a. Reorder point
- b. Safety stock
- c. Perpetual inventory
- d. Stock demands

*Guidance:* level 1

:: Fixed income analysis ::

The _____ , book yield or redemption yield of a bond or other fixed-interest security, such as gilts, is the internal rate of return earned by an investor who buys the bond today at the market price, assuming that the bond is held until maturity, and that all coupon and principal payments are made on schedule. _____ is the discount rate at which the sum of all future cash flows from the bond is equal to the current price of the bond. The YTM is often given in terms of Annual Percentage Rate , but more often market convention is followed. In a number of major markets the convention is to quote annualized yields with semi-annual compounding ; thus, for example, an annual effective yield of 10.25% would be quoted as 10.00%, because $1.05 \times 1.05 = 1.1025$ and $2 \times 5 = 10$.

Exam Probability: **Medium**

59. *Answer choices:*
<sub>(see index for correct answer)</sub>

- a. Fisher equation
- b. Chen model
- c. Option Adjusted Spread
- d. Yield to maturity

*Guidance:* level 1

# Human resource management

Human resource (HR) management is the strategic approach to the effective management of organization workers so that they help the business gain a competitive advantage. It is designed to maximize employee performance in service of an employer's strategic objectives. HR is primarily concerned with the management of people within organizations, focusing on policies and on systems. HR departments are responsible for overseeing employee-benefits design, employee recruitment, training and development, performance appraisal, and rewarding (e.g., managing pay and benefit systems). HR also concerns itself with organizational change and industrial relations, that is, the balancing of organizational practices with requirements arising from collective bargaining and from governmental laws.

---

:: Organizational theory ::

_____ is the process of creating, retaining, and transferring knowledge within an organization. An organization improves over time as it gains experience. From this experience, it is able to create knowledge. This knowledge is broad, covering any topic that could better an organization. Examples may include ways to increase production efficiency or to develop beneficial investor relations. Knowledge is created at four different units: individual, group, organizational, and inter organizational.

Exam Probability: **High**

1. *Answer choices:*
(see index for correct answer)

- a. Team Service Management
- b. Organizational learning
- c. Team leader
- d. Team effectiveness

*Guidance:* level 1

---

:: Foreign workers ::

A _____ or guest worker is a human who works in a country other than the one of which he or she is a citizen. Some _____ s are using a guest worker program in a country with more preferred job prospects than their home country. Guest workers are often either sent or invited to work outside their home country, or have acquired a job before they left their home country, whereas migrant workers often leave their home country without having a specific job at hand.

Exam Probability: **Medium**

2. *Answer choices:*
(see index for correct answer)

- a. Kalayaan
- b. Foreign workers in Saudi Arabia
- c. Foreign worker
- d. Migrant domestic workers

*Guidance:* level 1

---

:: ::

A _____ is the ability to carry out a task with determined results often within a given amount of time, energy, or both. _____ s can often be divided into domain-general and domain-specific _____ s. For example, in the domain of work, some general _____ s would include time management, teamwork and leadership, self-motivation and others, whereas domain-specific _____ s would be used only for a certain job. _____ usually requires certain environmental stimuli and situations to assess the level of _____ being shown and used.

Exam Probability: **Medium**

3. *Answer choices:*
(see index for correct answer)

- a. Skill
- b. process perspective
- c. co-culture
- d. similarity-attraction theory

*Guidance:* level 1

---

:: Employment discrimination ::

A _____ is a metaphor used to represent an invisible barrier that keeps a given demographic from rising beyond a certain level in a hierarchy.

4. *Answer choices:*
(see index for correct answer)

- a. Employment discrimination
- b. MacBride Principles
- c. New South Wales selection bias
- d. Employment Non-Discrimination Act

*Guidance:* level 1

:: ::

A _____ is a systematic way of determining the value/worth of a job in relation to other jobs in an organization. It tries to make a systematic comparison between jobs to assess their relative worth for the purpose of establishing a rational pay structure. _____ needs to be differentiated from job analysis. Job analysis is a systematic way of gathering information about a job. Every _____ method requires at least some basic job analysis in order to provide factual information about the jobs concerned. Thus, _____ begins with job analysis and ends at that point where the worth of a job is ascertained for achieving pay equity between jobs and different roles.

5. *Answer choices:*
(see index for correct answer)

- a. functional perspective
- b. Job evaluation
- c. cultural
- d. levels of analysis

*Guidance:* level 1

:: Human resource management ::

_____ or work sharing is an employment arrangement where typically two people are retained on a part-time or reduced-time basis to perform a job normally fulfilled by one person working full-time. Since all positions are shared thus leads to a net reduction in per-employee income. The people sharing the job work as a team to complete the job task and are equally responsible for the job workload. Compensation is apportioned between the workers. Working hours, pay and holidays are divided equally. The pay as you go system helps make deductions for national insurance and superannuations are made as a straightforward percentage.

Exam Probability: **Low**

6. *Answer choices:*
(see index for correct answer)

- a. Job sharing
- b. Competency-based management
- c. Upward communication
- d. Job enlargement

*Guidance:* level 1

:: Unemployment by country ::

Unemployment benefits are payments made by back authorized bodies to unemployed people. In the United States, benefits are funded by a compulsory governmental insurance system, not taxes on individual citizens. Depending on the jurisdiction and the status of the person, those sums may be small, covering only basic needs, or may compensate the lost time proportionally to the previous earned salary.

Exam Probability: **Low**

7. *Answer choices:*
(see index for correct answer)

- a. Unemployment in Spain
- b. Unemployment in Brazil
- c. Unemployment insurance

*Guidance:* level 1

:: Industrial agreements ::

A _____ , in labor relations, is a group of employees with a clear and identifiable community of interests who are represented by a single labor union in collective bargaining and other dealings with management. Examples would be non-management professors, law enforcement professionals, blue-collar workers, clerical and administrative employees, etc. Geographic location as well as the number of facilities included in _____ s can be at issue during representation cases.

Exam Probability: **Medium**

8. *Answer choices:*
(see index for correct answer)

- a. Bargaining unit
- b. Ex parte H.V. McKay
- c. Union security agreement
- d. Compromise agreement

*Guidance:* level 1

---

:: Business ethics ::

A _____ is a person who exposes any kind of information or activity that is deemed illegal, unethical, or not correct within an organization that is either private or public. The information of alleged wrongdoing can be classified in many ways: violation of company policy/rules, law, regulation, or threat to public interest/national security, as well as fraud, and corruption. Those who become _____ s can choose to bring information or allegations to surface either internally or externally. Internally, a _____ can bring his/her accusations to the attention of other people within the accused organization such as an immediate supervisor. Externally, a _____ can bring allegations to light by contacting a third party outside of an accused organization such as the media, government, law enforcement, or those who are concerned. _____ s, however, take the risk of facing stiff reprisal and retaliation from those who are accused or alleged of wrongdoing.

Exam Probability: **High**

9. *Answer choices:*
(see index for correct answer)

- a. Whistleblower
- b. Product stewardship

- c. Rules of the garage
- d. TG Soft

*Guidance:* level 1

---

:: Psychometrics ::

Electronic assessment, also known as e-assessment, _____ , computer assisted/mediated assessment and computer-based assessment, is the use of information technology in various forms of assessment such as educational assessment, health assessment, psychiatric assessment, and psychological assessment. This may utilize an online computer connected to a network. This definition embraces a wide range of student activity ranging from the use of a word processor to on-screen testing. Specific types of e-assessment include multiple choice, online/electronic submission, computerized adaptive testing and computerized classification testing.

Exam Probability: **High**

10. *Answer choices:*
(see index for correct answer)

- a. Visual analogue scale
- b. Online assessment
- c. Perceptual mapping
- d. Quantitative marketing research

*Guidance:* level 1

---

:: Human resource management ::

_____ is a core function of human resource management and it is related to the specification of contents, methods and relationship of jobs in order to satisfy technological and organizational requirements as well as the social and personal requirements of the job holder or the employee. Its principles are geared towards how the nature of a person's job affects their attitudes and behavior at work, particularly relating to characteristics such as skill variety and autonomy. The aim of a _____ is to improve job satisfaction, to improve through-put, to improve quality and to reduce employee problems .

Exam Probability: **High**

11. *Answer choices:*
(see index for correct answer)

- a. Employment testing
- b. Job design
- c. Training and development
- d. Dr. Marri Channa Reddy Human Resource Development Institute of Andhra Pradesh

*Guidance:* level 1

---

:: Labour relations ::

_____ is a form of protest in which people congregate outside a place of work or location where an event is taking place. Often, this is done in an attempt to dissuade others from going in , but it can also be done to draw public attention to a cause. Picketers normally endeavor to be non-violent. It can have a number of aims, but is generally to put pressure on the party targeted to meet particular demands or cease operations. This pressure is achieved by harming the business through loss of customers and negative publicity, or by discouraging or preventing workers or customers from entering the site and thereby preventing the business from operating normally.

Exam Probability: **Low**

12. *Answer choices:*
(see index for correct answer)

- a. Association of German Chambers of Industry and Commerce
- b. Lockout
- c. Union representative
- d. Picketing

*Guidance:* level 1

---

:: Occupational safety and health organizations ::

The _____ is the United States federal agency responsible for conducting research and making recommendations for the prevention of work-related injury and illness. NIOSH is part of the Centers for Disease Control and Prevention within the U.S. Department of Health and Human Services.

Exam Probability: **Medium**

13. *Answer choices:*

(see index for correct answer)

- a. Health and Safety Executive for Northern Ireland
- b. Migration and Health Research Center
- c. National Institute for Occupational Safety and Health
- d. American Society of Safety Engineers

*Guidance:* level 1

:: ::

_____ are interactive computer-mediated technologies that facilitate the creation and sharing of information, ideas, career interests and other forms of expression via virtual communities and networks. The variety of stand-alone and built-in _____ services currently available introduces challenges of definition; however, there are some common features.

Exam Probability: **Medium**

14. *Answer choices:*

(see index for correct answer)

- a. co-culture
- b. similarity-attraction theory
- c. functional perspective
- d. hierarchical perspective

*Guidance:* level 1

:: Employment compensation ::

A _____ is pay and benefits employees receive when they leave employment at a company unwillfully. In addition to their remaining regular pay, it may include some of the following.

Exam Probability: **High**

15. *Answer choices:*

(see index for correct answer)

- a. Severance package
- b. Defense Base Act
- c. Equal pay for equal work
- d. Pension insurance contract

:: ::

In business strategy, _____ is establishing a competitive advantage by having the lowest cost of operation in the industry. _____ is often driven by company efficiency, size, scale, scope and cumulative experience .A _____ strategy aims to exploit scale of production, well-defined scope and other economies , producing highly standardized products, using advanced technology.In recent years, more and more companies have chosen a strategic mix to achieve market leadership. These patterns consist of simultaneous _____ , superior customer service and product leadership. Walmart has succeeded across the world due to its _____ strategy. The company has cut down on exesses at every point of production and thus are able to provide the consumers with quality products at low prices.

Exam Probability: **Medium**

16. *Answer choices:*
(see index for correct answer)

- a. process perspective
- b. information systems assessment
- c. Cost leadership
- d. empathy

:: Management ::

In organizational studies, _____ is the efficient and effective development of an organization's resources when they are needed. Such resources may include financial resources, inventory, human skills, production resources, or information technology  and natural resources.

Exam Probability: **High**

17. *Answer choices:*
(see index for correct answer)

- a. Meeting system
- b. Resource management
- c. Association management company

- d. Leadership Series

---

:: United Kingdom labour law ::

The _____ was a series of programs, public work projects, financial reforms, and regulations enacted by President Franklin D. Roosevelt in the United States between 1933 and 1936. It responded to needs for relief, reform, and recovery from the Great Depression. Major federal programs included the Civilian Conservation Corps , the Civil Works Administration , the Farm Security Administration , the National Industrial Recovery Act of 1933 and the Social Security Administration . They provided support for farmers, the unemployed, youth and the elderly. The _____ included new constraints and safeguards on the banking industry and efforts to re-inflate the economy after prices had fallen sharply. _____ programs included both laws passed by Congress as well as presidential executive orders during the first term of the presidency of Franklin D. Roosevelt.

Exam Probability: **Medium**

18. *Answer choices:*
(see index for correct answer)

- a. Information and Consultation of Employees Regulations 2004
- b. Trade Boards Act 1918
- c. New Deal
- d. Working Time Regulations 1998

---

:: Management ::

A _____ is a method or technique that has been generally accepted as superior to any alternatives because it produces results that are superior to those achieved by other means or because it has become a standard way of doing things, e.g., a standard way of complying with legal or ethical requirements.

Exam Probability: **High**

19. *Answer choices:*
(see index for correct answer)

- a. Production flow analysis
- b. Dominant design
- c. Management styles
- d. Best practice

*Guidance:* level 1

---

:: Business ::

_____ is a trade policy that does not restrict imports or exports; it can also be understood as the free market idea applied to international trade. In government, _____ is predominantly advocated by political parties that hold liberal economic positions while economically left-wing and nationalist political parties generally support protectionism, the opposite of _____ .

Exam Probability: **Low**

20. *Answer choices:*
(see index for correct answer)

- a. E-lancing
- b. Corporate farming
- c. Ametek
- d. Legal governance, risk management, and compliance

*Guidance:* level 1

---

:: Trade union legislation ::

The _____ of 1935 is a foundational statute of United States labor law which guarantees the right of private sector employees to organize into trade unions, engage in collective bargaining, and take collective action such as strikes. The act was written by Senator Robert F. Wagner, passed by the 74th United States Congress, and signed into law by President Franklin D. Roosevelt.

Exam Probability: **High**

21. *Answer choices:*
(see index for correct answer)

- a. Trade Union Reform and Employment Rights Act 1993
- b. Trade Union Act 1984
- c. Labor Management Relations Act of 1947
- d. National Labor Relations Act

:: ::

_____ is a belief that hard work and diligence have a moral benefit and an inherent ability, virtue or value to strengthen character and individual abilities. It is a set of values centered on importance of work and manifested by determination or desire to work hard. Social ingrainment of this value is considered to enhance character through hard work that is respective to an individual's field of work.

Exam Probability: **Low**

22. *Answer choices:*
(see index for correct answer)

- a. Work ethic
- b. interpersonal communication
- c. hierarchical
- d. co-culture

:: Problem solving ::

In other words, _____ is a situation where a group of people meet to generate new ideas and solutions around a specific domain of interest by removing inhibitions. People are able to think more freely and they suggest as many spontaneous new ideas as possible. All the ideas are noted down and those ideas are not criticized and after _____ session the ideas are evaluated. The term was popularized by Alex Faickney Osborn in the 1953 book Applied Imagination.

Exam Probability: **Medium**

23. *Answer choices:*
(see index for correct answer)

- a. Convergent and divergent production
- b. Brainstorming
- c. Convergent thinking
- d. Project Euler

A _____ is an occupation founded upon specialized educational training, the purpose of which is to supply disinterested objective counsel and service to others, for a direct and definite compensation, wholly apart from expectation of other business gain. The term is a truncation of the term "liberal _____ ", which is, in turn, an Anglicization of the French term " _____ libérale". Originally borrowed by English users in the 19th century, it has been re-borrowed by international users from the late 20th, though the class overtones of the term do not seem to survive retranslation: "liberal _____ s" are, according to the European Union's Directive on Recognition of _____ al Qualifications "those practiced on the basis of relevant _____ al qualifications in a personal, responsible and _____ ally independent capacity by those providing intellectual and conceptual services in the interest of the client and the public".

Exam Probability: **High**

24. *Answer choices:*
(see index for correct answer)

- a. Profession
- b. corporate values
- c. Sarbanes-Oxley act of 2002
- d. process perspective

*Guidance:* level 1

:: Human resource management ::

_____ assesses whether a person performs a job well. _____ , studied academically as part of industrial and organizational psychology, also forms a part of human resources management. Performance is an important criterion for organizational outcomes and success. John P. Campbell describes _____ as an individual-level variable, or something a single person does. This differentiates it from more encompassing constructs such as organizational performance or national performance, which are higher-level variables.

Exam Probability: **High**

25. *Answer choices:*
(see index for correct answer)

- a. Job description management
- b. Organizational ethics
- c. Managerial assessment of proficiency
- d. Job performance

*Guidance:* level 1

---

:: Employment compensation ::

A _____ is the minimum income necessary for a worker to meet their basic needs. Needs are defined to include food, housing, and other essential needs such as clothing. The goal of a _____ is to allow a worker to afford a basic but decent standard of living. Due to the flexible nature of the term "needs", there is not one universally accepted measure of what a _____ is and as such it varies by location and household type.

Exam Probability: **High**

26. *Answer choices:*
(see index for correct answer)

- a. My Family Care
- b. Pay scale
- c. Living wage
- d. Prevailing wage

*Guidance:* level 1

---

:: ::

According to Torrington, a _____ is usually developed by conducting a job analysis, which includes examining the tasks and sequences of tasks necessary to perform the job. The analysis considers the areas of knowledge and skills needed for the job. A job usually includes several roles. According to Hall, the _____ might be broadened to form a person specification or may be known as "terms of reference". The person/job specification can be presented as a stand-alone document, but in practice it is usually included within the _____ . A _____ is often used by employers in the recruitment process.

Exam Probability: **Low**

27. *Answer choices:*

- a. levels of analysis
- b. hierarchical
- c. Job description
- d. Character

*Guidance:* level 1

---

:: Employment ::

_____ s are experiential learning opportunities, similar to internships but generally shorter, provided by partnerships between educational institutions and employers to give students short practical experiences in their field of study. In medicine it may refer to a visiting physician who is not part of the regular staff. In law, it usually refers to rigorous legal work opportunities undertaken by law students for law school credit and pay, similar to that of a junior attorney. It is derived from Latin externus and from English -ship.

Exam Probability: **Medium**

28. *Answer choices:*

- a. Monster Employment Index
- b. Externship
- c. Labour discrimination
- d. Fly-in fly-out

*Guidance:* level 1

---

:: ::

The _____ of 1938 29 U.S.C. § 203 is a United States labor law that creates the right to a minimum wage, and "time-and-a-half" overtime pay when people work over forty hours a week. It also prohibits most employment of minors in "oppressive child labor". It applies to employees engaged in interstate commerce or employed by an enterprise engaged in commerce or in the production of goods for commerce, unless the employer can claim an exemption from coverage.

Exam Probability: **Low**

29. *Answer choices:*
(see index for correct answer)

- a. personal values
- b. open system
- c. Fair Labor Standards Act
- d. deep-level diversity

*Guidance:* level 1

---

:: Human resource management ::

_____ is the strategic approach to the effective management of people in an organization so that they help the business to gain a competitive advantage. It is designed to maximize employee performance in service of an employer's strategic objectives. HR is primarily concerned with the management of people within organizations, focusing on policies and on systems. HR departments are responsible for overseeing employee-benefits design, employee recruitment, training and development, performance appraisal, and Reward management . HR also concerns itself with organizational change and industrial relations, that is, the balancing of organizational practices with requirements arising from collective bargaining and from governmental laws.

Exam Probability: **High**

30. *Answer choices:*
(see index for correct answer)

- a. Human resource management
- b. Technical performance measure
- c. CEO succession
- d. Training and development

*Guidance:* level 1

---

:: Multiple choice ::

The _____ is a standardized psychometric test of adult personality and psychopathology. Psychologists and other mental health professionals use various versions of the MMPI to help develop treatment plans; assist with differential diagnosis; help answer legal questions ; screen job candidates during the personnel selection process; or as part of a therapeutic assessment procedure.

31. *Answer choices:*

(see index for correct answer)

- a. Multiple choice
- b. Eysenck Personality Questionnaire
- c. Eddy Test
- d. Minnesota Multiphasic Personality Inventory

*Guidance:* level 1

---

:: Human resource management ::

_____ refers to the ratio of the number of job positions to the number of job applicants and is used in the context of selection and recruitment.

Exam Probability: **High**

32. *Answer choices:*

(see index for correct answer)

- a. Selection ratio
- b. Experticity
- c. Employment testing
- d. Corporate Equality Index

*Guidance:* level 1

---

:: Self ::

_____ is a conscious or subconscious process in which people attempt to influence the perceptions of other people about a person, object or event. They do so by regulating and controlling information in social interaction. It was first conceptualized by Erving Goffman in 1959 in The Presentation of Self in Everyday Life, and then was expanded upon in 1967. An example of _____ theory in play is in sports such as soccer. At an important game, a player would want to showcase themselves in the best light possible, because there are college recruiters watching. This person would have the flashiest pair of cleats and try and perform their best to show off their skills. Their main goal may be to impress the college recruiters in a way that maximizes their chances of being chosen for a college team rather than winning the game.

33. *Answer choices:*

(see index for correct answer)

- a. Self-presentation
- b. ecological self
- c. Impression management
- d. Egocentrism

*Guidance:* level 1

---

:: Personal finance ::

_____ is an arrangement in which a portion of an employee's income is paid out at a later date after which the income was earned. Examples of _____ include pensions, retirement plans, and employee stock options. The primary benefit of most _____ is the deferral of tax to the date at which the employee receives the income.

Exam Probability: **Low**

34. *Answer choices:*

(see index for correct answer)

- a. Coverdell Education Savings Account
- b. Certificate of life
- c. Debt management
- d. Deferred compensation

*Guidance:* level 1

---

:: ::

A _____ service is an online platform which people use to build social networks or social relationship with other people who share similar personal or career interests, activities, backgrounds or real-life connections.

Exam Probability: **High**

35. *Answer choices:*

(see index for correct answer)

- a. Character
- b. process perspective
- c. co-culture
- d. Social networking

:: ::

_____ was the plaintiff in the American employment discrimination case Ledbetter v. Goodyear Tire & Rubber Co. Congress passed a fair pay act in her name, the _____ Fair Pay Act of 2009. She has since become a women's equality activist, public speaker, and author. In 2011, Ledbetter was inducted into the National Women's Hall of Fame.

Exam Probability: **High**

36. *Answer choices:*
(see index for correct answer)

- a. Lilly Ledbetter
- b. levels of analysis
- c. empathy
- d. interpersonal communication

:: Human resource management ::

_____ is the corporate management term for the act of reorganizing the legal, ownership, operational, or other structures of a company for the purpose of making it more profitable, or better organized for its present needs. Other reasons for _____ include a change of ownership or ownership structure, demerger, or a response to a crisis or major change in the business such as bankruptcy, repositioning, or buyout. _____ may also be described as corporate _____ , debt _____ and financial _____ .

Exam Probability: **Low**

37. *Answer choices:*
(see index for correct answer)

- a. Organizational culture
- b. Job design
- c. Restructuring
- d. Recruitment process outsourcing

Greenberg introduced the concept of _____ with regard to how an employee judges the behaviour of the organization and the employee's resulting attitude and behaviour. .

Exam Probability: **High**

38. *Answer choices:*
(see index for correct answer)

- a. Organizational behavior management
- b. Satisficing
- c. Organizational justice
- d. Collaborative partnerships

*Guidance:* level 1

---

:: Occupational safety and health ::

A safety data sheet , _____ , or product safety data sheet is a document that lists information relating to occupational safety and health for the use of various substances and products. SDSs are a widely used system for cataloging information on chemicals, chemical compounds, and chemical mixtures. SDS information may include instructions for the safe use and potential hazards associated with a particular material or product, along with spill-handling procedures. SDS formats can vary from source to source within a country depending on national requirements.

Exam Probability: **High**

39. *Answer choices:*
(see index for correct answer)

- a. Job safety analysis
- b. Material safety data sheet
- c. Beryllium
- d. Alice Hamilton

*Guidance:* level 1

---

:: Nepotism ::

_____ is the granting of favour to relatives in various fields, including business, politics, entertainment, sports, religion and other activities. The term originated with the assignment of nephews to important positions by Catholic popes and bishops. Trading parliamentary employment for favors is a modern-day example of _____ . Criticism of _____ , however, can be found in ancient Indian texts such as the Kural literature.

Exam Probability: **Medium**

40. *Answer choices:*
(see index for correct answer)

- a. Ethnic nepotism
- b. Nepotism
- c. Monklandsgate
- d. Cronyism

*Guidance:* level 1

---

:: Employee relations ::

_____ ownership, or employee share ownership, is an ownership interest in a company held by the company's workforce. The ownership interest may be facilitated by the company as part of employees' remuneration or incentive compensation for work performed, or the company itself may be employee owned.

Exam Probability: **Low**

41. *Answer choices:*
(see index for correct answer)

- a. Industry Federation of the State of Rio de Janeiro
- b. Employee stock
- c. Fringe benefit
- d. Employee surveys

*Guidance:* level 1

---

:: Life skills ::

_____ , emotional leadership , emotional quotient and _____ quotient , is the capability of individuals to recognize their own emotions and those of others, discern between different feelings and label them appropriately, use emotional information to guide thinking and behavior, and manage and/or adjust emotions to adapt to environments or achieve one's goal.

Exam Probability: **Medium**

42. *Answer choices:*
(see index for correct answer)

- a. coping mechanism
- b. emotion work
- c. multiple intelligence
- d. Emotional intelligence

*Guidance:* level 1

:: Psychometrics ::

A _____ is a set of categories designed to elicit information about a quantitative or a qualitative attribute. In the social sciences, particularly psychology, common examples are the Likert response scale and 1-10 _____ s in which a person selects the number which is considered to reflect the perceived quality of a product.

Exam Probability: **Low**

43. *Answer choices:*
(see index for correct answer)

- a. Survey methodology
- b. Internal consistency
- c. Rating scale
- d. Idiographic image

*Guidance:* level 1

:: Management education ::

_____ is the implementation of government policy and also an academic discipline that studies this implementation and prepares civil servants for working in the public service. As a "field of inquiry with a diverse scope" whose fundamental goal is to "advance management and policies so that government can function". Some of the various definitions which have been offered for the term are: "the management of public programs"; the "translation of politics into the reality that citizens see every day"; and "the study of government decision making, the analysis of the policies themselves, the various inputs that have produced them, and the inputs necessary to produce alternative policies."

Exam Probability: **Low**

44. *Answer choices:*
(see index for correct answer)

- a. Venture Capital Investment Competition
- b. Entrepreneurship education
- c. Master of Business Engineering
- d. Public administration

*Guidance:* level 1

---

:: Human resource management ::

_____ is a method of job analysis that was developed by the Employment and Training Administration of the United States Department of Labor. FJA produces standardized occupational information specific to the performance of the work and the performer.

Exam Probability: **Low**

45. *Answer choices:*
(see index for correct answer)

- a. Resource-based view
- b. Functional job analysis
- c. Expense management
- d. Organizational ethics

*Guidance:* level 1

---

:: Labor rights ::

A _____ is a wrong or hardship suffered, real or supposed, which forms legitimate grounds of complaint. In the past, the word meant the infliction or cause of hardship.

Exam Probability: **Low**

46. *Answer choices:*
(see index for correct answer)

- a. China Labour Bulletin
- b. Right to work
- c. Labor rights
- d. Kate Mullany House

*Guidance:* level 1

---

:: Recruitment ::

_____ , also known as Recruitment communications and Recruitment agency, includes all communications used by an organization to attract talent to work within it. Recruitment advertisements may be the first impression of a company for many job seekers. In turn, the strength of employer branding in job postings can directly impact interest in job openings.

Exam Probability: **Medium**

47. *Answer choices:*
(see index for correct answer)

- a. Recruitment advertising
- b. Blind audition
- c. Social recruiting
- d. Military recruitment

*Guidance:* level 1

---

:: Unemployment ::

_____ is the support service provided by responsible organizations, keen to support individuals who are exiting the business – to help former employees transition to new jobs and help them re-orient themselves in the job market. A consultancy firm usually provides the _____ services which are paid for by the former employer and are achieved usually through practical advice, training materials and workshops. Some companies may offer psychological support.

Exam Probability: **High**

48. *Answer choices:*
(see index for correct answer)

- a. Outplacement
- b. Frictional unemployment
- c. Phillips curve
- d. Employment Promotion and Protection against Unemployment Convention, 1988

*Guidance:* level 1

---

:: Majority–minority relations ::

_____ , also known as reservation in India and Nepal, positive discrimination / action in the United Kingdom, and employment equity in Canada and South Africa, is the policy of promoting the education and employment of members of groups that are known to have previously suffered from discrimination. Historically and internationally, support for _____ has sought to achieve goals such as bridging inequalities in employment and pay, increasing access to education, promoting diversity, and redressing apparent past wrongs, harms, or hindrances.

Exam Probability: **High**

49. *Answer choices:*
(see index for correct answer)

- a. positive discrimination
- b. cultural dissonance
- c. cultural Relativism

*Guidance:* level 1

---

:: Behavior ::

_____ refers to behavior-change procedures that were employed during the 1970s and early 1980s. Based on methodological behaviorism, overt behavior was modified with presumed consequences, including artificial positive and negative reinforcement contingencies to increase desirable behavior, or administering positive and negative punishment and/or extinction to reduce problematic behavior. For the treatment of phobias, habituation and punishment were the basic principles used in flooding, a subcategory of desensitization.

Exam Probability: **High**

50. *Answer choices:*
(see index for correct answer)

- a. theory of reasoned action
- b. Behavior modification

*Guidance:* level 1

---

:: Behavioral and social facets of systemic risk ::

_____ is the difficulty in understanding an issue and effectively making decisions when one has too much information about that issue. Generally, the term is associated with the excessive quantity of daily information.

_____ most likely originated from information theory, which are studies in the storage, preservation, communication, compression, and extraction of information. The term, _____ , was first used in Bertram Gross' 1964 book, The Managing of Organizations, and it was further popularized by Alvin Toffler in his bestselling 1970 book Future Shock. Speier et al. stated.

Exam Probability: **Low**

51. *Answer choices:*
(see index for correct answer)

- a. vicious cycle
- b. virtuous circle
- c. Human reliability
- d. Information overload

*Guidance:* level 1

---

:: ::

_____ is a common standard in United States labor law arbitration that is used in labor union contracts in the United States as a form of job security.

Exam Probability: **Medium**

52. *Answer choices:*
(see index for correct answer)

- a. functional perspective
- b. hierarchical
- c. imperative
- d. deep-level diversity

*Guidance:* level 1

:: International trade ::

_____ or globalisation is the process of interaction and integration among people, companies, and governments worldwide. As a complex and multifaceted phenomenon, _____ is considered by some as a form of capitalist expansion which entails the integration of local and national economies into a global, unregulated market economy. _____ has grown due to advances in transportation and communication technology. With the increased global interactions comes the growth of international trade, ideas, and culture. _____ is primarily an economic process of interaction and integration that's associated with social and cultural aspects. However, conflicts and diplomacy are also large parts of the history of _____, and modern _____.

Exam Probability: **Low**

53. *Answer choices:*
(see index for correct answer)

- a. Common Fund for Commodities
- b. Portuguese India Armadas
- c. Globalization
- d. Trading nation

*Guidance:* level 1

:: Television terminology ::

Distance education or long- _____ is the education of students who may not always be physically present at a school. Traditionally, this usually involved correspondence courses wherein the student corresponded with the school via post. Today it involves online education. Courses that are conducted are either hybrid, blended or 100% _____ . Massive open online courses , offering large-scale interactive participation and open access through the World Wide Web or other network technologies, are recent developments in distance education. A number of other terms are used roughly synonymously with distance education.

Exam Probability: **Low**

54. *Answer choices:*
(see index for correct answer)

- a. nonprofit
- b. multiplexing
- c. Distance learning
- d. not-for-profit

*Guidance:* level 1

:: ::

In organizational behavior and industrial/organizational psychology, proactivity or _____ behavior by individuals refers to anticipatory, change-oriented and self-initiated behavior in situations. _____ behavior involves acting in advance of a future situation, rather than just reacting. It means taking control and making things happen rather than just adjusting to a situation or waiting for something to happen. _____ employees generally do not need to be asked to act, nor do they require detailed instructions.

Exam Probability: **Medium**

55. *Answer choices:*
(see index for correct answer)

- a. process perspective
- b. cultural
- c. Proactive
- d. hierarchical

*Guidance:* level 1

The _____ is a unit of the United States Department of Labor. It is the principal fact-finding agency for the U.S. government in the broad field of labor economics and statistics and serves as a principal agency of the U.S. Federal Statistical System. The BLS is a governmental statistical agency that collects, processes, analyzes, and disseminates essential statistical data to the American public, the U.S. Congress, other Federal agencies, State and local governments, business, and labor representatives. The BLS also serves as a statistical resource to the United States Department of Labor, and conducts research into how much families need to earn to be able to enjoy a decent standard of living.

Exam Probability: **Low**

56. *Answer choices:*
(see index for correct answer)

- a. Underearners Anonymous
- b. Average high cost multiple
- c. Bureau of Labor Statistics
- d. Federal Unemployment Tax Act

*Guidance:* level 1

---

_____ is the act of matching attitudes, beliefs, and behaviors to group norms or politics. Norms are implicit, specific rules, shared by a group of individuals, that guide their interactions with others. People often choose to conform to society rather than to pursue personal desires because it is often easier to follow the path others have made already, rather than creating a new one. This tendency to conform occurs in small groups and/or society as a whole, and may result from subtle unconscious influences , or direct and overt social pressure. _____ can occur in the presence of others, or when an individual is alone. For example, people tend to follow social norms when eating or watching television, even when alone.

Exam Probability: **Low**

57. *Answer choices:*
(see index for correct answer)

- a. Nut Island effect
- b. Civic virtue
- c. Organizational justice
- d. Group behaviour

*Guidance:* level 1

---

:: Personnel economics ::

In labor economics, the _____ hypothesis argues that wages, at least in some markets, form in a way that is not market-clearing. Specifically, it points to the incentive for managers to pay their employees more than the market-clearing wage in order to increase their productivity or efficiency, or reduce costs associated with turnover, in industries where the costs of replacing labor are high. This increased labor productivity and/or decreased costs pay for the higher wages.

Exam Probability: **Medium**

58. *Answer choices:*
(see index for correct answer)

- a. Efficiency wage
- b. Luxury tax
- c. Work self-efficacy

*Guidance:* level 1

---

:: Legal terms ::

_____ , a form of alternative dispute resolution , is a way to resolve disputes outside the courts. The dispute will be decided by one or more persons , which renders the " _____ award". An _____ award is legally binding on both sides and enforceable in the courts.

Exam Probability: **Medium**

59. *Answer choices:*
(see index for correct answer)

- a. Commodate
- b. Fundamental justice
- c. Third party complaint
- d. Argumentative

## Information systems

Information systems (IS) are formal, sociotechnical, organizational systems designed to collect, process, store, and distribute information. In a sociotechnical perspective Information Systems are composed by four components: technology, process, people and organizational structure.

---

:: Confidence tricks ::

_____ is the fraudulent attempt to obtain sensitive information such as usernames, passwords and credit card details by disguising oneself as a trustworthy entity in an electronic communication. Typically carried out by email spoofing or instant messaging, it often directs users to enter personal information at a fake website which matches the look and feel of the legitimate site.

Exam Probability: **High**

1. *Answer choices:*
(see index for correct answer)

- a. Moving scam
- b. Phishing
- c. Cackle-bladder
- d. Technical support scam

*Guidance:* level 1

---

:: Information technology management ::

_____ concerns a cycle of organizational activity: the acquisition of information from one or more sources, the custodianship and the distribution of that information to those who need it, and its ultimate disposition through archiving or deletion.

Exam Probability: **High**

2. *Answer choices:*
(see index for correct answer)

- a. Soluto
- b. Multichannel Group
- c. Change management
- d. Information management

*Guidance:* level 1

---

:: Computer security standards ::

The _____ for Information Technology Security Evaluation is an international standard for computer security certification. It is currently in version 3.1 revision 5.

Exam Probability: **High**

3. *Answer choices:*
(see index for correct answer)

- a. Common Criteria
- b. ITSEC
- c. Rainbow Series
- d. S/MIME

*Guidance:* level 1

---

:: Web security exploits ::

A _____ is a baked or cooked food that is small, flat and sweet. It usually contains flour, sugar and some type of oil or fat. It may include other ingredients such as raisins, oats, chocolate chips, nuts, etc.

Exam Probability: **Medium**

4. *Answer choices:*

(see index for correct answer)

- a. Content Security Policy
- b. XML external entity
- c. OWASP
- d. Reflected DOM Injection

*Guidance:* level 1

---

:: Ergonomics ::

_____ is the design of products, devices, services, or environments for people with disabilities. The concept of accessible design and practice of accessible development ensures both "direct access"  and "indirect access" meaning compatibility with a person's assistive technology .

Exam Probability: **Medium**

5. *Answer choices:*

(see index for correct answer)

- a. Computer desk
- b. Engineering psychology
- c. Computer-aided ergonomics
- d. F.lux

*Guidance:* level 1

---

:: Information technology management ::

_____ s or pop-ups are forms of online advertising on the World Wide Web. A pop-up is a graphical user interface  display area, usually a small window, that suddenly appears  in the foreground of the visual interface. The pop-up window containing an advertisement is usually generated by JavaScript that  uses cross-site scripting , sometimes with a secondary payload that uses Adobe Flash. They can also be generated by other vulnerabilities/security holes in browser security.

Exam Probability: **Low**

6. *Answer choices:*

(see index for correct answer)

- a. ESCM

- b. Wire data
- c. Pop-up ad
- d. Information repository

*Guidance:* level 1

---

:: Information science ::

The United States National Forum on _____ defines _____ as "... the hyper ability to know when there is a need for information, to be able to identify, locate, evaluate, and effectively use that information for the issue or problem at hand." The American Library Association defines "_____" as a set of abilities requiring individuals to "recognize when information is needed and have the ability to locate, evaluate, and use effectively the needed information. Other definitions incorporate aspects of "skepticism, judgement, free thinking, questioning, and understanding..." or incorporate competencies that an informed citizen of an information society ought to possess to participate intelligently and actively in that society.

Exam Probability: **Low**

7. *Answer choices:*
(see index for correct answer)

- a. The Royal School of Library and Information Science
- b. Information literacy
- c. Information architecture
- d. Information science

*Guidance:* level 1

---

:: Types of marketing ::

In microeconomics and management, _____ is an arrangement in which the supply chain of a company is owned by that company. Usually each member of the supply chain produces a different product or service, and the products combine to satisfy a common need. It is contrasted with horizontal integration, wherein a company produces several items which are related to one another. _____ has also described management styles that bring large portions of the supply chain not only under a common ownership, but also into one corporation .

Exam Probability: **Medium**

8. *Answer choices:*

(see index for correct answer)

- a. Vertical integration
- b. Pre-installed software
- c. Multi-domestic strategy
- d. Community marketing

*Guidance:* level 1

---

:: Multi-agent systems ::

A _____ is a number of Internet-connected devices, each of which is running one or more bots. _____ s can be used to perform distributed denial-of-service attack , steal data, send spam, and allows the attacker to access the device and its connection. The owner can control the _____ using command and control  software.  The word " _____ " is a combination of the words "robot" and "network". The term is usually used with a negative or malicious connotation.

Exam Probability: **Low**

9. *Answer choices:*

(see index for correct answer)

- a. Multi-agent planning
- b. Botnet
- c. Simple Network Management Protocol
- d. MASSIVE

*Guidance:* level 1

---

:: Computer networking ::

A backbone is a part of computer network that interconnects various pieces of network, providing a path for the exchange of information between different LANs or subnetworks. A backbone can tie together diverse networks in the same building, in different buildings in a campus environment, or over wide areas. Normally, the backbone's capacity is greater than the networks connected to it.

Exam Probability: **High**

10. *Answer choices:*

(see index for correct answer)

- a. Message switching
- b. Network cloaking
- c. Router
- d. Hierarchical internetworking model

---

:: Finance ::

_____ is a financial estimate intended to help buyers and owners determine the direct and indirect costs of a product or system. It is a management accounting concept that can be used in full cost accounting or even ecological economics where it includes social costs.

Exam Probability: **Medium**

11. *Answer choices:*
(see index for correct answer)

- a. Financial commons
- b. XBRLS
- c. Numbrs
- d. Total cost of ownership

---

:: Security compliance ::

_____ refers to the inability to withstand the effects of a hostile environment. A window of _____ is a time frame within which defensive measures are diminished, compromised or lacking.

Exam Probability: **Low**

12. *Answer choices:*
(see index for correct answer)

- a. Nikto Web Scanner
- b. Security Content Automation Protocol
- c. 201 CMR 17.00
- d. Information assurance vulnerability alert

---

:: ::

An _____ is system software that manages computer hardware and software resources and provides common services for computer programs.

Exam Probability: **Medium**

13. *Answer choices:*
(see index for correct answer)

- a. co culture
- b. open system
- c. interpersonal communication
- d. Operating system

*Guidance:* level 1

---

:: Web analytics ::

A click path or _____ is the sequence of hyperlinks one or more website visitors follows on a given site, presented in the order viewed. A visitor's click path may start within the website or at a separate 3rd party website, often a search engine results page, and it continues as a sequence of successive webpages visited by the user. Click paths take call data and can match it to ad sources, keywords, and/or referring domains, in order to capture data.

Exam Probability: **Medium**

14. *Answer choices:*
(see index for correct answer)

- a. Microsoft adCenter Analytics
- b. WebSideStory
- c. Open Web Analytics
- d. Clickstream

*Guidance:* level 1

---

:: Computing output devices ::

An _____ is any piece of computer hardware equipment which converts information into human-readable form.

15. *Answer choices:*
(see index for correct answer)

- a. Datapoint 3300
- b. Palette
- c. Output device
- d. DR37-P

*Guidance:* level 1

---

:: Intelligence (information gathering) ::

_____ comprises the strategies and technologies used by enterprises for the data analysis of business information. BI technologies provide historical, current and predictive views of business operations. Common functions of _____ technologies include reporting, online analytical processing, analytics, data mining, process mining, complex event processing, business performance management, benchmarking, text mining, predictive analytics and prescriptive analytics. BI technologies can handle large amounts of structured and sometimes unstructured data to help identify, develop and otherwise create new strategic business opportunities. They aim to allow for the easy interpretation of these big data. Identifying new opportunities and implementing an effective strategy based on insights can provide businesses with a competitive market advantage and long-term stability.

16. *Answer choices:*
(see index for correct answer)

- a. Military intelligence
- b. Signals intelligence
- c. Intelligence analysis management
- d. Company Level Intelligence Cell

*Guidance:* level 1

---

:: Process management ::

When used in the context of communication networks, such as Ethernet or packet radio, _____ or network _____ is the rate of successful message delivery over a communication channel. The data these messages belong to may be delivered over a physical or logical link, or it can pass through a certain network node. _____ is usually measured in bits per second , and sometimes in data packets per second  or data packets per time slot.

Exam Probability: **Medium**

17. *Answer choices:*
(see index for correct answer)

- a. Chemical plant cost indexes
- b. P and R measures
- c. Turnaround
- d. Business process modeling

*Guidance:* level 1

---

:: Management ::

A _____ describes the rationale of how an organization creates, delivers, and captures value, in economic, social, cultural or other contexts. The process of _____ construction and modification is also called _____ innovation and forms a part of business strategy.

Exam Probability: **High**

18. *Answer choices:*
(see index for correct answer)

- a. U-procedure and Theory U
- b. Product life-cycle management
- c. Narcissistic leadership
- d. Performance management

*Guidance:* level 1

---

:: Management ::

A _____ defines or constrains some aspect of business and always resolves to either true or false. _____ s are intended to assert business structure or to control or influence the behavior of the business. _____ s describe the operations, definitions and constraints that apply to an organization. _____ s can apply to people, processes, corporate behavior and computing systems in an organization, and are put in place to help the organization achieve its goals.

Exam Probability: **Medium**

19. *Answer choices:*
(see index for correct answer)

- a. Integrated master plan
- b. Business rule
- c. Pareto analysis
- d. Financial planning

*Guidance:* level 1

---

:: Data transmission ::

In telecommunication a _____ is the means of connecting one location to another for the purpose of transmitting and receiving digital information. It can also refer to a set of electronics assemblies, consisting of a transmitter and a receiver and the interconnecting data telecommunication circuit. These are governed by a link protocol enabling digital data to be transferred from a data source to a data sink.

Exam Probability: **High**

20. *Answer choices:*
(see index for correct answer)

- a. Transmission time
- b. RadioMail
- c. Data link
- d. Code word

*Guidance:* level 1

---

:: Information technology management ::

In information technology to _____ means to move from one place to another, information to detailed data by focusing in on something. In a GUI-environment, "drilling-down" may involve clicking on some representation in order to reveal more detail.

Exam Probability: **Low**

21. *Answer choices:*
(see index for correct answer)

- a. Records life-cycle
- b. Autonomic networking
- c. Drill down
- d. Knowledge balance sheet

*Guidance:* level 1

:: Marketing by medium ::

_____ , also called online marketing or Internet advertising or web advertising, is a form of marketing and advertising which uses the Internet to deliver promotional marketing messages to consumers. Many consumers find _____ disruptive and have increasingly turned to ad blocking for a variety of reasons. When software is used to do the purchasing, it is known as programmatic advertising.

Exam Probability: **Medium**

22. *Answer choices:*
(see index for correct answer)

- a. Viral marketing
- b. Social video marketing
- c. Online advertising
- d. Direct Text Marketing

*Guidance:* level 1

:: Information technology management ::

_____ is a good-practice framework created by international professional association ISACA for information technology management and IT governance. _____ provides an implementable "set of controls over information technology and organizes them around a logical framework of IT-related processes and enablers."

Exam Probability: **High**

23. *Answer choices:*
(see index for correct answer)

- a. COBIT
- b. Web operations
- c. Contract management
- d. OPIDIS

*Guidance:* level 1

---

:: Behavioral and social facets of systemic risk ::

_____ is the difficulty in understanding an issue and effectively making decisions when one has too much information about that issue. Generally, the term is associated with the excessive quantity of daily information. _____ most likely originated from information theory, which are studies in the storage, preservation, communication, compression, and extraction of information. The term, _____ , was first used in Bertram Gross' 1964 book, The Managing of Organizations, and it was further popularized by Alvin Toffler in his bestselling 1970 book Future Shock. Speier et al. stated.

Exam Probability: **Medium**

24. *Answer choices:*
(see index for correct answer)

- a. Psychological manipulation
- b. virtuous cycle
- c. Information overload
- d. Attention management

*Guidance:* level 1

---

:: Business ::

_____ is a sourcing model in which individuals or organizations obtain goods and services, including ideas and finances, from a large, relatively open and often rapidly-evolving group of internet users; it divides work between participants to achieve a cumulative result. The word _____ itself is a portmanteau of crowd and outsourcing, and was coined in 2005. As a mode of sourcing, _____ existed prior to the digital age .

Exam Probability: **High**

25. *Answer choices:*
(see index for correct answer)

- a. Shriram Properties
- b. Architecture of Interoperable Information Systems
- c. Operating subsidiary
- d. Crowdsourcing

*Guidance:* level 1

---

:: Data management ::

_____ , or IG, is the management of information at an organization. _____ balances the use and security of information. _____ helps with legal compliance, operational transparency, and reducing expenditures associated with legal discovery. An organization can establish a consistent and logical framework for employees to handle data through their _____ policies and procedures. These policies guide proper behavior regarding how organizations and their employees handle electronically stored information .

Exam Probability: **Low**

26. *Answer choices:*
(see index for correct answer)

- a. State transition network
- b. Ontology merging
- c. Information governance
- d. Automatic data processing equipment

*Guidance:* level 1

---

:: Service-oriented (business computing) ::

_____ is a software licensing and delivery model in which software is licensed on a subscription basis and is centrally hosted. It is sometimes referred to as "on-demand software", and was formerly referred to as "software plus services" by Microsoft. SaaS is typically accessed by users using a thin client, e.g. via a web browser. SaaS has become a common delivery model for many business applications, including office software, messaging software, payroll processing software, DBMS software, management software, CAD software, development software, gamification, virtualization, accounting, collaboration, customer relationship management , Management Information Systems , enterprise resource planning , invoicing, human resource management , talent acquisition, learning management systems, content management , Geographic Information Systems , and service desk management. SaaS has been incorporated into the strategy of nearly all leading enterprise software companies.

Exam Probability: **High**

27. *Answer choices:*
(see index for correct answer)

- a. JackBe
- b. Open Knowledge Initiative
- c. Mushroom Networks
- d. Software as a service

*Guidance:* level 1

:: ::

A _____ is an abstract model that organizes elements of data and standardizes how they relate to one another and to properties of the real world entities. For instance, a _____ may specify that the data element representing a car be composed of a number of other elements which, in turn, represent the color and size of the car and define its owner.

Exam Probability: **Low**

28. *Answer choices:*
(see index for correct answer)

- a. information systems assessment
- b. co-culture
- c. empathy
- d. Character

:: Automatic identification and data capture ::

_____ uses electromagnetic fields to automatically identify and track tags attached to objects. The tags contain electronically stored information. Passive tags collect energy from a nearby RFID reader's interrogating radio waves. Active tags have a local power source and may operate hundreds of meters from the RFID reader. Unlike a barcode, the tag need not be within the line of sight of the reader, so it may be embedded in the tracked object. RFID is one method of automatic identification and data capture .

Exam Probability: **Low**

29. *Answer choices:*
(see index for correct answer)

- a. Bokode
- b. Mobile data terminal
- c. Smart label
- d. Automated species identification

:: ::

_____ is software designed to perform a group of coordinated functions, tasks, or activities for the benefit of the user. Examples of an application include a word processor, a spreadsheet, an accounting application, a web browser, an email client,a media player, a file viewer, an aeronautical flight simulator, a console game or a photo editor. The collective noun _____ refers to all applications collectively. This contrasts with system software, which is mainly involved with running the computer.

Exam Probability: **Medium**

30. *Answer choices:*
(see index for correct answer)

- a. Application software
- b. cultural
- c. co-culture
- d. open system

:: ::

_____ is software designed to provide a platform for other software. Examples of _____ include operating systems like macOS, Ubuntu and Microsoft Windows, computational science software, game engines, industrial automation, and software as a service applications.

Exam Probability: **Low**

31. *Answer choices:*
(see index for correct answer)

- a. process perspective
- b. interpersonal communication
- c. surface-level diversity
- d. System software

:: ::

Within the Internet, _____ s are formed by the rules and procedures of the _____ System . Any name registered in the DNS is a _____ . _____ s are used in various networking contexts and for application-specific naming and addressing purposes. In general, a _____ represents an Internet Protocol resource, such as a personal computer used to access the Internet, a server computer hosting a web site, or the web site itself or any other service communicated via the Internet. In 2017, 330.6 million _____ s had been registered.

Exam Probability: **Medium**

32. *Answer choices:*
(see index for correct answer)

- a. deep-level diversity
- b. similarity-attraction theory
- c. Domain name
- d. information systems assessment

:: Industrial design ::

Across the many fields concerned with _____ , including information science, computer science, human-computer interaction, communication, and industrial design, there is little agreement over the meaning of the term " _____ ", although all are related to interaction with computers and other machines with a user interface.

Exam Probability: **High**

33. *Answer choices:*
(see index for correct answer)

- a. WikID
- b. Interactivity
- c. Chintz
- d. Paris Convention for the Protection of Industrial Property

*Guidance:* level 1

---

:: E-commerce ::

_____ is a type of performance-based marketing in which a business rewards one or more affiliates for each visitor or customer brought by the affiliate's own marketing efforts.

Exam Probability: **Medium**

34. *Answer choices:*
(see index for correct answer)

- a. Andy Dunn
- b. Free Shipping Day
- c. Demandware
- d. Dragonpay

*Guidance:* level 1

---

:: Human–computer interaction ::

_____ is the ease of use and learnability of a human-made object such as a tool or device. In software engineering, _____ is the degree to which a software can be used by specified consumers to achieve quantified objectives with effectiveness, efficiency, and satisfaction in a quantified context of use.

Exam Probability: **Medium**

35. *Answer choices:*
(see index for correct answer)

- a. Ben Shneiderman
- b. 3D interaction
- c. Social affordance
- d. Learner-generated context

*Guidance:* level 1

---

:: Policy ::

A _____ is a statement or a legal document that discloses some or all of the ways a party gathers, uses, discloses, and manages a customer or client's data. It fulfills a legal requirement to protect a customer or client's privacy. Personal information can be anything that can be used to identify an individual, not limited to the person's name, address, date of birth, marital status, contact information, ID issue, and expiry date, financial records, credit information, medical history, where one travels, and intentions to acquire goods and services. In the case of a business it is often a statement that declares a party's policy on how it collects, stores, and releases personal information it collects. It informs the client what specific information is collected, and whether it is kept confidential, shared with partners, or sold to other firms or enterprises. Privacy policies typically represent a broader, more generalized treatment, as opposed to data use statements, which tend to be more detailed and specific.

Exam Probability: **High**

36. *Answer choices:*
(see index for correct answer)

- a. Privacy policy
- b. Multifunctionality in agriculture
- c. Veterinary Feed Directive

- d. Wicked problem

Guidance: level 1

---

:: SQL ::

SQL is a domain-specific language used in programming and designed for managing data held in a relational database management system , or for stream processing in a relational data stream management system . It is particularly useful in handling structured data where there are relations between different entities/variables of the data. SQL offers two main advantages over older read/write APIs like ISAM or VSAM. First, it introduced the concept of accessing many records with one single command; and second, it eliminates the need to specify how to reach a record, e.g. with or without an index.

Exam Probability: **High**

37. *Answer choices:*
(see index for correct answer)

- a. SQL PL
- b. SQL/XML
- c. Structured query language
- d. Correlated subquery

Guidance: level 1

---

:: Business process ::

_____ is a discipline in operations management in which people use various methods to discover, model, analyze, measure, improve, optimize, and automate business processes. BPM focuses on improving corporate performance by managing business processes. Any combination of methods used to manage a company's business processes is BPM. Processes can be structured and repeatable or unstructured and variable. Though not required, enabling technologies are often used with BPM.

Exam Probability: **High**

38. *Answer choices:*
(see index for correct answer)

- a. Business logic
- b. Business process management

- c. Business operations
- d. Real-time enterprise

*Guidance:* level 1

---

:: ::

_____ are interactive computer-mediated technologies that facilitate the creation and sharing of information, ideas, career interests and other forms of expression via virtual communities and networks. The variety of stand-alone and built-in _____ services currently available introduces challenges of definition; however, there are some common features.

Exam Probability: **Medium**

39. *Answer choices:*
(see index for correct answer)

- a. information systems assessment
- b. Character
- c. hierarchical
- d. co-culture

*Guidance:* level 1

---

:: Fraud ::

_____ is the deliberate use of someone else's identity, usually as a method to gain a financial advantage or obtain credit and other benefits in the other person's name, and perhaps to the other person's disadvantage or loss. The person whose identity has been assumed may suffer adverse consequences, especially if they are held responsible for the perpetrator's actions.
_____ occurs when someone uses another's personally identifying information, like their name, identifying number, or credit card number, without their permission, to commit fraud or other crimes. The term _____ was coined in 1964. Since that time, the definition of _____ has been statutorily prescribed throughout both the U.K. and the United States as the theft of personally identifying information, generally including a person's name, date of birth, social security number, driver's license number, bank account or credit card numbers, PIN numbers, electronic signatures, fingerprints, passwords, or any other information that can be used to access a person's financial resources.

40. *Answer choices:*

(see index for correct answer)

- a. Fraud in the factum
- b. Wangiri
- c. Identity theft
- d. Employment fraud

*Guidance:* level 1

:: ::

A web _____ or Internet _____ is a software system that is designed to carry out web search , which means to search the World Wide Web in a systematic way for particular information specified in a web search query. The search results are generally presented in a line of results, often referred to as _____ results pages . The information may be a mix of web pages, images, videos, infographics, articles, research papers and other types of files. Some _____ s also mine data available in databases or open directories. Unlike web directories, which are maintained only by human editors, _____ s also maintain real-time information by running an algorithm on a web crawler.Internet content that is not capable of being searched by a web _____ is generally described as the deep web.

41. *Answer choices:*

(see index for correct answer)

- a. empathy
- b. Search engine
- c. process perspective
- d. personal values

*Guidance:* level 1

:: Supply chain management terms ::

In business and finance, _____ is a system of organizations, people, activities, information, and resources involved in moving a product or service from supplier to customer. _____ activities involve the transformation of natural resources, raw materials, and components into a finished product that is delivered to the end customer. In sophisticated _____ systems, used products may re-enter the _____ at any point where residual value is recyclable. _____ s link value chains.

Exam Probability: **Low**

42. *Answer choices:*
(see index for correct answer)

- a. Supply chain
- b. Stockout
- c. Overstock
- d. Supply-chain management

*Guidance:* level 1

---

:: Survey methodology ::

A _____ is the procedure of systematically acquiring and recording information about the members of a given population. The term is used mostly in connection with national population and housing _____ es; other common _____ es include agriculture, business, and traffic _____ es. The United Nations defines the essential features of population and housing _____ es as "individual enumeration, universality within a defined territory, simultaneity and defined periodicity", and recommends that population _____ es be taken at least every 10 years. United Nations recommendations also cover _____ topics to be collected, official definitions, classifications and other useful information to co-ordinate international practice.

Exam Probability: **Medium**

43. *Answer choices:*
(see index for correct answer)

- a. Public opinion
- b. Swiss Centre of Expertise in the Social Sciences
- c. Total survey error
- d. Census

:: ::

Collaborative software or _____ is application software designed to help people involved in a common task to achieve their goals. One of the earliest definitions of collaborative software is "intentional group processes plus software to support them".

Exam Probability: **Low**

44. *Answer choices:*
(see index for correct answer)

- a. personal values
- b. Groupware
- c. hierarchical perspective
- d. levels of analysis

:: ::

The _____ , commonly known as the Web, is an information system where documents and other web resources are identified by Uniform Resource Locators , which may be interlinked by hypertext, and are accessible over the Internet.
The resources of the WWW may be accessed by users by a software application called a web browser.

Exam Probability: **Low**

45. *Answer choices:*
(see index for correct answer)

- a. process perspective
- b. corporate values
- c. World Wide Web
- d. deep-level diversity

:: E-commerce ::

A _____ is a plastic payment card that can be used instead of cash when making purchases. It is similar to a credit card, but unlike a credit card, the money is immediately transferred directly from the cardholder's bank account when performing a transaction.

Exam Probability: **Medium**

46. *Answer choices:*
(see index for correct answer)

- a. Variable pricing
- b. Electronic Commerce Regulations 2002
- c. ITransact
- d. Over-the-top content

*Guidance:* level 1

:: Marketing by medium ::

_____ or viral advertising is a business strategy that uses existing social networks to promote a product. Its name refers to how consumers spread information about a product with other people in their social networks, much in the same way that a virus spreads from one person to another. It can be delivered by word of mouth or enhanced by the network effects of the Internet and mobile networks.

Exam Probability: **Low**

47. *Answer choices:*
(see index for correct answer)

- a. Social video marketing
- b. Social intelligence architect
- c. Viral marketing
- d. Online advertising

*Guidance:* level 1

:: Virtual reality ::

A _____ is a computer-based simulated environment which may be populated by many users who can create a personal avatar, and simultaneously and independently explore the _____ , participate in its activities and communicate with others. These avatars can be textual, two or three-dimensional graphical representations, or live video avatars with auditory and touch sensations. In general, _____ s allow for multiple users but single player computer games, such as Skyrim, can also be considered a type of _____ .

Exam Probability: **Medium**

48. *Answer choices:*
(see index for correct answer)

- a. Leadwerks Engine
- b. Virtual world
- c. Typhoon
- d. Computer simulation

*Guidance:* level 1

---

:: Data ::

_____ is viewed by many disciplines as a modern equivalent of visual communication. It involves the creation and study of the visual representation of data.

Exam Probability: **Low**

49. *Answer choices:*
(see index for correct answer)

- a. Empress Embedded Database
- b. Infonomics
- c. Data visualization
- d. Data acquisition

*Guidance:* level 1

---

:: Computing input devices ::

In computing, an _____ is a piece of computer hardware equipment used to provide data and control signals to an information processing system such as a computer or information appliance. Examples of _____ s include keyboards, mouse, scanners, digital cameras and joysticks. Audio _____ s may be used for purposes including speech recognition. Many companies are utilizing speech recognition to help assist users to use their device.

Exam Probability: **High**

50. *Answer choices:*
(see index for correct answer)

- a. Doxie
- b. FaceVsion
- c. Input device
- d. Light pen

*Guidance:* level 1

:: Information systems ::

A _____ manages the creation and modification of digital content. It typically supports multiple users in a collaborative environment.

Exam Probability: **Low**

51. *Answer choices:*
(see index for correct answer)

- a. Content management system
- b. Ucode system
- c. CGA
- d. Railway costing

*Guidance:* level 1

:: Supply chain management ::

ERP is usually referred to as a category of business management software — typically a suite of integrated applications—that an organization can use to collect, store, manage, and interpret data from these many business activities.

52. *Answer choices:*
(see index for correct answer)

- a. Reverse auction
- b. TXT e-solutions
- c. Enterprise resource planning
- d. JDA Software

*Guidance:* level 1

:: Network analyzers ::

A _____ , meaning "meat eater" , is an organism that derives its energy and nutrient requirements from a diet consisting mainly or exclusively of animal tissue, whether through predation or scavenging. Animals that depend solely on animal flesh for their nutrient requirements are called obligate _____ s while those that also consume non-animal food are called facultative _____ s. Omnivores also consume both animal and non-animal food, and, apart from the more general definition, there is no clearly defined ratio of plant to animal material that would distinguish a facultative _____ from an omnivore. A _____ at the top of the food chain, not preyed upon by other animals, is termed an apex predator.

Exam Probability: **Medium**

53. *Answer choices:*
(see index for correct answer)

- a. Weplab
- b. Carnivore
- c. Monitor mode
- d. PathPing

*Guidance:* level 1

:: Information science ::

In discourse-based grammatical theory, _____ is any tracking of referential information by speakers. Information may be new, just introduced into the conversation; given, already active in the speakers' consciousness; or old, no longer active. The various types of activation, and how these are defined, are model-dependent.

54. *Answer choices:*
(see index for correct answer)

- a. Information flow
- b. Actionable information logistics
- c. Cultural informatics
- d. Jason Farradane

*Guidance:* level 1

---

:: Information technology management ::

The term _____ is used to refer to periods when a system is unavailable. _____ or outage duration refers to a period of time that a system fails to provide or perform its primary function. Reliability, availability, recovery, and unavailability are related concepts. The unavailability is the proportion of a time-span that a system is unavailable or offline. This is usually a result of the system failing to function because of an unplanned event, or because of routine maintenance .

Exam Probability: **Medium**

55. *Answer choices:*
(see index for correct answer)

- a. ITIL security management
- b. Test effort
- c. ISO/IEC 19770
- d. Downtime

*Guidance:* level 1

---

:: Market research ::

_____ s are many different distantly related animals that typically have a long cylindrical tube-like body and no limbs. _____ s vary in size from microscopic to over 1 metre in length for marine polychaete _____ s , 6.7 metres for the African giant earth _____ , Microchaetus rappi, and 58 metres for the marine nemertean _____ , Lineus longissimus. Various types of _____ occupy a small variety of parasitic niches, living inside the bodies of other animals. Free-living _____ species do not live on land, but instead, live in marine or freshwater environments, or underground by burrowing.In biology, " _____ " refers to an obsolete taxon, vermes, used by Carolus Linnaeus and Jean-Baptiste Lamarck for all non-arthropod invertebrate animals, now seen to be paraphyletic. The name stems from the Old English word wyrm. Most animals called " _____ s" are invertebrates, but the term is also used for the amphibian caecilians and the slow _____ Anguis, a legless burrowing lizard. Invertebrate animals commonly called " _____ s" include annelids , nematodes , platyhelminthes , marine nemertean _____ s , marine Chaetognatha , priapulid _____ s, and insect larvae such as grubs and maggots.

Exam Probability: **Medium**

56. *Answer choices:*
(see index for correct answer)

- a. Customer advisory council
- b. Location intelligence
- c. Worm
- d. Early adopter

*Guidance:* level 1

---

:: Information retrieval ::

_____ is the practice of making content from multiple enterprise-type sources, such as databases and intranets, searchable to a defined audience .

Exam Probability: **Medium**

57. *Answer choices:*
(see index for correct answer)

- a. Search-based application
- b. Clairlib
- c. Subsetting

- d. Enterprise search

Guidance: level 1

:: ::

The _____ of 1996 was enacted by the 104th United States Congress and signed by President Bill Clinton in 1996. It was created primarily to modernize the flow of healthcare information, stipulate how Personally Identifiable Information maintained by the healthcare and healthcare insurance industries should be protected from fraud and theft, and address limitations on healthcare insurance coverage.

Exam Probability: **Medium**

58. *Answer choices:*
(see index for correct answer)

- a. Health Insurance Portability and Accountability Act
- b. Character
- c. Sarbanes-Oxley act of 2002
- d. cultural

Guidance: level 1

:: Infographics ::

A _____ is a graphical representation of data, in which "the data is represented by symbols, such as bars in a bar _____ , lines in a line _____ , or slices in a pie _____ ". A _____ can represent tabular numeric data, functions or some kinds of qualitative structure and provides different info.

Exam Probability: **High**

59. *Answer choices:*
(see index for correct answer)

- a. Ionogram
- b. Statistical graphics
- c. The Way Things Work
- d. Moose

Guidance: level 1

## Marketing

Marketing is the study and management of exchange relationships. Marketing is the business process of creating relationships with and satisfying customers. With its focus on the customer, marketing is one of the premier components of business management.

Marketing is defined by the American Marketing Association as "the activity, set of institutions, and processes for creating, communicating, delivering, and exchanging offerings that have value for customers, clients, partners, and society at large."

---

:: Network theory ::

A _____ is a social structure made up of a set of social actors , sets of dyadic ties, and other social interactions between actors. The _____ perspective provides a set of methods for analyzing the structure of whole social entities as well as a variety of theories explaining the patterns observed in these structures. The study of these structures uses _____ analysis to identify local and global patterns, locate influential entities, and examine network dynamics.

Exam Probability: **Medium**

1. *Answer choices:*
(see index for correct answer)

- a. Centrality
- b. Fitness model
- c. Social network
- d. Narrative network

*Guidance:* level 1

---

:: ::

_____ or commercialisation is the process of introducing a new product or production method into commerce—making it available on the market. The term often connotes especially entry into the mass market , but it also includes a move from the laboratory into commerce. Many technologies begin in a research and development laboratory or in an inventor's workshop and may not be practical for commercial use in their infancy . The "development" segment of the "research and development" spectrum requires time and money as systems are engineered with a view to making the product or method a paying commercial proposition. The product launch of a new product is the final stage of new product development - at this point advertising, sales promotion, and other marketing efforts encourage commercial adoption of the product or method. Beyond _____ can lie consumerization .

Exam Probability: **High**

2. *Answer choices:*
(see index for correct answer)

- a. imperative
- b. corporate values
- c. Commercialization
- d. levels of analysis

*Guidance:* level 1

---

:: Commodities ::

In economics, a _____ is an economic good or service that has full or substantial fungibility: that is, the market treats instances of the good as equivalent or nearly so with no regard to who produced them. Most commodities are raw materials, basic resources, agricultural, or mining products, such as iron ore, sugar, or grains like rice and wheat. Commodities can also be mass-produced unspecialized products such as chemicals and computer memory.

Exam Probability: **Low**

3. *Answer choices:*
(see index for correct answer)

- a. Commoditization
- b. IRely
- c. Commodity money
- d. Commodity pathway diversion

:: Generally Accepted Accounting Principles ::

Expenditure is an outflow of money to another person or group to pay for an item or service, or for a category of costs. For a tenant, rent is an _____ . For students or parents, tuition is an _____ . Buying food, clothing, furniture or an automobile is often referred to as an _____ . An _____ is a cost that is "paid" or "remitted", usually in exchange for something of value. Something that seems to cost a great deal is "expensive". Something that seems to cost little is "inexpensive". " _____ s of the table" are _____ s of dining, refreshments, a feast, etc.

Exam Probability: **High**

4. *Answer choices:*

(see index for correct answer)

- a. Indian Accounting Standards
- b. Normal balance
- c. Expense
- d. Earnings before interest, taxes, depreciation, and amortization

:: Market research ::

_____ refers to a collection of methods that managers use to analyze an organization's internal and external environment to understand the organization's capabilities, customers, and business environment. The _____ consists of several methods of analysis: The 5Cs Analysis, SWOT analysis and Porter five forces analysis. A Marketing Plan is created to guide businesses on how to communicate the benefits of their products to the needs of potential customer. The _____ is the second step in the marketing plan and is a critical step in establishing a long term relationship with customers.

Exam Probability: **High**

5. *Answer choices:*

(see index for correct answer)

- a. Ecological model of competition
- b. INDEX

- c. Innovation game
- d. Nielsen SoundScan

Guidance: level 1

:: ::

A _____ is an organized collection of data, generally stored and accessed electronically from a computer system. Where _____ s are more complex they are often developed using formal design and modeling techniques.

Exam Probability: **Medium**

6. *Answer choices:*
(see index for correct answer)

- a. personal values
- b. information systems assessment
- c. Database
- d. process perspective

Guidance: level 1

:: Financial economics ::

In management, business value is an informal term that includes all forms of value that determine the health and well-being of the firm in the long run. Business value expands concept of value of the firm beyond economic value to include other forms of value such as employee value, _____ , supplier value, channel partner value, alliance partner value, managerial value, and societal value. Many of these forms of value are not directly measured in monetary terms.

Exam Probability: **Medium**

7. *Answer choices:*
(see index for correct answer)

- a. Lookback option
- b. Forward price
- c. Capital asset
- d. Cyclical asymmetry

Guidance: level 1

In production, research, retail, and accounting, a _____ is the value of money that has been used up to produce something or deliver a service, and hence is not available for use anymore. In business, the _____ may be one of acquisition, in which case the amount of money expended to acquire it is counted as _____ . In this case, money is the input that is gone in order to acquire the thing. This acquisition _____ may be the sum of the _____ of production as incurred by the original producer, and further _____ s of transaction as incurred by the acquirer over and above the price paid to the producer. Usually, the price also includes a mark-up for profit over the _____ of production.

Exam Probability: **Low**

8. *Answer choices:*

- a. cultural
- b. interpersonal communication
- c. similarity-attraction theory
- d. Cost

*Guidance:* level 1

---

_____ is the production of products for use or sale using labour and machines, tools, chemical and biological processing, or formulation. The term may refer to a range of human activity, from handicraft to high tech, but is most commonly applied to industrial design, in which raw materials are transformed into finished goods on a large scale. Such finished goods may be sold to other manufacturers for the production of other, more complex products, such as aircraft, household appliances, furniture, sports equipment or automobiles, or sold to wholesalers, who in turn sell them to retailers, who then sell them to end users and consumers.

Exam Probability: **Medium**

9. *Answer choices:*

- a. deep-level diversity

- b. imperative
- c. Manufacturing
- d. surface-level diversity

*Guidance:* level 1

---

:: Market research ::

_____ , an acronym for Information through Disguised Experimentation is an annual market research fair conducted by the students of IIM-Lucknow. Students create games and use various other simulated environments to capture consumers' subconscious thoughts. This innovative method of market research removes the sensitization effect that might bias peoples answers to questions. This ensures that the most truthful answers are captured to research questions. The games are designed in such a way that the observers can elicit all the required information just by observing and noting down the behaviour and the responses of the participants.

Exam Probability: **Low**

10. *Answer choices:*
(see index for correct answer)

- a. AbsolutData
- b. Friday night death slot
- c. Coolhunting
- d. Competitor analysis

*Guidance:* level 1

---

:: Marketing ::

_____ is research conducted for a problem that has not been studied more clearly, intended to establish priorities, develop operational definitions and improve the final research design. _____ helps determine the best research design, data-collection method and selection of subjects. It should draw definitive conclusions only with extreme caution. Given its fundamental nature, _____ often relies on techniques such as.

Exam Probability: **Low**

11. *Answer choices:*
(see index for correct answer)

- a. Mass marketing
- b. Consumer complaint
- c. Predatory pricing
- d. Exploratory research

---

:: Management ::

_____ is the organizational discipline which focuses on the practical application of marketing orientation, techniques and methods inside enterprises and organizations and on the management of a firm's marketing resources and activities.

Exam Probability: **Medium**

12. *Answer choices:*
(see index for correct answer)

- a. Document automation
- b. Project team builder
- c. Marketing management
- d. Vasa syndrome

---

:: Generally Accepted Accounting Principles ::

In accounting, _____ is the income that a business have from its normal business activities, usually from the sale of goods and services to customers. _____ is also referred to as sales or turnover. Some companies receive _____ from interest, royalties, or other fees. _____ may refer to business income in general, or it may refer to the amount, in a monetary unit, earned during a period of time, as in "Last year, Company X had _____ of $42 million". Profits or net income generally imply total _____ minus total expenses in a given period. In accounting, in the balance statement it is a subsection of the Equity section and _____ increases equity, it is often referred to as the "top line" due to its position on the income statement at the very top. This is to be contrasted with the "bottom line" which denotes net income .

Exam Probability: **High**

13. *Answer choices:*

(see index for correct answer)

- a. Gross profit
- b. Access to finance
- c. Revenue
- d. Fixed investment

*Guidance:* level 1

---

:: ::

Bloomberg Businessweek is an American weekly business magazine published since 2009 by Bloomberg L.P. Businessweek, founded in 1929, aimed to provide information and interpretation about events in the business world. The magazine is headquartered in New York City. Megan Murphy served as editor from November 2016; she stepped down from the role in January 2018 and Joel Weber was appointed in her place. The magazine is published 47 times a year.

Exam Probability: **Medium**

14. *Answer choices:*

(see index for correct answer)

- a. interpersonal communication
- b. Business Week
- c. Sarbanes-Oxley act of 2002
- d. Character

*Guidance:* level 1

---

:: Management occupations ::

_____ ship is the process of designing, launching and running a new business, which is often initially a small business. The people who create these businesses are called _____ s.

Exam Probability: **High**

15. *Answer choices:*

(see index for correct answer)

- a. Functional manager
- b. Entrepreneur
- c. Comprador
- d. Apparatchik

:: Survey methodology ::

_____ is often used to assess thoughts, opinions, and feelings. Surveys can be specific and limited, or they can have more global, widespread goals. Psychologists and sociologists often use surveys to analyze behavior, while it is also used to meet the more pragmatic needs of the media, such as, in evaluating political candidates, public health officials, professional organizations, and advertising and marketing directors. A survey consists of a predetermined set of questions that is given to a sample. With a representative sample, that is, one that is representative of the larger population of interest, one can describe the attitudes of the population from which the sample was drawn. Further, one can compare the attitudes of different populations as well as look for changes in attitudes over time. A good sample selection is key as it allows one to generalize the findings from the sample to the population, which is the whole purpose of _____ .

Exam Probability: **Low**

16. *Answer choices:*
(see index for correct answer)

- a. Survey research
- b. Swiss Centre of Expertise in the Social Sciences
- c. World Association for Public Opinion Research
- d. Total survey error

:: ::

_____ is the provision of service to customers before, during and after a purchase. The perception of success of such interactions is dependent on employees "who can adjust themselves to the personality of the guest". _____ concerns the priority an organization assigns to _____ relative to components such as product innovation and pricing. In this sense, an organization that values good _____ may spend more money in training employees than the average organization or may proactively interview customers for feedback.

17. *Answer choices:*

(see index for correct answer)

- a. cultural
- b. hierarchical
- c. imperative
- d. process perspective

*Guidance:* level 1

---

:: Data analysis ::

_____ is a process of inspecting, cleansing, transforming, and modeling data with the goal of discovering useful information, informing conclusions, and supporting decision-making. _____ has multiple facets and approaches, encompassing diverse techniques under a variety of names, and is used in different business, science, and social science domains. In today's business world, _____ plays a role in making decisions more scientific and helping businesses operate more effectively.

Exam Probability: **High**

18. *Answer choices:*

(see index for correct answer)

- a. Oversampling and undersampling in data analysis
- b. German tank problem
- c. Ariel Beresniak
- d. Topological data analysis

*Guidance:* level 1

---

:: Production economics ::

In microeconomics, _____ are the cost advantages that enterprises obtain due to their scale of operation , with cost per unit of output decreasing with increasing scale.

Exam Probability: **Low**

19. *Answer choices:*

(see index for correct answer)

- a. Marginal product
- b. Value and Capital
- c. Synergy
- d. Capacity utilization

*Guidance:* level 1

---

:: Logistics ::

_____ is generally the detailed organization and implementation of a complex operation. In a general business sense, _____ is the management of the flow of things between the point of origin and the point of consumption in order to meet requirements of customers or corporations. The resources managed in _____ may include tangible goods such as materials, equipment, and supplies, as well as food and other consumable items. The _____ of physical items usually involves the integration of information flow, materials handling, production, packaging, inventory, transportation, warehousing, and often security.

Exam Probability: **Medium**

20. *Answer choices:*
(see index for correct answer)

- a. TI-HI
- b. Global Data Synchronization Network
- c. Logistics
- d. Biomedical Equipment Technician

*Guidance:* level 1

---

:: Monopoly (economics) ::

The _____ of 1890 was a United States antitrust law that regulates competition among enterprises, which was passed by Congress under the presidency of Benjamin Harrison.

Exam Probability: **Medium**

21. *Answer choices:*
(see index for correct answer)

- a. Sherman Antitrust Act
- b. Special 301 Report
- c. Chamberlinian monopolistic competition

- d. Natural monopoly

Guidance: level 1

---

:: ::

_____ is the means to see, hear, or become aware of something or someone through our fundamental senses. The term _____ derives from the Latin word perceptio, and is the organization, identification, and interpretation of sensory information in order to represent and understand the presented information, or the environment.

Exam Probability: **Low**

22. *Answer choices:*
(see index for correct answer)

- a. Character
- b. deep-level diversity
- c. Sarbanes-Oxley act of 2002
- d. empathy

Guidance: level 1

---

:: Retailing ::

A _____ is a retail establishment offering a wide range of consumer goods in different product categories known as "departments". In modern major cities, the _____ made a dramatic appearance in the middle of the 19th century, and permanently reshaped shopping habits, and the definition of service and luxury. Similar developments were under way in London , in Paris and in New York .

Exam Probability: **Medium**

23. *Answer choices:*
(see index for correct answer)

- a. Chain store
- b. Diffusion line
- c. Omni-channel Retailing
- d. Department store

Guidance: level 1

:: Public relations ::

_____ is the public visibility or awareness for any product, service or company. It may also refer to the movement of information from its source to the general public, often but not always via the media. The subjects of _____ include people , goods and services, organizations, and works of art or entertainment.

Exam Probability: **Low**

24. *Answer choices:*
(see index for correct answer)

- a. Publicity
- b. Sparkpr
- c. Media monitoring service
- d. Litigation public relations

*Guidance:* level 1

---

:: Advertising ::

A _____ is a large outdoor advertising structure , typically found in high-traffic areas such as alongside busy roads. _____ s present large advertisements to passing pedestrians and drivers. Typically showing witty slogans and distinctive visuals, _____ s are highly visible in the top designated market areas.

Exam Probability: **High**

25. *Answer choices:*
(see index for correct answer)

- a. Cidade Limpa
- b. Retail media
- c. VigLink
- d. Billboard

*Guidance:* level 1

---

:: Commercial item transport and distribution ::

In commerce, supply-chain management , the management of the flow of goods and services, involves the movement and storage of raw materials, of work-in-process inventory, and of finished goods from point of origin to point of consumption. Interconnected or interlinked networks, channels and node businesses combine in the provision of products and services required by end customers in a supply chain. Supply-chain management has been defined  as the "design, planning, execution, control, and monitoring of supply-chain activities with the objective of creating net value, building a competitive infrastructure, leveraging worldwide logistics, synchronizing supply with demand and measuring performance globally."SCM practice draws heavily from the areas of industrial engineering, systems engineering, operations management, logistics, procurement, information technology, and marketing  and strives for an integrated approach. Marketing channels play an important role in supply-chain management. Current research in supply-chain management is concerned with topics related to sustainability and risk management, among others. Some suggest that the "people dimension" of SCM, ethical issues, internal integration, transparency/visibility, and human capital/talent management are topics that have, so far, been underrepresented on the research agenda.

Exam Probability: **High**

26. *Answer choices:*
(see index for correct answer)

- a. Zeppelin
- b. Supply chain management
- c. Wholesale fashion distribution
- d. Courier software

*Guidance:* level 1

:: ::

An _____ is an area of the production, distribution, or trade, and consumption of goods and services by different agents. Understood in its broadest sense, 'The _____ is defined as a social domain that emphasize the practices, discourses, and material expressions associated with the production, use, and management of resources'. Economic agents can be individuals, businesses, organizations, or governments. Economic transactions occur when two parties agree to the value or price of the transacted good or service, commonly expressed in a certain currency. However, monetary transactions only account for a small part of the economic domain.

Exam Probability: **Low**

27. *Answer choices:*
(see index for correct answer)

- a. corporate values
- b. hierarchical
- c. information systems assessment
- d. Economy

*Guidance:* level 1

:: ::

_____ is the act of conveying meanings from one entity or group to another through the use of mutually understood signs, symbols, and semiotic rules.

Exam Probability: **Medium**

28. *Answer choices:*
(see index for correct answer)

- a. information systems assessment
- b. cultural
- c. Communication
- d. similarity-attraction theory

*Guidance:* level 1

:: Retailing ::

_____ is the process of selling consumer goods or services to customers through multiple channels of distribution to earn a profit. _____ ers satisfy demand identified through a supply chain. The term " _____ er" is typically applied where a service provider fills the small orders of a large number of individuals, who are end-users, rather than large orders of a small number of wholesale, corporate or government clientele. Shopping generally refers to the act of buying products. Sometimes this is done to obtain final goods, including necessities such as food and clothing; sometimes it takes place as a recreational activity. Recreational shopping often involves window shopping and browsing: it does not always result in a purchase.

Exam Probability: **High**

29. *Answer choices:*
(see index for correct answer)

- a. Consignment
- b. People counter
- c. Junk shop
- d. Retail

*Guidance:* level 1

:: Advertising techniques ::

In promotion and of advertising, a _____ or show consists of a person's written or spoken statement extolling the virtue of a product. The term " _____ " most commonly applies to the sales-pitches attributed to ordinary citizens, whereas the word "endorsement" usually applies to pitches by celebrities. _____ s can be part of communal marketing. Sometimes, the cartoon character can be a _____ in a commercial.

Exam Probability: **Low**

30. *Answer choices:*
(see index for correct answer)

- a. Soft sell
- b. Trojan horse
- c. Roll-in
- d. Dolly Dimples

*Guidance:* level 1

_____ Corporation is an American multinational technology company with headquarters in Redmond, Washington. It develops, manufactures, licenses, supports and sells computer software, consumer electronics, personal computers, and related services. Its best known software products are the _____ Windows line of operating systems, the _____ Office suite, and the Internet Explorer and Edge Web browsers. Its flagship hardware products are the Xbox video game consoles and the _____ Surface lineup of touchscreen personal computers. As of 2016, it is the world's largest software maker by revenue, and one of the world's most valuable companies. The word " _____ " is a portmanteau of "microcomputer" and "software". _____ is ranked No. 30 in the 2018 Fortune 500 rankings of the largest United States corporations by total revenue.

Exam Probability: **High**

31. *Answer choices:*
(see index for correct answer)

- a. information systems assessment
- b. hierarchical perspective
- c. Microsoft
- d. levels of analysis

*Guidance:* level 1

---

_____ s  are formal, sociotechnical, organizational systems designed to collect, process, store, and distribute information. In a sociotechnical perspective, _____ s are composed by four components: task, people, structure , and technology.

Exam Probability: **High**

32. *Answer choices:*
(see index for correct answer)

- a. Information system
- b. co-culture
- c. information systems assessment
- d. process perspective

:: Auctioneering ::

An _____ is a process of buying and selling goods or services by offering them up for bid, taking bids, and then selling the item to the highest bidder. The open ascending price _____ is arguably the most common form of _____ in use today. Participants bid openly against one another, with each subsequent bid required to be higher than the previous bid. An _____ eer may announce prices, bidders may call out their bids themselves , or bids may be submitted electronically with the highest current bid publicly displayed. In a Dutch _____ , the _____ eer begins with a high asking price for some quantity of like items; the price is lowered until a participant is willing to accept the _____ eer`s price for some quantity of the goods in the lot or until the seller`s reserve price is met. While _____ s are most associated in the public imagination with the sale of antiques, paintings, rare collectibles and expensive wines, _____ s are also used for commodities, livestock, radio spectrum and used cars. In economic theory, an _____ may refer to any mechanism or set of trading rules for exchange.

Exam Probability: **Low**

33. *Answer choices:*
(see index for correct answer)

- a. Name Your Own Price
- b. Vickrey auction
- c. Auction
- d. Auction chant

:: ::

In _____ relations and communication science, _____ s are groups of individual people, and the _____ is the totality of such groupings. This is a different concept to the sociological concept of the Öffentlichkeit or _____ sphere. The concept of a _____ has also been defined in political science, psychology, marketing, and advertising. In _____ relations and communication science, it is one of the more ambiguous concepts in the field. Although it has definitions in the theory of the field that have been formulated from the early 20th century onwards, it has suffered in more recent years from being blurred, as a result of conflation of the idea of a _____ with the notions of audience, market segment, community, constituency, and stakeholder.

Exam Probability: **Medium**

34. *Answer choices:*
(see index for correct answer)

- a. cultural
- b. similarity-attraction theory
- c. Public
- d. open system

*Guidance:* level 1

---

:: Market research ::

_____ is "the process or set of processes that links the producers, customers, and end users to the marketer through information used to identify and define marketing opportunities and problems; generate, refine, and evaluate marketing actions; monitor marketing performance; and improve understanding of marketing as a process. _____ specifies the information required to address these issues, designs the method for collecting information, manages and implements the data collection process, analyzes the results, and communicates the findings and their implications."

Exam Probability: **High**

35. *Answer choices:*
(see index for correct answer)

- a. Sagacity segmentation
- b. Product forecasting
- c. Qualitative marketing research

- d. Marketing research

*Guidance:* level 1

---

:: Human resource management ::

_____ encompasses values and behaviors that contribute to the unique social and psychological environment of a business. The _____ influences the way people interact, the context within which knowledge is created, the resistance they will have towards certain changes, and ultimately the way they share knowledge. _____ represents the collective values, beliefs and principles of organizational members and is a product of factors such as history, product, market, technology, strategy, type of employees, management style, and national culture; culture includes the organization's vision, values, norms, systems, symbols, language, assumptions, environment, location, beliefs and habits.

Exam Probability: **Medium**

36. *Answer choices:*
(see index for correct answer)

- a. The Giving of Orders
- b. Organizational orientations
- c. Incentive program
- d. Talent supply chain management

*Guidance:* level 1

---

:: Health promotion ::

_____ is a form of advertising, it has been a large industry for some time now. Originally with newspapers and billboards, but now we have advanced to huge LCD screens and online advertisement on social medias and websites. The most common use of _____ in today's society is through social media.. It has the primary goal of achieving "social good". Traditional commercial marketing aims are primarily financial, though they can have positive social affects as well. In the context of public health, _____ would promote general health, raise awareness and induce changes in behaviour. To see _____ as only the use of standard commercial marketing practices to achieve non-commercial goals is an oversimplified view.

**37.** *Answer choices:*
(see index for correct answer)

- a. Eberhard Wenzel
- b. Social marketing
- c. NHS Health Scotland
- d. Choosing Wisely

*Guidance:* level 1

---

:: Product management ::

A _____ , trade mark, or trade-mark is a recognizable sign, design, or expression which identifies products or services of a particular source from those of others, although _____ s used to identify services are usually called service marks. The _____ owner can be an individual, business organization, or any legal entity. A _____ may be located on a package, a label, a voucher, or on the product itself. For the sake of corporate identity, _____ s are often displayed on company buildings. It is legally recognized as a type of intellectual property.

Exam Probability: **High**

**38.** *Answer choices:*
(see index for correct answer)

- a. Brand equity
- b. Control chart
- c. Trademark
- d. Dwinell-Wright Company

*Guidance:* level 1

---

:: ::

In financial markets, a share is a unit used as mutual funds, limited partnerships, and real estate investment trusts. The owner of _____ in the corporation/company is a shareholder of the corporation. A share is an indivisible unit of capital, expressing the ownership relationship between the company and the shareholder. The denominated value of a share is its face value, and the total of the face value of issued _____ represent the capital of a company, which may not reflect the market value of those _____ .

Exam Probability: **Medium**

39. *Answer choices:*
(see index for correct answer)

- a. co-culture
- b. interpersonal communication
- c. functional perspective
- d. Shares

*Guidance:* level 1

:: Business terms ::

A _____ is a short statement of why an organization exists, what its overall goal is, identifying the goal of its operations: what kind of product or service it provides, its primary customers or market, and its geographical region of operation. It may include a short statement of such fundamental matters as the organization's values or philosophies, a business's main competitive advantages, or a desired future state—the "vision".

Exam Probability: **Medium**

40. *Answer choices:*
(see index for correct answer)

- a. Mission statement
- b. strategic plan
- c. Owner Controlled Insurance Program
- d. back office

*Guidance:* level 1

:: Commerce ::

_____ relates to "the exchange of goods and services, especially on a large scale". It includes legal, economic, political, social, cultural and technological systems that operate in a country or in international trade.

Exam Probability: **High**

41. *Answer choices:*

- a. Quickbrowse
- b. Shipping list
- c. Social dumping
- d. Commerce

*Guidance:* level 1

:: Management ::

In business, a _____ is the attribute that allows an organization to outperform its competitors. A _____ may include access to natural resources, such as high-grade ores or a low-cost power source, highly skilled labor, geographic location, high entry barriers, and access to new technology.

Exam Probability: **High**

42. *Answer choices:*

- a. Competitive advantage
- b. Personal offshoring
- c. Dynamic enterprise modeling
- d. Libertarian management

*Guidance:* level 1

:: Business models ::

A _____ , _____ company or daughter company is a company that is owned or controlled by another company, which is called the parent company, parent, or holding company. The _____ can be a company, corporation, or limited liability company. In some cases it is a government or state-owned enterprise. In some cases, particularly in the music and book publishing industries, subsidiaries are referred to as imprints.

Exam Probability: **High**

43. *Answer choices:*
(see index for correct answer)

- a. InnovationXchange
- b. Business Model Canvas
- c. Independent business
- d. Technology push

*Guidance:* level 1

:: Marketing ::

_____ is a market strategy in which a firm decides to ignore market segment differences and appeal the whole market with one offer or one strategy, which supports the idea of broadcasting a message that will reach the largest number of people possible. Traditionally _____ has focused on radio, television and newspapers as the media used to reach this broad audience. By reaching the largest audience possible, exposure to the product is maximized, and in theory this would directly correlate with a larger number of sales or buys into the product.

Exam Probability: **Medium**

44. *Answer choices:*
(see index for correct answer)

- a. Enterprise marketing management
- b. Market sector
- c. Penetration pricing
- d. Mass marketing

*Guidance:* level 1

:: ::

A _____ consists of one people who live in the same dwelling and share meals. It may also consist of a single family or another group of people. A dwelling is considered to contain multiple _____ s if meals or living spaces are not shared. The _____ is the basic unit of analysis in many social, microeconomic and government models, and is important to economics and inheritance.

Exam Probability: **Medium**

45. *Answer choices:*
(see index for correct answer)

- a. Household
- b. co-culture
- c. empathy
- d. Character

*Guidance:* level 1

---

:: Brand management ::

Marketing communications uses different marketing channels and tools in combination: Marketing communication channels focus on any way a business communicates a message to its desired market, or the market in general. A marketing communication tool can be anything from: advertising, personal selling, direct marketing, sponsorship, communication, and promotion to public relations.

Exam Probability: **High**

46. *Answer choices:*
(see index for correct answer)

- a. Integrated marketing
- b. Brand preference
- c. The Co-operative brand
- d. Brand awareness

*Guidance:* level 1

---

:: ::

The _____ is a U.S. business-focused, English-language international daily newspaper based in New York City. The Journal, along with its Asian and European editions, is published six days a week by Dow Jones & Company, a division of News Corp. The newspaper is published in the broadsheet format and online. The Journal has been printed continuously since its inception on July 8, 1889, by Charles Dow, Edward Jones, and Charles Bergstresser.

Exam Probability: **Medium**

47. *Answer choices:*
(see index for correct answer)

- a. Wall Street Journal
- b. cultural
- c. personal values
- d. Character

*Guidance:* level 1

---

:: Advertising ::

_____ is the behavioral and cognitive process of selectively concentrating on a discrete aspect of information, whether deemed subjective or objective, while ignoring other perceivable information. It is a state of arousal. It is the taking possession by the mind in clear and vivid form of one out of what seem several simultaneous objects or trains of thought. Focalization, the concentration of consciousness, is of its essence. _____ has also been described as the allocation of limited cognitive processing resources.

Exam Probability: **Low**

48. *Answer choices:*
(see index for correct answer)

- a. Attention
- b. International Standardized Commercial Identifier
- c. Brand Development Index
- d. Screenvision

*Guidance:* level 1

---

:: ::

_____ is the study and management of exchange relationships. _____ is the business process of creating relationships with and satisfying customers. With its focus on the customer, _____ is one of the premier components of business management.

Exam Probability: **High**

49. *Answer choices:*
(see index for correct answer)

- a. Marketing
- b. co-culture
- c. process perspective
- d. cultural

*Guidance:* level 1

---

:: Cognitive dissonance ::

In the field of psychology, _____ is the mental discomfort experienced by a person who holds two or more contradictory beliefs, ideas, or values. This discomfort is triggered by a situation in which a person's belief clashes with new evidence perceived by the person. When confronted with facts that contradict beliefs, ideals, and values, people will try to find a way to resolve the contradiction to reduce their discomfort.

Exam Probability: **Low**

50. *Answer choices:*
(see index for correct answer)

- a. Self-refuting idea
- b. Cognitive dissonance
- c. Double standard
- d. Doublespeak

*Guidance:* level 1

---

:: Marketing ::

The _____ is a foundation model for businesses. The _____ has been defined as the "set of marketing tools that the firm uses to pursue its marketing objectives in the target market". Thus the _____ refers to four broad levels of marketing decision, namely: product, price, place, and promotion. Marketing practice has been occurring for millennia, but marketing theory emerged in the early twentieth century. The contemporary _____, or the 4 Ps, which has become the dominant framework for marketing management decisions, was first published in 1960. In services marketing, an extended _____ is used, typically comprising 7 Ps, made up of the original 4 Ps extended by process, people, and physical evidence. Occasionally service marketers will refer to 8 Ps, comprising these 7 Ps plus performance.

Exam Probability: **Low**

51. *Answer choices:*
(see index for correct answer)

- a. Marketing mix
- b. Law of primacy in persuasion
- c. Market orientation
- d. Fourth screen

*Guidance:* level 1

:: Progressive Era in the United States ::

The Clayton Antitrust Act of 1914 , was a part of United States antitrust law with the goal of adding further substance to the U.S. antitrust law regime; the _____ sought to prevent anticompetitive practices in their incipiency. That regime started with the Sherman Antitrust Act of 1890, the first Federal law outlawing practices considered harmful to consumers . The _____ specified particular prohibited conduct, the three-level enforcement scheme, the exemptions, and the remedial measures.

Exam Probability: **High**

52. *Answer choices:*
(see index for correct answer)

- a. pragmatism
- b. Mann Act
- c. Clayton Act

---

:: Marketing ::

_____ , sometimes called trigger-based or event-driven marketing, is a marketing strategy that uses two-way communication channels to allow consumers to connect with a company directly. Although this exchange can take place in person, in the last decade it has increasingly taken place almost exclusively online through email, social media, and blogs.

Exam Probability: **Medium**

53. *Answer choices:*
(see index for correct answer)

- a. MaxDiff
- b. Interactive marketing
- c. Impulse purchase
- d. Marketing mix

---

:: Cultural appropriation ::

_____ is a social and economic order that encourages the acquisition of goods and services in ever-increasing amounts. With the industrial revolution, but particularly in the 20th century, mass production led to an economic crisis: there was overproduction—the supply of goods would grow beyond consumer demand, and so manufacturers turned to planned obsolescence and advertising to manipulate consumer spending. In 1899, a book on _____ published by Thorstein Veblen, called The Theory of the Leisure Class, examined the widespread values and economic institutions emerging along with the widespread "leisure time" in the beginning of the 20th century. In it Veblen "views the activities and spending habits of this leisure class in terms of conspicuous and vicarious consumption and waste. Both are related to the display of status and not to functionality or usefulness."

Exam Probability: **High**

54. *Answer choices:*
(see index for correct answer)

- a. Racial fetishism

- b. The Rebel Sell
- c. Consumerism
- d. Plastic Paddy

*Guidance:* level 1

---

:: Product development ::

_____ is the understanding of the dynamics of the product in order to showcase the best qualities and maximum features of the product. Marketers spend a lot of time and research in order to target their attended audience. Marketers will look into a _____ before marketing a product towards their customers.

Exam Probability: **High**

55. *Answer choices:*
(see index for correct answer)

- a. Product concept
- b. Product optimization
- c. Design brief
- d. Material selection

*Guidance:* level 1

---

:: Management ::

A _____ is a promise of value to be delivered, communicated, and acknowledged. It is also a belief from the customer about how value will be delivered, experienced and acquired.

Exam Probability: **Low**

56. *Answer choices:*
(see index for correct answer)

- a. Value proposition
- b. Public sector consulting
- c. Inside job
- d. Adhocracy

*Guidance:* level 1

---

:: Marketing terminology ::

_____ is used in marketing to describe the inability to assess the value gained from engaging in an activity using any tangible evidence. It is often used to describe services where there is no tangible product that the customer can purchase, that can be seen or touched.

Exam Probability: **Medium**

57. *Answer choices:*
(see index for correct answer)

- a. Intangibility
- b. Relative market share
- c. Target rating point
- d. Channel value proposition

*Guidance:* level 1

:: ::

Employment is a relationship between two parties, usually based on a contract where work is paid for, where one party, which may be a corporation, for profit, not-for-profit organization, co-operative or other entity is the employer and the other is the employee. Employees work in return for payment, which may be in the form of an hourly wage, by piecework or an annual salary, depending on the type of work an employee does or which sector she or he is working in. Employees in some fields or sectors may receive gratuities, bonus payment or stock options. In some types of employment, employees may receive benefits in addition to payment. Benefits can include health insurance, housing, disability insurance or use of a gym. Employment is typically governed by employment laws, regulations or legal contracts.

Exam Probability: **Low**

58. *Answer choices:*
(see index for correct answer)

- a. deep-level diversity
- b. process perspective
- c. Personnel
- d. information systems assessment

*Guidance:* level 1

In computing, a _____ , also known as an enterprise _____ , is a system used for reporting and data analysis, and is considered a core component of business intelligence. DWs are central repositories of integrated data from one or more disparate sources. They store current and historical data in one single place that are used for creating analytical reports for workers throughout the enterprise.

Exam Probability: **Low**

59. *Answer choices:*

(see index for correct answer)

- a. Semantic warehousing
- b. Data binding
- c. Data profiling
- d. Data warehouse

*Guidance:* level 1

## Manufacturing

Manufacturing is the production of merchandise for use or sale using labor and machines, tools, chemical and biological processing, or formulation. The term may refer to a range of human activity, from handicraft to high tech, but is most commonly applied to industrial design , in which raw materials are transformed into finished goods on a large scale. Such finished goods may be sold to other manufacturers for the production of other, more complex products, such as aircraft, household appliances, furniture, sports equipment or automobiles, or sold to wholesalers, who in turn sell them to retailers, who then sell them to end users and consumers.

:: ::

In production, research, retail, and accounting, a _____ is the value of money that has been used up to produce something or deliver a service, and hence is not available for use anymore. In business, the _____ may be one of acquisition, in which case the amount of money expended to acquire it is counted as _____ . In this case, money is the input that is gone in order to acquire the thing. This acquisition _____ may be the sum of the _____ of production as incurred by the original producer, and further _____ s of transaction as incurred by the acquirer over and above the price paid to the producer. Usually, the price also includes a mark-up for profit over the _____ of production.

Exam Probability: **High**

1. *Answer choices:*

(see index for correct answer)

- a. corporate values
- b. hierarchical
- c. functional perspective
- d. cultural

*Guidance:* level 1

_____ is the process of finding an estimate, or approximation, which is a value that is usable for some purpose even if input data may be incomplete, uncertain, or unstable. The value is nonetheless usable because it is derived from the best information available. Typically, _____ involves "using the value of a statistic derived from a sample to estimate the value of a corresponding population parameter". The sample provides information that can be projected, through various formal or informal processes, to determine a range most likely to describe the missing information. An estimate that turns out to be incorrect will be an overestimate if the estimate exceeded the actual result, and an underestimate if the estimate fell short of the actual result.

Exam Probability: **Low**

2. *Answer choices:*
(see index for correct answer)

- a. Character
- b. co-culture
- c. Estimation
- d. interpersonal communication

*Guidance:* level 1

:: Natural resources ::

_____ s are resources that exist without actions of humankind. This includes all valued characteristics such as magnetic, gravitational, electrical properties and forces etc. On Earth it includes sunlight, atmosphere, water, land along with all vegetation, crops and animal life that naturally subsists upon or within the heretofore identified characteristics and substances.

Exam Probability: **Medium**

3. *Answer choices:*
(see index for correct answer)

- a. QEMSCAN
- b. Ferrallitisation
- c. Soil
- d. Natural resource

*Guidance:* level 1

_____ uses statistical sampling to determine whether to accept or reject a production lot of material. It has been a common quality control technique used in industry. It is usually done as products leaves the factory, or in some cases even within the factory. Most often a producer supplies a consumer a number of items and a decision to accept or reject the items is made by determining the number of defective items in a sample from the lot. The lot is accepted if the number of defects falls below where the acceptance number or otherwise the lot is rejected.

Exam Probability: **High**

4. *Answer choices:*
(see index for correct answer)

- a. Response rate
- b. Recall bias
- c. Stratified sampling
- d. Sample

*Guidance:* level 1

In work place, _____ or job _____ means good ranking with the hypothesized conception of requirements of a role. There are two types of job _____ s: contextual and task. Task _____ is related to cognitive ability while contextual _____ is dependent upon personality. Task _____ are behavioral roles that are recognized in job descriptions and by remuneration systems, they are directly related to organizational _____, whereas, contextual _____ are value based and additional behavioral roles that are not recognized in job descriptions and covered by compensation; they are extra roles that are indirectly related to organizational _____. Citizenship _____ like contextual _____ means a set of individual activity/contribution that supports the organizational culture.

Exam Probability: **Low**

5. *Answer choices:*
(see index for correct answer)

- a. Shelf-ready packaging
- b. 463L master pallet
- c. Performance
- d. Oxygen transmission rate

---

:: ::

An _____ is a company that produces parts and equipment that may be marketed by another manufacturer. For example, Foxconn, a Taiwanese electronics contract manufacturing company, which produces a variety of parts and equipment for companies such as Apple Inc., Dell, Google, Huawei, Nintendo, etc., is the largest OEM company in the world by both scale and revenue.

Exam Probability: **Medium**

6. *Answer choices:*
(see index for correct answer)

- a. Character
- b. co-culture
- c. Sarbanes-Oxley act of 2002
- d. Original equipment manufacturer

---

:: Production and manufacturing ::

_____ is a systematic method to improve the "value" of goods or products and services by using an examination of function. Value, as defined, is the ratio of function to cost. Value can therefore be manipulated by either improving the function or reducing the cost. It is a primary tenet of _____ that basic functions be preserved and not be reduced as a consequence of pursuing value improvements.

Exam Probability: **Low**

7. *Answer choices:*
(see index for correct answer)

- a. Business Planning and Control System
- b. Value engineering
- c. Profibus
- d. Production part approval process

:: Business planning ::

_____ is a critical component to the successful delivery of any project, programme or activity. A stakeholder is any individual, group or organization that can affect, be affected by, or perceive itself to be affected by a programme.

Exam Probability: **High**

8. *Answer choices:*

(see index for correct answer)

- a. Open Options Corporation
- b. Community Futures
- c. Stakeholder management
- d. Business war games

:: Project management ::

In economics and business decision-making, a sunk cost is a cost that has already been incurred and cannot be recovered.

Exam Probability: **High**

9. *Answer choices:*

(see index for correct answer)

- a. Theory X and Theory Y
- b. PM Declaration of Interdependence
- c. Scope
- d. Sunk costs

:: Supply chain management terms ::

In business and finance, _____ is a system of organizations, people, activities, information, and resources involved in moving a product or service from supplier to customer. _____ activities involve the transformation of natural resources, raw materials, and components into a finished product that is delivered to the end customer. In sophisticated _____ systems, used products may re-enter the _____ at any point where residual value is recyclable. _____ s link value chains.

Exam Probability: **Low**

10. *Answer choices:*
(see index for correct answer)

- a. Final assembly schedule
- b. Supply chain
- c. Cool Chain Quality Indicator
- d. Last mile

*Guidance:* level 1

---

:: Computer memory companies ::

_____ Corporation is a Japanese multinational conglomerate headquartered in Tokyo, Japan. Its diversified products and services include information technology and communications equipment and systems, electronic components and materials, power systems, industrial and social infrastructure systems, consumer electronics, household appliances, medical equipment, office equipment, as well as lighting and logistics.

Exam Probability: **High**

11. *Answer choices:*
(see index for correct answer)

- a. Toshiba
- b. Strontium Technology
- c. GeIL
- d. M-Systems

*Guidance:* level 1

---

:: Auditing ::

_____ is the process of systematic examination of a quality system carried out by an internal or external _____ or or an audit team. It is an important part of an organization's quality management system and is a key element in the ISO quality system standard, ISO 9001.

Exam Probability: **Low**

12. *Answer choices:*
(see index for correct answer)

- a. Quality audit
- b. Audit working papers
- c. Joint audit
- d. Auditor General Act

*Guidance:* level 1

---

:: Building materials ::

_____ is an alloy of iron and carbon, and sometimes other elements. Because of its high tensile strength and low cost, it is a major component used in buildings, infrastructure, tools, ships, automobiles, machines, appliances, and weapons.

Exam Probability: **High**

13. *Answer choices:*
(see index for correct answer)

- a. Tadelakt
- b. Porcelain tile
- c. Shake
- d. Hyparrhenia hirta

*Guidance:* level 1

---

:: ::

A _____ consists of an orchestrated and repeatable pattern of business activity enabled by the systematic organization of resources into processes that transform materials, provide services, or process information. It can be depicted as a sequence of operations, the work of a person or group, the work of an organization of staff, or one or more simple or complex mechanisms.

Exam Probability: **Medium**

14. *Answer choices:*
(see index for correct answer)

- a. co-culture
- b. Workflow
- c. imperative
- d. corporate values

*Guidance:* level 1

:: Finance ::

_____ is a financial estimate intended to help buyers and owners determine the direct and indirect costs of a product or system. It is a management accounting concept that can be used in full cost accounting or even ecological economics where it includes social costs.

Exam Probability: **High**

15. *Answer choices:*
(see index for correct answer)

- a. Legal Cost Finance
- b. Political arbitrage
- c. Quantum finance
- d. In-house lending

*Guidance:* level 1

:: Business process ::

A committee is a body of one or more persons that is subordinate to a deliberative assembly. Usually, the assembly sends matters into a committee as a way to explore them more fully than would be possible if the assembly itself were considering them. Committees may have different functions and their type of work differ depending on the type of the organization and its needs.

Exam Probability: **Medium**

16. *Answer choices:*
(see index for correct answer)

- a. Intention mining
- b. Dynamic business process management
- c. Business logic
- d. Steering committee

*Guidance:* level 1

---

:: Packaging materials ::

_____ is a thin material produced by pressing together moist fibres of cellulose pulp derived from wood, rags or grasses, and drying them into flexible sheets.It is a versatile material with many uses, including writing, printing, packaging, cleaning, decorating, and a number of industrial and construction processes. _____ s are essential in legal or non-legal documentation.

Exam Probability: **High**

17. *Answer choices:*
(see index for correct answer)

- a. Filament tape
- b. Tear tape
- c. Bubble wrap
- d. Inflatable air cushion

*Guidance:* level 1

---

:: Management ::

_____ is the discipline of strategically planning for, and managing, all interactions with third party organizations that supply goods and/or services to an organization in order to maximize the value of those interactions. In practice, SRM entails creating closer, more collaborative relationships with key suppliers in order to uncover and realize new value and reduce risk of failure.

Exam Probability: **Low**

18. *Answer choices:*
(see index for correct answer)

- a. Supply network
- b. Supplier relationship management
- c. Goals Breakdown Structure
- d. Authoritarian leadership style

*Guidance:* level 1

:: Management ::

_____ is a formal technique useful where many possible courses of action are competing for attention. In essence, the problem-solver estimates the benefit delivered by each action, then selects a number of the most effective actions that deliver a total benefit reasonably close to the maximal possible one.

Exam Probability: **Medium**

19. *Answer choices:*
(see index for correct answer)

- a. Pareto analysis
- b. Control
- c. Advisory board
- d. Management by exception

*Guidance:* level 1

:: Decision theory ::

_____ is a method developed in Japan beginning in 1966 to help transform the voice of the customer into engineering characteristics for a product. Yoji Akao, the original developer, described QFD as a "method to transform qualitative user demands into quantitative parameters, to deploy the functions forming quality, and to deploy methods for achieving the design quality into subsystems and component parts, and ultimately to specific elements of the manufacturing process." The author combined his work in quality assurance and quality control points with function deployment used in value engineering.

Exam Probability: **Low**

20. *Answer choices:*
(see index for correct answer)

- a. Choice-supportive bias
- b. Bulk Dispatch Lapse
- c. Quality function deployment
- d. Mean-preserving spread

*Guidance:* level 1

---

:: Management ::

_____ is the identification, evaluation, and prioritization of risks followed by coordinated and economical application of resources to minimize, monitor, and control the probability or impact of unfortunate events or to maximize the realization of opportunities.

Exam Probability: **Medium**

21. *Answer choices:*
(see index for correct answer)

- a. Target operating model
- b. Stakeholder
- c. Risk management
- d. Managerial prerogative

*Guidance:* level 1

---

:: ::

_____ refers to the confirmation of certain characteristics of an object, person, or organization. This confirmation is often, but not always, provided by some form of external review, education, assessment, or audit. Accreditation is a specific organization's process of _____ . According to the National Council on Measurement in Education, a _____ test is a credentialing test used to determine whether individuals are knowledgeable enough in a given occupational area to be labeled "competent to practice" in that area.

Exam Probability: **High**

22. *Answer choices:*
(see index for correct answer)

- a. surface-level diversity
- b. hierarchical perspective
- c. interpersonal communication
- d. empathy

*Guidance:* level 1

---

:: Management ::

_____ is a category of business activity made possible by software tools that aim to provide customers with both independence from vendors and better means for engaging with vendors. These same tools can also apply to individuals' relations with other institutions and organizations.

Exam Probability: **High**

23. *Answer choices:*
(see index for correct answer)

- a. Vasa syndrome
- b. Remedial action
- c. Product Development and Systems Engineering Consortium
- d. Event chain methodology

*Guidance:* level 1

---

:: Management ::

A supply-chain network is an evolution of the basic supply chain. Due to rapid technological advancement, organisations with a basic supply chain can develop this chain into a more complex structure involving a higher level of interdependence and connectivity between more organisations, this constitutes a supply-chain network.

Exam Probability: **Low**

24. *Answer choices:*

(see index for correct answer)

- a. Facilitator
- b. Communications management
- c. Public sector consulting
- d. Supply chain network

*Guidance:* level 1

---

:: Semiconductor companies ::

_____ Corporation is a Japanese multinational conglomerate corporation headquartered in Konan, Minato, Tokyo. Its diversified business includes consumer and professional electronics, gaming, entertainment and financial services. The company owns the largest music entertainment business in the world, the largest video game console business and one of the largest video game publishing businesses, and is one of the leading manufacturers of electronic products for the consumer and professional markets, and a leading player in the film and television entertainment industry. _____ was ranked 97th on the 2018 Fortune Global 500 list.

Exam Probability: **High**

25. *Answer choices:*

(see index for correct answer)

- a. VeriSilicon
- b. Conemtech
- c. Inotera
- d. Sony

*Guidance:* level 1

---

:: Information technology management ::

_____ within quality management systems and information technology systems is a process—either formal or informal—used to ensure that changes to a product or system are introduced in a controlled and coordinated manner. It reduces the possibility that unnecessary changes will be introduced to a system without forethought, introducing faults into the system or undoing changes made by other users of software. The goals of a _____ procedure usually include minimal disruption to services, reduction in back-out activities, and cost-effective utilization of resources involved in implementing change.

Exam Probability: **High**

26. *Answer choices:*
(see index for correct answer)

- a. Acceptable use policy
- b. Change control
- c. EDIFACT
- d. Computer-aided facility management

*Guidance:* level 1

:: Quality assurance ::

Organizations that issue credentials or certify third parties against official standards are themselves formally accredited by _____ bodies ; hence they are sometimes known as "accredited certification bodies". The _____ process ensures that their certification practices are acceptable, typically meaning that they are competent to test and certify third parties, behave ethically and employ suitable quality assurance.

Exam Probability: **Low**

27. *Answer choices:*
(see index for correct answer)

- a. Healthcare Facilities Accreditation Program
- b. Quality Assurance Agency for Higher Education
- c. Accreditation
- d. Commission on Accreditation of Rehabilitation Facilities

*Guidance:* level 1

:: Manufacturing ::

A _____ is an object used to extend the ability of an individual to modify features of the surrounding environment. Although many animals use simple _____ s, only human beings, whose use of stone _____ s dates back hundreds of millennia, use _____ s to make other _____ s. The set of _____ s needed to perform different tasks that are part of the same activity is called gear or equipment.

Exam Probability: **High**

28. *Answer choices:*

(see index for correct answer)

- a. EMO
- b. B2MML
- c. Agile manufacturing
- d. Fusing

*Guidance:* level 1

---

:: Goods ::

In most contexts, the concept of _____ denotes the conduct that should be preferred when posed with a choice between possible actions. _____ is generally considered to be the opposite of evil, and is of interest in the study of morality, ethics, religion and philosophy. The specific meaning and etymology of the term and its associated translations among ancient and contemporary languages show substantial variation in its inflection and meaning depending on circumstances of place, history, religious, or philosophical context.

Exam Probability: **Low**

29. *Answer choices:*

(see index for correct answer)

- a. Anti-rival good
- b. Search good
- c. Intermediate good
- d. Superior good

*Guidance:* level 1

---

:: ::

Some scenarios associate "this kind of planning" with learning "life skills".Schedules are necessary, or at least useful, in situations where individuals need to know what time they must be at a specific location to receive a specific service, and where people need to accomplish a set of goals within a set time period.

Exam Probability: **Low**

30. *Answer choices:*
(see index for correct answer)

- a. open system
- b. Scheduling
- c. levels of analysis
- d. similarity-attraction theory

*Guidance:* level 1

:: ::

The _____ is a project plan of how the production budget will be spent over a given timescale, for every phase of a business project.

Exam Probability: **Medium**

31. *Answer choices:*
(see index for correct answer)

- a. empathy
- b. functional perspective
- c. Production schedule
- d. surface-level diversity

*Guidance:* level 1

:: ::

_____ is a kind of action that occur as two or more objects have an effect upon one another. The idea of a two-way effect is essential in the concept of _____ , as opposed to a one-way causal effect. A closely related term is interconnectivity, which deals with the _____ s of _____ s within systems: combinations of many simple _____ s can lead to surprising emergent phenomena. _____ has different tailored meanings in various sciences. Changes can also involve _____ .

Exam Probability: **Medium**

32. *Answer choices:*
(see index for correct answer)

- a. surface-level diversity
- b. similarity-attraction theory
- c. personal values
- d. functional perspective

*Guidance:* level 1

---

:: Production economics ::

_____ is the creation of a whole that is greater than the simple sum of its parts. The term _____ comes from the Attic Greek word sea synergia from synergos, , meaning "working together".

Exam Probability: **High**

33. *Answer choices:*
(see index for correct answer)

- a. Returns to scale
- b. Capitalist mode of production
- c. Synergy
- d. Production theory

*Guidance:* level 1

---

:: Infographics ::

The _____ is a form used to collect data in real time at the location where the data is generated. The data it captures can be quantitative or qualitative. When the information is quantitative, the _____ is sometimes called a tally sheet.

Exam Probability: **Low**

34. *Answer choices:*
(see index for correct answer)

- a. Statistical graphics
- b. Check sheet
- c. U.S. Route shield
- d. National Fire Protection Association

*Guidance:* level 1

:: ::

In sales, commerce and economics, a _____ is the recipient of a good, service, product or an idea - obtained from a seller, vendor, or supplier via a financial transaction or exchange for money or some other valuable consideration.

Exam Probability: **Low**

35. *Answer choices:*
(see index for correct answer)

- a. Customer
- b. interpersonal communication
- c. personal values
- d. corporate values

*Guidance:* level 1

:: Project management ::

A _____ is a source or supply from which a benefit is produced and it has some utility. _____ s can broadly be classified upon their availability—they are classified into renewable and non-renewable _____ s.Examples of non renewable _____ s are coal ,crude oil natural gas nuclear energy etc. Examples of renewable _____ s are air,water,wind,solar energy etc. They can also be classified as actual and potential on the basis of level of development and use, on the basis of origin they can be classified as biotic and abiotic, and on the basis of their distribution, as ubiquitous and localized . An item becomes a _____ with time and developing technology. Typically, _____ s are materials, energy, services, staff, knowledge, or other assets that are transformed to produce benefit and in the process may be consumed or made unavailable. Benefits of _____ utilization may include increased wealth, proper functioning of a system, or enhanced well-being. From a human perspective a natural _____ is anything obtained from the environment to satisfy human needs and wants. From a broader biological or ecological perspective a _____ satisfies the needs of a living organism .

Exam Probability: **High**

36. *Answer choices:*
(see index for correct answer)

- a. Association for Project Management
- b. PM Declaration of Interdependence
- c. Multidisciplinary approach
- d. Project workforce management

*Guidance:* level 1

:: Outsourcing ::

A _____ is a document that solicits proposal, often made through a bidding process, by an agency or company interested in procurement of a commodity, service, or valuable asset, to potential suppliers to submit business proposals. It is submitted early in the procurement cycle, either at the preliminary study, or procurement stage.

Exam Probability: **Low**

37. *Answer choices:*
(see index for correct answer)

- a. Service-level agreement
- b. service level agreement
- c. IQor
- d. Strategic sourcing

---

:: Commercial item transport and distribution ::

_____ in logistics and supply chain management is an organization's use of third-party businesses to outsource elements of its distribution, warehousing, and fulfillment services.

Exam Probability: **Low**

38. *Answer choices:*

- a. Intermodal freight transport
- b. Australia standard pallets
- c. Third-party logistics
- d. NORPASS

---

:: Lean manufacturing ::

_____ is a Japanese term that means "mistake-proofing" or "inadvertent error prevention". A _____ is any mechanism in any process that helps an equipment operator avoid mistakes . Its purpose is to eliminate product defects by preventing, correcting, or drawing attention to human errors as they occur. The concept was formalised, and the term adopted, by Shigeo Shingo as part of the Toyota Production System. It was originally described as baka-yoke, but as this means "fool-proofing" the name was changed to the milder _____ .

Exam Probability: **High**

39. *Answer choices:*

- a. Poka-yoke
- b. Lean software development
- c. Lean accounting
- d. Kanban board

---

:: ::

_____ is the process of making predictions of the future based on past and present data and most commonly by analysis of trends. A commonplace example might be estimation of some variable of interest at some specified future date. Prediction is a similar, but more general term. Both might refer to formal statistical methods employing time series, cross-sectional or longitudinal data, or alternatively to less formal judgmental methods. Usage can differ between areas of application: for example, in hydrology the terms "forecast" and "_____" are sometimes reserved for estimates of values at certain specific future times, while the term "prediction" is used for more general estimates, such as the number of times floods will occur over a long period.

Exam Probability: **Low**

40. *Answer choices:*
(see index for correct answer)

- a. surface-level diversity
- b. Sarbanes-Oxley act of 2002
- c. Forecasting
- d. information systems assessment

---

:: Direct marketing ::

_____ Inc. is an American privately owned multi-level marketing company. According to Direct Selling News, _____ was the sixth largest network marketing company in the world in 2018, with a wholesale volume of US$3.25 billion. _____ is based in Addison, Texas, outside Dallas. The company was founded by _____ Ash in 1963. Richard Rogers, _____'s son, is the chairman, and David Holl is president and was named CEO in 2006.

Exam Probability: **High**

41. *Answer choices:*
(see index for correct answer)

- a. Boardroom, Inc.
- b. Inktel

- c. Mary Kay
- d. Flyer

*Guidance:* level 1

---

:: Software testing ::

_____ 1 was the first artificial Earth satellite. The Soviet Union launched it into an elliptical low Earth orbit on 4 October 1957, orbiting for three weeks before its batteries died, then silently for two more months before falling back into the atmosphere. It was a 58 cm diameter polished metal sphere, with four external radio antennas to broadcast radio pulses. Its radio signal was easily detectable even by radio amateurs, and the 65° inclination and duration of its orbit made its flight path cover virtually the entire inhabited Earth. This surprise success precipitated the American _____ crisis and triggered the Space Race, a part of the Cold War. The launch was the beginning of a new era of political, military, technological, and scientific developments.

Exam Probability: **Medium**

42. *Answer choices:*
(see index for correct answer)

- a. Sputnik
- b. Google Guice
- c. Regression testing
- d. Bug bash

*Guidance:* level 1

---

:: Production and manufacturing ::

Automatic _____ in continuous production processes is a combination of control engineering and chemical engineering disciplines that uses industrial control systems to achieve a production level of consistency, economy and safety which could not be achieved purely by human manual control. It is implemented widely in industries such as oil refining, pulp and paper manufacturing, chemical processing and power generating plants.

Exam Probability: **High**

43. *Answer choices:*

- a. Process control
- b. Critical to quality
- c. Citect
- d. Zero Defects

*Guidance:* level 1

---

:: Quality assurance ::

The _____ is a United States-based nonprofit tax-exempt 501 organization that accredits more than 21,000 US health care organizations and programs. The international branch accredits medical services from around the world. A majority of US state governments recognize _____ accreditation as a condition of licensure for the receipt of Medicaid and Medicare reimbursements.

Exam Probability: **High**

44. *Answer choices:*

- a. HP Quality Center
- b. Certified Quality Engineer
- c. Joint Commission
- d. Strengthening the reporting of observational studies in epidemiology

*Guidance:* level 1

---

:: Metrics ::

_____ is a computer model developed by the University of Idaho, that uses Landsat satellite data to compute and map evapotranspiration . _____ calculates ET as a residual of the surface energy balance, where ET is estimated by keeping account of total net short wave and long wave radiation at the vegetation or soil surface, the amount of heat conducted into soil, and the amount of heat convected into the air above the surface. The difference in these three terms represents the amount of energy absorbed during the conversion of liquid water to vapor, which is ET. _____ expresses near-surface temperature gradients used in heat convection as indexed functions of radio _____ surface temperature, thereby eliminating the need for absolutely accurate surface temperature and the need for air-temperature measurements.

Exam Probability: **Low**

45. *Answer choices:*
(see index for correct answer)

- a. Accommodation index
- b. Key Risk Indicator
- c. Software Metrics Metamodel
- d. Full-time equivalent

*Guidance:* level 1

---

:: Project management ::

_____ is a process of setting goals, planning and/or controlling the organizing and leading the execution of any type of activity, such as.

Exam Probability: **Low**

46. *Answer choices:*
(see index for correct answer)

- a. Defense Acquisition Workforce Improvement Act
- b. Project management 2.0
- c. Management process
- d. Theme-centered interaction

*Guidance:* level 1

---

:: Lean manufacturing ::

_____ is the Sino-Japanese word for "improvement". In business, _____ refers to activities that continuously improve all functions and involve all employees from the CEO to the assembly line workers. It also applies to processes, such as purchasing and logistics, that cross organizational boundaries into the supply chain. It has been applied in healthcare, psychotherapy, life-coaching, government, and banking.

Exam Probability: **High**

47. *Answer choices:*
(see index for correct answer)

- a. Kaizen
- b. Lean Six Sigma
- c. Lean software development
- d. Lean laboratory

*Guidance:* level 1

---

:: Business process ::

A _____ or business method is a collection of related, structured activities or tasks by people or equipment which in a specific sequence produce a service or product for a particular customer or customers. _____ es occur at all organizational levels and may or may not be visible to the customers. A _____ may often be visualized as a flowchart of a sequence of activities with interleaving decision points or as a process matrix of a sequence of activities with relevance rules based on data in the process. The benefits of using _____ es include improved customer satisfaction and improved agility for reacting to rapid market change. Process-oriented organizations break down the barriers of structural departments and try to avoid functional silos.

Exam Probability: **High**

48. *Answer choices:*
(see index for correct answer)

- a. Desktop outsourcing
- b. Business process validation
- c. Extended Enterprise Modeling Language
- d. Leverage-point modeling

*Guidance:* level 1

:: Production and manufacturing ::

_____ is a comprehensive and rigorous industrial process by which a previously sold, leased, used, worn or non-functional product or part is returned to a 'like-new' or 'better-than-new' condition, from both a quality and performance perspective, through a controlled, reproducible and sustainable process.

49. *Answer choices:*
(see index for correct answer)

- a. Rolled throughput yield
- b. Economic dispatch
- c. ERPNEXT
- d. Remanufacturing

*Guidance:* level 1

:: Unit operations ::

_____ is a discipline of thermal engineering that concerns the generation, use, conversion, and exchange of thermal energy between physical systems. _____ is classified into various mechanisms, such as thermal conduction, thermal convection, thermal radiation, and transfer of energy by phase changes. Engineers also consider the transfer of mass of differing chemical species, either cold or hot, to achieve _____ . While these mechanisms have distinct characteristics, they often occur simultaneously in the same system.

50. *Answer choices:*
(see index for correct answer)

- a. Theoretical plate
- b. Separation process
- c. Heat transfer
- d. Sedimentation coefficient

*Guidance:* level 1

:: Management accounting ::

_____ are costs that are not directly accountable to a cost object .
_____ may be either fixed or variable. _____ include administration,
personnel and security costs. These are those costs which are not directly
related to production. Some _____ may be overhead. But some overhead
costs can be directly attributed to a project and are direct costs.

Exam Probability: **High**

51. *Answer choices:*
(see index for correct answer)

- a. Certified Management Accountants of Canada
- b. Target income sales
- c. Total benefits of ownership
- d. Constraints accounting

*Guidance:* level 1

---

:: Waste ::

_____ are unwanted or unusable materials. _____ is any substance
which is discarded after primary use, or is worthless, defective and of no use.
A by-product by contrast is a joint product of relatively minor economic value.
A _____ product may become a by-product, joint product or resource
through an invention that raises a _____ product's value above zero.

Exam Probability: **Low**

52. *Answer choices:*
(see index for correct answer)

- a. Industrial waste
- b. Sawdust
- c. Tailings
- d. Waste

*Guidance:* level 1

---

:: ::

_____ is the production of products for use or sale using labour and machines, tools, chemical and biological processing, or formulation. The term may refer to a range of human activity, from handicraft to high tech, but is most commonly applied to industrial design, in which raw materials are transformed into finished goods on a large scale. Such finished goods may be sold to other manufacturers for the production of other, more complex products, such as aircraft, household appliances, furniture, sports equipment or automobiles, or sold to wholesalers, who in turn sell them to retailers, who then sell them to end users and consumers.

Exam Probability: **Low**

53. *Answer choices:*
(see index for correct answer)

- a. similarity-attraction theory
- b. cultural
- c. Character
- d. Manufacturing

*Guidance:* level 1

---

:: Non-parametric statistics ::

A _____ is an accurate representation of the distribution of numerical data. It is an estimate of the probability distribution of a continuous variable and was first introduced by Karl Pearson. It differs from a bar graph, in the sense that a bar graph relates two variables, but a _____ relates only one. To construct a _____ , the first step is to "bin" the range of values—that is, divide the entire range of values into a series of intervals—and then count how many values fall into each interval. The bins are usually specified as consecutive, non-overlapping intervals of a variable. The bins must be adjacent, and are often of equal size.

Exam Probability: **Medium**

54. *Answer choices:*
(see index for correct answer)

- a. Semiparametric regression
- b. Order of a kernel
- c. Coefficient of concordance
- d. Histogram

:: Accounting source documents ::

A _____ is a commercial document and first official offer issued by a buyer to a seller indicating types, quantities, and agreed prices for products or services. It is used to control the purchasing of products and services from external suppliers. _____ s can be an essential part of enterprise resource planning system orders.

Exam Probability: **Medium**

55. *Answer choices:*
(see index for correct answer)

- a. Banknote
- b. Credit memorandum
- c. Invoice
- d. Air waybill

:: Quality ::

The _____ , formerly the _____ Control , is a knowledge-based global community of quality professionals, with nearly 80,000 members dedicated to promoting and advancing quality tools, principles, and practices in their workplaces and communities.

Exam Probability: **Medium**

56. *Answer choices:*
(see index for correct answer)

- a. Ringtest
- b. Root cause
- c. Society for Software Quality
- d. American Society for Quality

:: Packaging materials ::

_____ is a non-crystalline, amorphous solid that is often transparent and has widespread practical, technological, and decorative uses in, for example, window panes, tableware, and optoelectronics. The most familiar, and historically the oldest, types of manufactured _____ are "silicate _____ es" based on the chemical compound silica , the primary constituent of sand. The term _____ , in popular usage, is often used to refer only to this type of material, which is familiar from use as window _____ and in _____ bottles. Of the many silica-based _____ es that exist, ordinary glazing and container _____ is formed from a specific type called soda-lime _____ , composed of approximately 75% silicon dioxide , sodium oxide  from sodium carbonate , calcium oxide , also called lime, and several minor additives.

Exam Probability: **Low**

57. *Answer choices:*
(see index for correct answer)

- a. Tissue paper
- b. Glass
- c. Mycobond
- d. Unica

*Guidance:* level 1

---

:: Management ::

_____ is an iterative four-step management method used in business for the control and continuous improvement of processes and products. It is also known as the Deming circle/cycle/wheel, the Shewhart cycle, the control circle/cycle, or plan–do–study–act . Another version of this _____ cycle is O _____ . The added "O" stands for observation or as some versions say: "Observe the current condition." This emphasis on observation and current condition has currency with the literature on lean manufacturing and the Toyota Production System. The _____ cycle, with Ishikawa's changes, can be traced back to S. Mizuno of the Tokyo Institute of Technology in 1959.

Exam Probability: **Medium**

58. *Answer choices:*
(see index for correct answer)

- a. Strategic management
- b. Certified Energy Manager
- c. PDCA
- d. Enterprise planning system

*Guidance:* level 1

---

:: Casting (manufacturing) ::

A _____ is a regularity in the world, man-made design, or abstract ideas. As such, the elements of a _____ repeat in a predictable manner. A geometric _____ is a kind of _____ formed of geometric shapes and typically repeated like a wallpaper design.

Exam Probability: **High**

59. *Answer choices:*
(see index for correct answer)

- a. Fusible core injection molding
- b. Permeability
- c. Hydrogen gas porosity
- d. Pattern

*Guidance:* level 1

---

## Commerce

Commerce relates to "the exchange of goods and services, especially on a large scale." It includes legal, economic, political, social, cultural and technological systems that operate in any country or internationally.

:: ::

In logic and philosophy, an _____ is a series of statements , called the premises or premisses , intended to determine the degree of truth of another statement, the conclusion. The logical form of an _____ in a natural language can be represented in a symbolic formal language, and independently of natural language formally defined " _____ s" can be made in math and computer science.

Exam Probability: **Medium**

1. *Answer choices:*
(see index for correct answer)

- a. personal values
- b. deep-level diversity
- c. hierarchical perspective
- d. functional perspective

*Guidance:* level 1

:: ::

_____ , in general use, is a devotion and faithfulness to a nation, cause, philosophy, country, group, or person. Philosophers disagree on what can be an object of _____ , as some argue that _____ is strictly interpersonal and only another human being can be the object of _____ . The definition of _____ in law and political science is the fidelity of an individual to a nation, either one's nation of birth, or one's declared home nation by oath .

Exam Probability: **High**

2. *Answer choices:*

(see index for correct answer)

- a. surface-level diversity
- b. hierarchical
- c. Loyalty
- d. interpersonal communication

*Guidance:* level 1

---

:: E-commerce ::

_____ is the business-to-business or business-to-consumer or business-to-government purchase and sale of supplies, work, and services through the Internet as well as other information and networking systems, such as electronic data interchange and enterprise resource planning.

Exam Probability: **Medium**

3. *Answer choices:*

(see index for correct answer)

- a. Government-to-citizen
- b. Onbuy
- c. Product finder
- d. E-procurement

*Guidance:* level 1

---

:: Commerce ::

_____ , also known as duty _____ is defined by the United States Customs and Border Protection as the refund of certain duties, internal and revenue taxes and certain fees collected upon the importation of goods. Such refunds are only allowed upon the exportation or destruction of goods under U.S. Customs and Border Protection supervision. Duty _____ is an export promotions program sanctioned by the World Trade Organization and allows the refund of certain duties taxes and fees paid upon importation which was established in 1789 in order to promote U.S. innovation and manufacturing across the global market.

Exam Probability: **High**

4. *Answer choices:*
(see index for correct answer)

- a. Return merchandise authorization
- b. Requisition
- c. Drawback
- d. Group buying

*Guidance:* level 1

---

:: ::

_____ is the social science that studies the production, distribution, and consumption of goods and services.

Exam Probability: **High**

5. *Answer choices:*
(see index for correct answer)

- a. co-culture
- b. Economics
- c. similarity-attraction theory
- d. corporate values

*Guidance:* level 1

---

:: Auctioneering ::

A _____ is one of several similar kinds of auctions. Most commonly, it means an auction in which the auctioneer begins with a high asking price, and lowers it until some participant accepts the price, or it reaches a predetermined reserve price. This has also been called a clock auction or open-outcry descending-price auction. This type of auction is good for auctioning goods quickly, since a sale never requires more than one bid. Strategically, it`s similar to a first-price sealed-bid auction.

Exam Probability: **Low**

6. *Answer choices:*

(see index for correct answer)

- a. Calor licitantis
- b. Dutch auction
- c. Vickrey auction
- d. Online auction

*Guidance:* level 1

---

:: International trade ::

_____ involves the transfer of goods or services from one person or entity to another, often in exchange for money. A system or network that allows _____ is called a market.

Exam Probability: **Medium**

7. *Answer choices:*

(see index for correct answer)

- a. International Standards of Accounting and Reporting
- b. Extraterritorial income exclusion
- c. Trade
- d. Agreement on Technical Barriers to Trade

*Guidance:* level 1

---

:: ::

Business Model Canvas is a strategic management and lean startup template for developing new or documenting existing business models. It is a visual chart with elements describing a firm's or product's value proposition, infrastructure, customers, and finances. It assists firms in aligning their activities by illustrating potential trade-offs.

Exam Probability: **Low**

8. *Answer choices:*
(see index for correct answer)

- a. open system
- b. Cost structure
- c. process perspective
- d. interpersonal communication

*Guidance:* level 1

---

:: Human resource management ::

An organizational chart is a diagram that shows the structure of an organization and the relationships and relative ranks of its parts and positions/jobs. The term is also used for similar diagrams, for example ones showing the different elements of a field of knowledge or a group of languages.

Exam Probability: **Low**

9. *Answer choices:*
(see index for correct answer)

- a. Organization chart
- b. Employee value proposition
- c. Attendance management
- d. Selection ratio

*Guidance:* level 1

---

:: Export and import control ::

" _____ " means the Government Service which is responsible for the administration of _____ law and the collection of duties and taxes and which also has the responsibility for the application of other laws and regulations relating to the importation, exportation, movement or storage of goods.

Exam Probability: **Low**

10. *Answer choices:*
(see index for correct answer)

- a. Export Management and Compliance Program
- b. Export Control Classification Number
- c. Customs
- d. Customs Modernization Act

*Guidance:* level 1

---

:: Insolvency ::

_____ is a legal process through which people or other entities who cannot repay debts to creditors may seek relief from some or all of their debts. In most jurisdictions, _____ is imposed by a court order, often initiated by the debtor.

Exam Probability: **Low**

11. *Answer choices:*
(see index for correct answer)

- a. Insolvency
- b. Preferential creditor
- c. George Samuel Ford
- d. Conservatorship

*Guidance:* level 1

---

:: Game theory ::

To _____ is to make a deal between different parties where each party gives up part of their demand. In arguments, _____ is a concept of finding agreement through communication, through a mutual acceptance of terms—often involving variations from an original goal or desires.

Exam Probability: **High**

12. *Answer choices:*
(see index for correct answer)

- a. Differential game
- b. Keynesian beauty contest
- c. Aggregative game
- d. Compromise

*Guidance:* level 1

:: Management accounting ::

_____ s are costs that change as the quantity of the good or service that a business produces changes. _____ s are the sum of marginal costs over all units produced. They can also be considered normal costs. Fixed costs and _____ s make up the two components of total cost. Direct costs are costs that can easily be associated with a particular cost object. However, not all _____ s are direct costs. For example, variable manufacturing overhead costs are _____ s that are indirect costs, not direct costs. _____ s are sometimes called unit-level costs as they vary with the number of units produced.

Exam Probability: **High**

13. *Answer choices:*
(see index for correct answer)

- a. Target costing
- b. Management accounting in supply chains
- c. Variable cost
- d. Standard cost

*Guidance:* level 1

:: Stock market ::

_____ is freedom from, or resilience against, potential harm caused by others. Beneficiaries of _____ may be of persons and social groups, objects and institutions, ecosystems or any other entity or phenomenon vulnerable to unwanted change by its environment.

Exam Probability: **Medium**

14. *Answer choices:*
(see index for correct answer)

- a. Stock
- b. Microcap stock
- c. Security
- d. Mosaic theory

*Guidance:* level 1

---

:: ::

In Western musical notation, the staff or stave is a set of five horizontal lines and four spaces that each represent a different musical pitch or in the case of a percussion staff, different percussion instruments. Appropriate music symbols, depending on the intended effect, are placed on the staff according to their corresponding pitch or function. Musical notes are placed by pitch, percussion notes are placed by instrument, and rests and other symbols are placed by convention.

Exam Probability: **High**

15. *Answer choices:*
(see index for correct answer)

- a. Sarbanes-Oxley act of 2002
- b. personal values
- c. cultural
- d. Staff position

*Guidance:* level 1

---

:: E-commerce ::

An _____ , or automated clearinghouse, is an electronic network for financial transactions, generally domestic low value payments. An ACH is a computer-based clearing house and settlement facility established to process the exchange of electronic transactions between participating financial institutions. It is a form of clearing house that is specifically for payments and may support both credit transfers and direct debits.

Exam Probability: **Low**

16. *Answer choices:*

(see index for correct answer)

- a. Blogshop
- b. Global Product Classification
- c. ProStores
- d. PaySafe

*Guidance:* level 1

---

:: Budgets ::

A _____ is a financial plan for a defined period, often one year. It may also include planned sales volumes and revenues, resource quantities, costs and expenses, assets, liabilities and cash flows. Companies, governments, families and other organizations use it to express strategic plans of activities or events in measurable terms.

Exam Probability: **Medium**

17. *Answer choices:*

(see index for correct answer)

- a. Programme budgeting
- b. Participatory budgeting
- c. Budget
- d. Railway Budget

*Guidance:* level 1

---

:: Management occupations ::

_____ ship is the process of designing, launching and running a new business, which is often initially a small business. The people who create these businesses are called _____ s.

Exam Probability: **Medium**

18. *Answer choices:*
(see index for correct answer)

- a. Entrepreneur
- b. Hayward
- c. General counsel
- d. General partner

*Guidance:* level 1

:: Data interchange standards ::

_____ is the concept of businesses electronically communicating information that was traditionally communicated on paper, such as purchase orders and invoices. Technical standards for EDI exist to facilitate parties transacting such instruments without having to make special arrangements.

Exam Probability: **High**

19. *Answer choices:*
(see index for correct answer)

- a. Domain Application Protocol
- b. Uniform Communication Standard
- c. Interaction protocol
- d. Electronic data interchange

*Guidance:* level 1

:: ::

_____ is the production of products for use or sale using labour and machines, tools, chemical and biological processing, or formulation. The term may refer to a range of human activity, from handicraft to high tech, but is most commonly applied to industrial design, in which raw materials are transformed into finished goods on a large scale. Such finished goods may be sold to other manufacturers for the production of other, more complex products, such as aircraft, household appliances, furniture, sports equipment or automobiles, or sold to wholesalers, who in turn sell them to retailers, who then sell them to end users and consumers.

Exam Probability: **High**

20. *Answer choices:*
(see index for correct answer)

- a. hierarchical
- b. imperative
- c. Manufacturing
- d. process perspective

*Guidance:* level 1

---

:: Debt ::

_____ , in finance and economics, is payment from a borrower or deposit-taking financial institution to a lender or depositor of an amount above repayment of the principal sum , at a particular rate. It is distinct from a fee which the borrower may pay the lender or some third party. It is also distinct from dividend which is paid by a company to its shareholders from its profit or reserve, but not at a particular rate decided beforehand, rather on a pro rata basis as a share in the reward gained by risk taking entrepreneurs when the revenue earned exceeds the total costs.

Exam Probability: **High**

21. *Answer choices:*
(see index for correct answer)

- a. Least developed country
- b. Interest
- c. Debt management plan
- d. gearing

*Guidance:* level 1

An _____ is an area of the production, distribution, or trade, and consumption of goods and services by different agents. Understood in its broadest sense, 'The _____ is defined as a social domain that emphasize the practices, discourses, and material expressions associated with the production, use, and management of resources'. Economic agents can be individuals, businesses, organizations, or governments. Economic transactions occur when two parties agree to the value or price of the transacted good or service, commonly expressed in a certain currency. However, monetary transactions only account for a small part of the economic domain.

Exam Probability: **High**

22. *Answer choices:*
(see index for correct answer)

- a. Character
- b. corporate values
- c. process perspective
- d. co-culture

*Guidance:* level 1

:: Industry ::

A _____ is a set of sequential operations established in a factory where materials are put through a refining process to produce an end-product that is suitable for onward consumption; or components are assembled to make a finished article.

Exam Probability: **High**

23. *Answer choices:*
(see index for correct answer)

- a. Industrialisation
- b. Consciousness Industry
- c. Production line
- d. Boilery

*Guidance:* level 1

_____ is an internet portal launched in 1995 that provides a variety of content including news and weather, a metasearch engine, a web-based email, instant messaging, stock quotes, and a customizable user homepage. It is currently operated by IAC Applications of IAC, and _____ Networks. In the U.S., the main _____ site has long been a personal start page called My _____ . _____ also operates an e-mail service, although it is no longer open for new customers.

Exam Probability: **Low**

24. *Answer choices:*
(see index for correct answer)

- a. Dot-com company
- b. Urbanfetch
- c. Excite
- d. Dot-com bubble

*Guidance:* level 1

---

:: Organizational structure ::

An _____ defines how activities such as task allocation, coordination, and supervision are directed toward the achievement of organizational aims.

Exam Probability: **High**

25. *Answer choices:*
(see index for correct answer)

- a. Organization of the New York City Police Department
- b. Blessed Unrest
- c. Followership
- d. Organizational structure

*Guidance:* level 1

---

:: Payment systems ::

A _____ is any system used to settle financial transactions through the transfer of monetary value. This includes the institutions, instruments, people, rules, procedures, standards, and technologies that make it exchange possible. A common type of _____ is called an operational network that links bank accounts and provides for monetary exchange using bank deposits. Some _____ s also include credit mechanisms, which are essentially a different aspect of payment.

Exam Probability: **High**

26. *Answer choices:*

(see index for correct answer)

- a. Debit card cashback
- b. Interac e-Transfer
- c. Payment system
- d. TIPANET

*Guidance:* level 1

---

:: Real estate ::

_____ s serve several societal needs – primarily as shelter from weather, security, living space, privacy, to store belongings, and to comfortably live and work. A _____ as a shelter represents a physical division of the human habitat and the outside .

Exam Probability: **High**

27. *Answer choices:*

(see index for correct answer)

- a. Building
- b. Crown land
- c. Communal land
- d. Load factor

*Guidance:* level 1

---

:: ::

_____ s are formal, sociotechnical, organizational systems designed to collect, process, store, and distribute information. In a sociotechnical perspective, _____ s are composed by four components: task, people, structure, and technology.

Exam Probability: **Medium**

28. *Answer choices:*
(see index for correct answer)

- a. cultural
- b. similarity-attraction theory
- c. Information system
- d. levels of analysis

*Guidance:* level 1

---

:: Business law ::

A _____ is a business entity created by two or more parties, generally characterized by shared ownership, shared returns and risks, and shared governance. Companies typically pursue _____ s for one of four reasons: to access a new market, particularly emerging markets; to gain scale efficiencies by combining assets and operations; to share risk for major investments or projects; or to access skills and capabilities.

Exam Probability: **Low**

29. *Answer choices:*
(see index for correct answer)

- a. Process agent
- b. Trusted Computing
- c. Installment sale
- d. Joint venture

*Guidance:* level 1

---

:: Commerce ::

A _____ is an employee within a company, business or other organization who is responsible at some level for buying or approving the acquisition of goods and services needed by the company. Responsible for buying the best quality products, goods and services for their company at the most competitive prices, _____ s work in a wide range of sectors for many different organizations. The position responsibilities may be the same as that of a buyer or purchasing agent, or may include wider supervisory or managerial responsibilities. A _____ may oversee the acquisition of materials needed for production, general supplies for offices and facilities, equipment, or construction contracts. A _____ often supervises purchasing agents and buyers, but in small companies the _____ may also be the purchasing agent or buyer. The _____ position may also carry the title "Procurement Manager" or in the public sector, "Procurement Officer". He or she can come from both an Engineering or Economics background.

Exam Probability: **High**

30. *Answer choices:*
(see index for correct answer)

- a. Hauls
- b. Purchasing manager
- c. Safe harbor
- d. Defective on arrival

*Guidance:* level 1

:: Commercial item transport and distribution ::

A _____ , forwarder, or forwarding agent, also known as a non-vessel operating common carrier , is a person or company that organizes shipments for individuals or corporations to get goods from the manufacturer or producer to a market, customer or final point of distribution. Forwarders contract with a carrier or often multiple carriers to move the goods. A forwarder does not move the goods but acts as an expert in the logistics network. These carriers can use a variety of shipping modes, including ships, airplanes, trucks, and railroads, and often do utilize multiple modes for a single shipment. For example, the _____ may arrange to have cargo moved from a plant to an airport by truck, flown to the destination city, then moved from the airport to a customer's building by another truck.

31. *Answer choices:*
(see index for correct answer)

- a. Wharf
- b. Freight forwarder
- c. Consignor
- d. Sidelifter

*Guidance:* level 1

:: ::

A _____ , or also known as foreman, overseer, facilitator, monitor, area coordinator, or sometimes gaffer, is the job title of a low level management position that is primarily based on authority over a worker or charge of a workplace. A _____ can also be one of the most senior in the staff at the place of work, such as a Professor who oversees a PhD dissertation. Supervision, on the other hand, can be performed by people without this formal title, for example by parents. The term _____ itself can be used to refer to any personnel who have this task as part of their job description.

32. *Answer choices:*
(see index for correct answer)

- a. hierarchical perspective
- b. levels of analysis
- c. Supervisor
- d. empathy

*Guidance:* level 1

:: Accounting source documents ::

An _____ , bill or tab is a commercial document issued by a seller to a buyer, relating to a sale transaction and indicating the products, quantities, and agreed prices for products or services the seller had provided the buyer.

33. *Answer choices:*
(see index for correct answer)

- a. Credit memo
- b. Superbill
- c. Invoice
- d. Remittance advice

*Guidance:* level 1

---

:: ::

A _____ consists of one people who live in the same dwelling and share meals. It may also consist of a single family or another group of people. A dwelling is considered to contain multiple _____ s if meals or living spaces are not shared. The _____ is the basic unit of analysis in many social, microeconomic and government models, and is important to economics and inheritance.

Exam Probability: **High**

34. *Answer choices:*

(see index for correct answer)

- a. empathy
- b. co-culture
- c. Household
- d. imperative

*Guidance:* level 1

---

:: Securities (finance) ::

A _____ is a container that is traditionally constructed from stiff fibers, and can be made from a range of materials, including wood splints, runners, and cane. While most _____ s are made from plant materials, other materials such as horsehair, baleen, or metal wire can be used. _____ s are generally woven by hand. Some _____ s are fitted with a lid, while others are left open on top.

Exam Probability: **Low**

35. *Answer choices:*

(see index for correct answer)

- a. Share transmission
- b. Indirect holding system
- c. Look-through approach

- d. Principal at risk notes

*Guidance:* level 1

---

:: ::

A federation is a political entity characterized by a union of partially self-governing provinces, states, or other regions under a central _____ . In a federation, the self-governing status of the component states, as well as the division of power between them and the central government, is typically constitutionally entrenched and may not be altered by a unilateral decision of either party, the states or the federal political body. Alternatively, federation is a form of government in which sovereign power is formally divided between a central authority and a number of constituent regions so that each region retains some degree of control over its internal affairs. It is often argued that federal states where the central government has the constitutional authority to suspend a constituent state's government by invoking gross mismanagement or civil unrest, or to adopt national legislation that overrides or infringe on the constituent states' powers by invoking the central government's constitutional authority to ensure "peace and good government" or to implement obligations contracted under an international treaty, are not truly federal states.

Exam Probability: **Low**

36. *Answer choices:*
(see index for correct answer)

- a. personal values
- b. Sarbanes-Oxley act of 2002
- c. cultural
- d. levels of analysis

*Guidance:* level 1

---

:: Marketing analytics ::

_____ is a long-term, forward-looking approach to planning with the fundamental goal of achieving a sustainable competitive advantage. Strategic planning involves an analysis of the company's strategic initial situation prior to the formulation, evaluation and selection of market-oriented competitive position that contributes to the company's goals and marketing objectives.

37. *Answer choices:*

(see index for correct answer)

- a. Marketing performance measurement and management
- b. Perceptual map
- c. Marketing mix modeling
- d. Marketing strategy

*Guidance:* level 1

:: Asset ::

In financial accounting, an _____ is any resource owned by the business. Anything tangible or intangible that can be owned or controlled to produce value and that is held by a company to produce positive economic value is an _____ . Simply stated, _____ s represent value of ownership that can be converted into cash . The balance sheet of a firm records the monetary value of the _____ s owned by that firm. It covers money and other valuables belonging to an individual or to a business.

38. *Answer choices:*

(see index for correct answer)

- a. Fixed asset
- b. Current asset

*Guidance:* level 1

:: E-commerce ::

_____ is a United States-based payment gateway service provider allowing merchants to accept credit card and electronic check payments through their website and over an Internet Protocol connection. Founded in 1996, _____ is now a subsidiary of Visa Inc. Its service permits customers to enter credit card and shipping information directly onto a web page, in contrast to some alternatives that require the customer to sign up for a payment service before performing a transaction.

Exam Probability: **Low**

39. *Answer choices:*
(see index for correct answer)

- a. Digital ticket
- b. Authorize.Net
- c. The Cluetrain Manifesto
- d. IBill

*Guidance:* level 1

---

:: Scientific method ::

In the social sciences and life sciences, a _____ is a research method involving an up-close, in-depth, and detailed examination of a subject of study , as well as its related contextual conditions.

Exam Probability: **Medium**

40. *Answer choices:*
(see index for correct answer)

- a. Case study
- b. Causal research
- c. pilot project
- d. explanatory research

*Guidance:* level 1

---

:: Business law ::

The _____ , first published in 1952, is one of a number of Uniform Acts that have been established as law with the goal of harmonizing the laws of sales and other commercial transactions across the United States of America through UCC adoption by all 50 states, the District of Columbia, and the Territories of the United States.

Exam Probability: **High**

41. *Answer choices:*

(see index for correct answer)

- a. Interest of the company
- b. Uniform Commercial Code
- c. Limited liability
- d. Inslaw

*Guidance:* level 1

:: ::

_____ is the practice of deliberately managing the spread of information between an individual or an organization and the public. _____ may include an organization or individual gaining exposure to their audiences using topics of public interest and news items that do not require direct payment. This differentiates it from advertising as a form of marketing communications. _____ is the idea of creating coverage for clients for free, rather than marketing or advertising. But now, advertising is also a part of greater PR Activities.An example of good _____ would be generating an article featuring a client, rather than paying for the client to be advertised next to the article. The aim of _____ is to inform the public, prospective customers, investors, partners, employees, and other stakeholders and ultimately persuade them to maintain a positive or favorable view about the organization, its leadership, products, or political decisions. _____ professionals typically work for PR and marketing firms, businesses and companies, government, and public officials as PIOs and nongovernmental organizations, and nonprofit organizations. Jobs central to _____ include account coordinator, account executive, account supervisor, and media relations manager.

Exam Probability: **Medium**

42. *Answer choices:*

(see index for correct answer)

- a. deep-level diversity
- b. Public relations
- c. co-culture
- d. Character

*Guidance:* level 1

---

:: Fraud ::

In law, _____ is intentional deception to secure unfair or unlawful gain, or to deprive a victim of a legal right. _____ can violate civil law, a criminal law, or it may cause no loss of money, property or legal right but still be an element of another civil or criminal wrong. The purpose of _____ may be monetary gain or other benefits, for example by obtaining a passport, travel document, or driver's license, or mortgage _____, where the perpetrator may attempt to qualify for a mortgage by way of false statements.

Exam Probability: **High**

43. *Answer choices:*

(see index for correct answer)

- a. Workers Resistance
- b. Fraud
- c. Senior Medicare Patrols
- d. Phone cloning

*Guidance:* level 1

---

:: ::

In marketing jargon, product lining is offering several related products for sale individually. Unlike product bundling, where several products are combined into one group, which is then offered for sale as a units, product lining involves offering the products for sale separately. A line can comprise related products of various sizes, types, colors, qualities, or prices. Line depth refers to the number of subcategories a category has. Line consistency refers to how closely related the products that make up the line are. Line vulnerability refers to the percentage of sales or profits that are derived from only a few products in the line.

Exam Probability: **Medium**

44. *Answer choices:*
(see index for correct answer)

- a. hierarchical
- b. Product mix
- c. empathy
- d. imperative

*Guidance:* level 1

---

:: Commercial item transport and distribution ::

A _____ in common law countries is a person or company that transports goods or people for any person or company and that is responsible for any possible loss of the goods during transport. A _____ offers its services to the general public under license or authority provided by a regulatory body. The regulatory body has usually been granted "ministerial authority" by the legislation that created it. The regulatory body may create, interpret, and enforce its regulations upon the _____ with independence and finality, as long as it acts within the bounds of the enabling legislation.

Exam Probability: **Low**

45. *Answer choices:*
(see index for correct answer)

- a. Refrigerator truck
- b. Skid mount
- c. Livestock transportation
- d. Blue Water Trucking

*Guidance:* level 1

_____ is the study and management of exchange relationships. _____ is the business process of creating relationships with and satisfying customers. With its focus on the customer, _____ is one of the premier components of business management.

Exam Probability: **Medium**

46. *Answer choices:*

(see index for correct answer)

- a. interpersonal communication
- b. deep-level diversity
- c. process perspective
- d. personal values

*Guidance:* level 1

:: Income ::

In business and accounting, net income is an entity's income minus cost of goods sold, expenses and taxes for an accounting period. It is computed as the residual of all revenues and gains over all expenses and losses for the period, and has also been defined as the net increase in shareholders' equity that results from a company's operations. In the context of the presentation of financial statements, the IFRS Foundation defines net income as synonymous with profit and loss. The difference between revenue and the cost of making a product or providing a service, before deducting overheads, payroll, taxation, and interest payments. This is different from operating income .

Exam Probability: **High**

47. *Answer choices:*

(see index for correct answer)

- a. Aggregate expenditure
- b. Implied level of government service
- c. Bottom line
- d. Giganomics

*Guidance:* level 1

In legal terminology, a _____ is any formal legal document that sets out the facts and legal reasons that the filing party or parties believes are sufficient to support a claim against the party or parties against whom the claim is brought that entitles the plaintiff to a remedy . For example, the Federal Rules of Civil Procedure that govern civil litigation in United States courts provide that a civil action is commenced with the filing or service of a pleading called a _____ . Civil court rules in states that have incorporated the Federal Rules of Civil Procedure use the same term for the same pleading.

Exam Probability: **High**

48. *Answer choices:*
(see index for correct answer)

- a. process perspective
- b. imperative
- c. Complaint
- d. surface-level diversity

*Guidance:* level 1

---

:: Marketing by medium ::

_____ , also called online marketing or Internet advertising or web advertising, is a form of marketing and advertising which uses the Internet to deliver promotional marketing messages to consumers. Many consumers find _____ disruptive and have increasingly turned to ad blocking for a variety of reasons. When software is used to do the purchasing, it is known as programmatic advertising.

Exam Probability: **Medium**

49. *Answer choices:*
(see index for correct answer)

- a. New media marketing
- b. Online advertising
- c. Digital marketing
- d. Social intelligence architect

*Guidance:* level 1

A _____ is an individual or institution that legally owns one or more shares of stock in a public or private corporation. _____ s may be referred to as members of a corporation. Legally, a person is not a _____ in a corporation until their name and other details are entered in the corporation's register of _____ s or members.

Exam Probability: **High**

50. *Answer choices:*
(see index for correct answer)

- a. interpersonal communication
- b. functional perspective
- c. Sarbanes-Oxley act of 2002
- d. cultural

*Guidance:* level 1

:: Project management ::

In political science, an _____ is a means by which a petition signed by a certain minimum number of registered voters can force a government to choose to either enact a law or hold a public vote in parliament in what is called indirect _____ , or under direct _____ , the proposition is immediately put to a plebiscite or referendum, in what is called a Popular initiated Referendum or citizen-initiated referendum).

Exam Probability: **High**

51. *Answer choices:*
(see index for correct answer)

- a. Project team
- b. Initiative
- c. Legal matter management
- d. Project sponsorship

*Guidance:* level 1

:: Debt ::

_____ is the trust which allows one party to provide money or resources to another party wherein the second party does not reimburse the first party immediately , but promises either to repay or return those resources at a later date. In other words, _____ is a method of making reciprocity formal, legally enforceable, and extensible to a large group of unrelated people.

Exam Probability: **Low**

52. *Answer choices:*
(see index for correct answer)

- a. Asset protection
- b. Debt relief
- c. Credit
- d. Museum of Foreign Debt

*Guidance:* level 1

:: ::

In Christian denominations that practice infant baptism, confirmation is seen as the sealing of Christianity created in baptism. Those being _____ are known as confirmands. In some denominations, such as the Anglican Communion and Methodist Churches, confirmation bestows full membership in a local congregation upon the recipient. In others, such as the Roman Catholic Church, Confirmation "renders the bond with the Church more perfect", because, while a baptized person is already a member, "reception of the sacrament of Confirmation is necessary for the completion of baptismal grace".

Exam Probability: **High**

53. *Answer choices:*
(see index for correct answer)

- a. open system
- b. functional perspective
- c. Confirmed
- d. co-culture

*Guidance:* level 1

:: ::

In international relations, _____ is – from the perspective of governments – a voluntary transfer of resources from one country to another.

Exam Probability: **Low**

54. *Answer choices:*
(see index for correct answer)

- a. Sarbanes-Oxley act of 2002
- b. cultural
- c. co-culture
- d. functional perspective

*Guidance:* level 1

---

:: Commercial item transport and distribution ::

Wholesaling or distributing is the sale of goods or merchandise to retailers; to industrial, commercial, institutional, or other professional business users; or to other _____ rs and related subordinated services. In general, it is the sale of goods to anyone other than a standard consumer.

Exam Probability: **High**

55. *Answer choices:*
(see index for correct answer)

- a. Wholesale
- b. MC Freight Systems
- c. Warehouse receipt
- d. Steam wagon

*Guidance:* level 1

---

:: ::

_____ is the administration of an organization, whether it is a business, a not-for-profit organization, or government body. _____ includes the activities of setting the strategy of an organization and coordinating the efforts of its employees to accomplish its objectives through the application of available resources, such as financial, natural, technological, and human resources. The term " _____ " may also refer to those people who manage an organization.

Exam Probability: **Low**

56. *Answer choices:*
(see index for correct answer)

- a. functional perspective
- b. deep-level diversity
- c. Management
- d. co-culture

*Guidance:* level 1

:: ::

_____ is getting a diploma or academic degree or the ceremony that is sometimes associated with it, in which students become graduates. The date of _____ is often called _____ day. The _____ ceremony itself is also called commencement, convocation or invocation.

Exam Probability: **Medium**

57. *Answer choices:*
(see index for correct answer)

- a. imperative
- b. Graduation
- c. process perspective
- d. corporate values

*Guidance:* level 1

:: Dot-com bubble ::

Yahoo! _____ was a web hosting service. It was founded in November 1994 by David Bohnett and John Rezner, and was called Beverly Hills Internet for a very short time before being named _____ .

58. *Answer choices:*

- a. Dot com party
- b. Dot-com company
- c. Lycos
- d. GeoCities

:: Auctioneering ::

Unlike sealed-bid auctions , an _____ is "open" or fully transparent, as the identity of all bidders is disclosed to each other during the auction. More generally, an auction mechanism is considered "English" if it involves an iterative process of adjusting the price in a direction that is unfavorable to the bidders . In contrast, a Dutch auction would adjust the price in a direction that favored the bidders .

59. *Answer choices:*

- a. Call for bids
- b. English auction
- c. Dutch auction
- d. Forward auction

## Business ethics

Business ethics (also known as corporate ethics) is a form of applied ethics or professional ethics, that examines ethical principles and moral or ethical problems that can arise in a business environment. It applies to all aspects of business conduct and is relevant to the conduct of individuals and entire organizations. These ethics originate from individuals, organizational statements or from the legal system. These norms, values, ethical, and unethical practices are what is used to guide business. They help those businesses maintain a better connection with their stakeholders.

:: ::

The _____ to Fight AIDS, Tuberculosis and Malaria is an international financing organization that aims to "attract, leverage and invest additional resources to end the epidemics of HIV/AIDS, tuberculosis and malaria to support attainment of the Sustainable Development Goals established by the United Nations." A public-private partnership, the organization maintains its secretariat in Geneva, Switzerland. The organization began operations in January 2002. Microsoft founder Bill Gates was one of the first private foundations among many bilateral donors to provide seed money for the partnership.

Exam Probability: **Medium**

1. *Answer choices:*

(see index for correct answer)

- a. personal values
- b. cultural
- c. open system
- d. empathy

*Guidance:* level 1

:: ::

Bernard Lawrence _____ is an American former market maker, investment advisor, financier, fraudster, and convicted felon, who is currently serving a federal prison sentence for offenses related to a massive Ponzi scheme. He is the former non-executive chairman of the NASDAQ stock market, the confessed operator of the largest Ponzi scheme in world history, and the largest financial fraud in U.S. history. Prosecutors estimated the fraud to be worth $64.8 billion based on the amounts in the accounts of _____ `s 4,800 clients as of November 30, 2008.

Exam Probability: **High**

2. *Answer choices:*

(see index for correct answer)

- a. hierarchical perspective
- b. Madoff
- c. information systems assessment
- d. co-culture

*Guidance:* level 1

:: Professional ethics ::

In the mental health field, a _____ is a situation where multiple roles exist between a therapist, or other mental health practitioner, and a client. _____ s are also referred to as multiple relationships, and these two terms are used interchangeably in the research literature. The American Psychological Association  Ethical Principles of Psychologists and Code of Conduct  is a resource that outlines ethical standards and principles to which practitioners are expected to adhere. Standard 3.05 of the APA ethics code outlines the definition of multiple relationships. Dual or multiple relationships occur when.

Exam Probability: **Low**

3. *Answer choices:*

(see index for correct answer)

- a. Dual relationship
- b. Continuous professional development
- c. professional conduct

*Guidance:* level 1

_____ is a form of reverence gained by a leader who has strong interpersonal relationship skills. _____ , as an aspect of personal power, becomes particularly important as organizational leadership becomes increasingly about collaboration and influence, rather than command and control.

Exam Probability: **Low**

4. *Answer choices:*
(see index for correct answer)

- a. need for power
- b. Hard power
- c. Expert power

*Guidance:* level 1

---

A _____ organization , also known as a non-business entity, not-for-profit organization, or _____ institution, is dedicated to furthering a particular social cause or advocating for a shared point of view. In economic terms, it is an organization that uses its surplus of the revenues to further achieve its ultimate objective, rather than distributing its income to the organization's shareholders, leaders, or members. _____ s are tax exempt or charitable, meaning they do not pay income tax on the money that they receive for their organization. They can operate in religious, scientific, research, or educational settings.

Exam Probability: **Low**

5. *Answer choices:*
(see index for correct answer)

- a. Satellite television
- b. Nonprofit
- c. multiplexing
- d. not-for-profit

*Guidance:* level 1

---

_____ or statute law is written law set down by a body of legislature or by a singular legislator . This is as opposed to oral or customary law; or regulatory law promulgated by the executive or common law of the judiciary. Statutes may originate with national, state legislatures or local municipalities.

Exam Probability: **Low**

6. *Answer choices:*

(see index for correct answer)

- a. Statute of repose
- b. Statutory law
- c. ratification
- d. incorporation by reference

*Guidance:* level 1

:: ::

_____ is the introduction of contaminants into the natural environment that cause adverse change. _____ can take the form of chemical substances or energy, such as noise, heat or light. Pollutants, the components of _____ , can be either foreign substances/energies or naturally occurring contaminants. _____ is often classed as point source or nonpoint source _____ .In 2015, _____ killed 9 million people in the world.

Exam Probability: **Medium**

7. *Answer choices:*

(see index for correct answer)

- a. personal values
- b. similarity-attraction theory
- c. Pollution
- d. imperative

*Guidance:* level 1

:: ::

The _____ , founded in 1912, is a private, nonprofit organization whose self-described mission is to focus on advancing marketplace trust, consisting of 106 independently incorporated local BBB organizations in the United States and Canada, coordinated under the Council of _____ s in Arlington, Virginia.

Exam Probability: **Low**

8. *Answer choices:*
(see index for correct answer)

- a. hierarchical perspective
- b. Better Business Bureau
- c. imperative
- d. Sarbanes-Oxley act of 2002

*Guidance:* level 1

:: ::

Cannabis, also known as _____ among other names, is a psychoactive drug from the Cannabis plant used for medical or recreational purposes. The main psychoactive part of cannabis is tetrahydrocannabinol , one of 483 known compounds in the plant, including at least 65 other cannabinoids. Cannabis can be used by smoking, vaporizing, within food, or as an extract.

Exam Probability: **Low**

9. *Answer choices:*
(see index for correct answer)

- a. Character
- b. corporate values
- c. surface-level diversity
- d. personal values

*Guidance:* level 1

:: Leadership ::

_____ is a theory of leadership where a leader works with teams to identify needed change, creating a vision to guide the change through inspiration, and executing the change in tandem with committed members of a group; it is an integral part of the Full Range Leadership Model. _____ serves to enhance the motivation, morale, and job performance of followers through a variety of mechanisms; these include connecting the follower's sense of identity and self to a project and to the collective identity of the organization; being a role model for followers in order to inspire them and to raise their interest in the project; challenging followers to take greater ownership for their work, and understanding the strengths and weaknesses of followers, allowing the leader to align followers with tasks that enhance their performance.

Exam Probability: **Low**

10. *Answer choices:*
(see index for correct answer)

- a. BTS Group
- b. Meta-leadership
- c. Servant leadership
- d. Transformational leadership

*Guidance:* level 1

---

:: Fraud ::

In the United States, _____ is the claiming of Medicare health care reimbursement to which the claimant is not entitled. There are many different types of _____ , all of which have the same goal: to collect money from the Medicare program illegitimately.

Exam Probability: **High**

11. *Answer choices:*
(see index for correct answer)

- a. Credit card fraud
- b. Customer not present
- c. Hitler Diaries
- d. Voice phishing

*Guidance:* level 1

Competition law is a law that promotes or seeks to maintain market competition by regulating anti-competitive conduct by companies. Competition law is implemented through public and private enforcement. Competition law is known as "_____ law" in the United States for historical reasons, and as "anti-monopoly law" in China and Russia. In previous years it has been known as trade practices law in the United Kingdom and Australia. In the European Union, it is referred to as both _____ and competition law.

Exam Probability: **Medium**

12. *Answer choices:*
(see index for correct answer)

- a. co-culture
- b. Antitrust
- c. interpersonal communication
- d. Sarbanes-Oxley act of 2002

*Guidance:* level 1

---

:: Utilitarianism ::

_____ is a school of thought that argues that the pursuit of pleasure and intrinsic goods are the primary or most important goals of human life. A hedonist strives to maximize net pleasure . However upon finally gaining said pleasure, happiness may remain stationary.

Exam Probability: **High**

13. *Answer choices:*
(see index for correct answer)

- a. Felicific calculus
- b. Informed judge
- c. Mere addition paradox
- d. Telishment

*Guidance:* level 1

---

_____ ism is a form of government characterized by strong central power and limited political freedoms. Individual freedoms are subordinate to the state and there is no constitutional accountability and rule of law under an _____ regime. _____ regimes can be autocratic with power concentrated in one person or it can be more spread out between multiple officials and government institutions. Juan Linz's influential 1964 description of _____ ism characterized _____ political systems by four qualities.

Exam Probability: **Medium**

14. *Answer choices:*
(see index for correct answer)

- a. deep-level diversity
- b. Authoritarian
- c. cultural
- d. empathy

*Guidance:* level 1

:: Renewable energy ::

A _____ is a fuel that is produced through contemporary biological processes, such as agriculture and anaerobic digestion, rather than a fuel produced by geological processes such as those involved in the formation of fossil fuels, such as coal and petroleum, from prehistoric biological matter. If the source biomatter can regrow quickly, the resulting fuel is said to be a form of renewable energy.

Exam Probability: **High**

15. *Answer choices:*
(see index for correct answer)

- a. Biofuel
- b. The Fourth Revolution: Energy
- c. Tidal power
- d. GREEN Cell Shipping

*Guidance:* level 1

:: Market-based policy instruments ::

Cause marketing is defined as a type of corporate social responsibility, in which a company's promotional campaign has the dual purpose of increasing profitability while bettering society.

Exam Probability: **High**

16. *Answer choices:*
(see index for correct answer)

- a. Pigovian
- b. Time-based currency
- c. Cobra effect
- d. Cause-related marketing

*Guidance:* level 1

---

:: Corporate scandals ::

Exxon Mobil Corporation, doing business as _____ , is an American multinational oil and gas corporation headquartered in Irving, Texas. It is the largest direct descendant of John D. Rockefeller's Standard Oil Company, and was formed on November 30, 1999 by the merger of Exxon and Mobil . _____ 's primary brands are Exxon, Mobil, Esso, and _____ Chemical.

Exam Probability: **Medium**

17. *Answer choices:*
(see index for correct answer)

- a. Barings Bank
- b. Stanford International Bank
- c. Eurest Support Services
- d. Harken Energy scandal

*Guidance:* level 1

---

:: Business ethics ::

_____ is an area of applied ethics which deals with the moral principles behind the operation and regulation of marketing. Some areas of _____ overlap with media ethics.

18. *Answer choices:*

- a. Evolution of corporate social responsibility in India
- b. Electronic retailing self-regulation program
- c. Philosophy of business
- d. Sexual harassment

*Guidance:* level 1

:: ::

_____ is a non-governmental environmental organization with offices in over 39 countries and an international coordinating body in Amsterdam, the Netherlands. _____ was founded in 1971 by Irving Stowe, and Dorothy Stowe, Canadian and US ex-pat environmental activists. _____ states its goal is to "ensure the ability of the Earth to nurture life in all its diversity" and focuses its campaigning on worldwide issues such as climate change, deforestation, overfishing, commercial whaling, genetic engineering, and anti-nuclear issues. It uses direct action, lobbying, research, and ecotage to achieve its goals. The global organization does not accept funding from governments, corporations, or political parties, relying on three million individual supporters and foundation grants. _____ has a general consultative status with the United Nations Economic and Social Council and is a founding member of the INGO Accountability Charter, an international non-governmental organization that intends to foster accountability and transparency of non-governmental organizations.

19. *Answer choices:*

- a. co-culture
- b. Greenpeace
- c. imperative
- d. surface-level diversity

*Guidance:* level 1

:: Data management ::

_____ is a form of intellectual property that grants the creator of an original creative work an exclusive legal right to determine whether and under what conditions this original work may be copied and used by others, usually for a limited term of years. The exclusive rights are not absolute but limited by limitations and exceptions to _____ law, including fair use. A major limitation on _____ on ideas is that _____ protects only the original expression of ideas, and not the underlying ideas themselves.

Exam Probability: **Low**

20. *Answer choices:*
(see index for correct answer)

- a. VMDS
- b. CERF
- c. Serializability
- d. Enterprise Objects Framework

*Guidance:* level 1

---

:: ::

The Ethics & Compliance Initiative was formed in 2015 and consists of three nonprofit organizations: the Ethics Research Center, the Ethics & Compliance Association, and the Ethics & Compliance Certification Institute. Based in Arlington, Virginia, United States, ECI is devoted to the advancement of high ethical standards and practices in public and private institutions, and provides research about ethical standards, workplace integrity, and compliance practices and processes.

Exam Probability: **Medium**

21. *Answer choices:*
(see index for correct answer)

- a. Ethics Resource Center
- b. functional perspective
- c. co-culture
- d. Character

*Guidance:* level 1

---

:: Labor rights ::

The _____ is the concept that people have a human _____ , or engage in productive employment, and may not be prevented from doing so. The _____ is enshrined in the Universal Declaration of Human Rights and recognized in international human rights law through its inclusion in the International Covenant on Economic, Social and Cultural Rights, where the _____ emphasizes economic, social and cultural development.

22. *Answer choices:*
(see index for correct answer)

- a. Swift raids
- b. The Hyatt 100
- c. Labor rights
- d. Right to work

*Guidance:* level 1

:: Progressive Era in the United States ::

The Clayton Antitrust Act of 1914 , was a part of United States antitrust law with the goal of adding further substance to the U.S. antitrust law regime; the _____ sought to prevent anticompetitive practices in their incipiency. That regime started with the Sherman Antitrust Act of 1890, the first Federal law outlawing practices considered harmful to consumers . The _____ specified particular prohibited conduct, the three-level enforcement scheme, the exemptions, and the remedial measures.

23. *Answer choices:*
(see index for correct answer)

- a. Clayton Act
- b. pragmatism
- c. Mann Act

*Guidance:* level 1

:: Coal ::

_____ is a combustible black or brownish-black sedimentary rock, formed as rock strata called _____ seams. _____ is mostly carbon with variable amounts of other elements; chiefly hydrogen, sulfur, oxygen, and nitrogen. _____ is formed if dead plant matter decays into peat and over millions of years the heat and pressure of deep burial converts the peat into _____ . Vast deposits of _____ originates in former wetlands—called _____ forests—that covered much of the Earth's tropical land areas during the late Carboniferous and Permian times.

Exam Probability: **Low**

24. *Answer choices:*
(see index for correct answer)

- a. Sub-bituminous coal
- b. Coal
- c. Pulverised fuel ash
- d. Black coal equivalent

*Guidance:* level 1

---

:: Supply chain management terms ::

In business and finance, _____ is a system of organizations, people, activities, information, and resources involved in moving a product or service from supplier to customer. _____ activities involve the transformation of natural resources, raw materials, and components into a finished product that is delivered to the end customer. In sophisticated _____ systems, used products may re-enter the _____ at any point where residual value is recyclable. _____ s link value chains.

Exam Probability: **Low**

25. *Answer choices:*
(see index for correct answer)

- a. Stockout
- b. Overstock
- c. Capital spare
- d. Work in process

*Guidance:* level 1

---

:: ::

_____ is an eight-block-long street running roughly northwest to southeast from Broadway to South Street, at the East River, in the Financial District of Lower Manhattan in New York City. Over time, the term has become a metonym for the financial markets of the United States as a whole, the American financial services industry, or New York–based financial interests.

Exam Probability: **Medium**

26. *Answer choices:*
(see index for correct answer)

- a. Wall Street
- b. hierarchical perspective
- c. surface-level diversity
- d. similarity-attraction theory

*Guidance:* level 1

---

:: Occupational safety and health ::

_____ is a chemical element with symbol Pb and atomic number 82. It is a heavy metal that is denser than most common materials. _____ is soft and malleable, and also has a relatively low melting point. When freshly cut, _____ is silvery with a hint of blue; it tarnishes to a dull gray color when exposed to air. _____ has the highest atomic number of any stable element and three of its isotopes are endpoints of major nuclear decay chains of heavier elements.

Exam Probability: **High**

27. *Answer choices:*
(see index for correct answer)

- a. Canadian Registered Safety Professional
- b. Lead
- c. Latex allergy
- d. Flame arrester

*Guidance:* level 1

---

:: Majority–minority relations ::

It was established as axiomatic in anthropological research by Franz Boas in the first few decades of the 20th century and later popularized by his students. Boas first articulated the idea in 1887: "civilization is not something absolute, but ... is relative, and ... our ideas and conceptions are true only so far as our civilization goes". However, Boas did not coin the term.

Exam Probability: **Low**

28. *Answer choices:*
(see index for correct answer)

- a. Affirmative action
- b. positive discrimination
- c. Cultural relativism

*Guidance:* level 1

---

:: International trade ::

_____ involves the transfer of goods or services from one person or entity to another, often in exchange for money. A system or network that allows _____ is called a market.

Exam Probability: **Medium**

29. *Answer choices:*
(see index for correct answer)

- a. Gravity model of trade
- b. International Trade Awards
- c. Northwest Cattle Project
- d. Trade

*Guidance:* level 1

---

:: Business ::

_____ , or built-in obsolescence, in industrial design and economics is a policy of planning or designing a product with an artificially limited useful life, so that it becomes obsolete after a certain period of time. The rationale behind this strategy is to generate long-term sales volume by reducing the time between repeat purchases .

30. *Answer choices:*
(see index for correct answer)

- a. Number
- b. Legal governance, risk management, and compliance
- c. Door-to-door
- d. Planned obsolescence

*Guidance:* level 1

:: ::

An _____ is the release of a liquid petroleum hydrocarbon into the environment, especially the marine ecosystem, due to human activity, and is a form of pollution. The term is usually given to marine _____ s, where oil is released into the ocean or coastal waters, but spills may also occur on land. _____ s may be due to releases of crude oil from tankers, offshore platforms, drilling rigs and wells, as well as spills of refined petroleum products and their by-products, heavier fuels used by large ships such as bunker fuel, or the spill of any oily refuse or waste oil.

31. *Answer choices:*
(see index for correct answer)

- a. process perspective
- b. deep-level diversity
- c. Oil spill
- d. co-culture

*Guidance:* level 1

:: ::

_____ is a product prepared from the leaves of the _____ plant by curing them. The plant is part of the genus Nicotiana and of the Solanaceae family. While more than 70 species of _____ are known, the chief commercial crop is N. tabacum. The more potent variant N. rustica is also used around the world.

Exam Probability: **Medium**

32. *Answer choices:*

(see index for correct answer)

- a. Tobacco
- b. interpersonal communication
- c. information systems assessment
- d. Sarbanes-Oxley act of 2002

*Guidance:* level 1

:: ::

A _____ is the ability to carry out a task with determined results often within a given amount of time, energy, or both. _____ s can often be divided into domain-general and domain-specific _____ s. For example, in the domain of work, some general _____ s would include time management, teamwork and leadership, self-motivation and others, whereas domain-specific _____ s would be used only for a certain job. _____ usually requires certain environmental stimuli and situations to assess the level of _____ being shown and used.

Exam Probability: **Low**

33. *Answer choices:*

(see index for correct answer)

- a. Skill
- b. imperative
- c. deep-level diversity
- d. hierarchical

*Guidance:* level 1

:: ::

_____ is "property consisting of land and the buildings on it, along with its natural resources such as crops, minerals or water; immovable property of this nature; an interest vested in this an item of real property, buildings or housing in general. Also: the business of _____ ; the profession of buying, selling, or renting land, buildings, or housing." It is a legal term used in jurisdictions whose legal system is derived from English common law, such as India, England, Wales, Northern Ireland, United States, Canada, Pakistan, Australia, and New Zealand.

Exam Probability: **Medium**

34. *Answer choices:*
(see index for correct answer)

- a. hierarchical
- b. personal values
- c. information systems assessment
- d. corporate values

*Guidance:* level 1

---

:: Environmental economics ::

_____ is the process of people maintaining change in a balanced environment, in which the exploitation of resources, the direction of investments, the orientation of technological development and institutional change are all in harmony and enhance both current and future potential to meet human needs and aspirations. For many in the field, _____ is defined through the following interconnected domains or pillars: environment, economic and social, which according to Fritjof Capra is based on the principles of Systems Thinking. Sub-domains of sustainable development have been considered also: cultural, technological and political. While sustainable development may be the organizing principle for _____ for some, for others, the two terms are paradoxical . Sustainable development is the development that meets the needs of the present without compromising the ability of future generations to meet their own needs. Brundtland Report for the World Commission on Environment and Development introduced the term of sustainable development.

Exam Probability: **High**

35. *Answer choices:*
(see index for correct answer)

- a. Eco-costs
- b. National Round Table on the Environment and the Economy
- c. First Green Bank
- d. Sustainability

*Guidance:* level 1

---

:: Monopoly (economics) ::

The _____ of 1890 was a United States antitrust law that regulates competition among enterprises, which was passed by Congress under the presidency of Benjamin Harrison.

Exam Probability: **High**

36. *Answer choices:*

(see index for correct answer)

- a. Sherman Antitrust Act
- b. Natural monopoly
- c. Coercive monopoly
- d. Monopsony

*Guidance:* level 1

---

:: Euthenics ::

_____ is an ethical framework and suggests that an entity, be it an organization or individual, has an obligation to act for the benefit of society at large. _____ is a duty every individual has to perform so as to maintain a balance between the economy and the ecosystems. A trade-off may exist between economic development, in the material sense, and the welfare of the society and environment, though this has been challenged by many reports over the past decade. _____ means sustaining the equilibrium between the two. It pertains not only to business organizations but also to everyone whose any action impacts the environment. This responsibility can be passive, by avoiding engaging in socially harmful acts, or active, by performing activities that directly advance social goals. _____ must be intergenerational since the actions of one generation have consequences on those following.

Exam Probability: **Low**

37. *Answer choices:*

(see index for correct answer)

- a. Social responsibility
- b. Euthenics
- c. Family and consumer science
- d. Minnie Cumnock Blodgett

---

:: Natural gas ::

_____ is a naturally occurring hydrocarbon gas mixture consisting primarily of methane, but commonly including varying amounts of other higher alkanes, and sometimes a small percentage of carbon dioxide, nitrogen, hydrogen sulfide, or helium. It is formed when layers of decomposing plant and animal matter are exposed to intense heat and pressure under the surface of the Earth over millions of years. The energy that the plants originally obtained from the sun is stored in the form of chemical bonds in the gas.

Exam Probability: **Medium**

38. *Answer choices:*
(see index for correct answer)

- a. Renewable natural gas
- b. Gas Safe Register
- c. Clathrate hydrate
- d. ISO 15971

---

:: ::

In ecology, a _____ is the type of natural environment in which a particular species of organism lives. It is characterized by both physical and biological features. A species' _____ is those places where it can find food, shelter, protection and mates for reproduction.

Exam Probability: **Medium**

39. *Answer choices:*
(see index for correct answer)

- a. hierarchical perspective
- b. Character
- c. levels of analysis

- d. Habitat

---

:: Financial regulatory authorities of the United States ::

The _____ is an agency of the United States government responsible for consumer protection in the financial sector. CFPB`s jurisdiction includes banks, credit unions, securities firms, payday lenders, mortgage-servicing operations, foreclosure relief services, debt collectors and other financial companies operating in the United States.

Exam Probability: **Low**

40. *Answer choices:*

- a. National Credit Union Administration
- b. Consumer Financial Protection Bureau
- c. Securities Investor Protection Corporation
- d. Federal Reserve Board

---

:: ::

The Federal National Mortgage Association , commonly known as _____ , is a United States government-sponsored enterprise and, since 1968, a publicly traded company. Founded in 1938 during the Great Depression as part of the New Deal, the corporation`s purpose is to expand the secondary mortgage market by securitizing mortgage loans in the form of mortgage-backed securities , allowing lenders to reinvest their assets into more lending and in effect increasing the number of lenders in the mortgage market by reducing the reliance on locally based savings and loan associations . Its brother organization is the Federal Home Loan Mortgage Corporation , better known as Freddie Mac. As of 2018, _____ is ranked #21 on the Fortune 500 rankings of the largest United States corporations by total revenue.

Exam Probability: **Medium**

41. *Answer choices:*

- a. functional perspective
- b. Fannie Mae
- c. personal values
- d. similarity-attraction theory

Guidance: level 1

---

:: Public relations terminology ::

_____ , also called "green sheen", is a form of spin in which green PR or green marketing is deceptively used to promote the perception that an organization's products, aims or policies are environmentally friendly. Evidence that an organization is _____ often comes from pointing out the spending differences: when significantly more money or time has been spent advertising being "green" , than is actually spent on environmentally sound practices. _____ efforts can range from changing the name or label of a product to evoke the natural environment on a product that contains harmful chemicals to multimillion-dollar marketing campaigns portraying highly polluting energy companies as eco-friendly.Publicized accusations of _____ have contributed to the term's increasing use.

Exam Probability: **Medium**

42. *Answer choices:*
(see index for correct answer)

- a. Junk science
- b. PR Gallery
- c. Greenwashing
- d. Crisis communication

Guidance: level 1

---

:: ::

_____ , O.S.A. was a German professor of theology, composer, priest, monk, and a seminal figure in the Protestant Reformation.

Exam Probability: **Low**

43. *Answer choices:*
(see index for correct answer)

- a. Martin Luther

- b. information systems assessment
- c. personal values
- d. levels of analysis

Guidance: level 1

---

:: ::

The _____ of 1906 was the first of a series of significant consumer protection laws which was enacted by Congress in the 20th century and led to the creation of the Food and Drug Administration. Its main purpose was to ban foreign and interstate traffic in adulterated or mislabeled food and drug products, and it directed the U.S. Bureau of Chemistry to inspect products and refer offenders to prosecutors. It required that active ingredients be placed on the label of a drug's packaging and that drugs could not fall below purity levels established by the United States Pharmacopeia or the National Formulary. The Jungle by Upton Sinclair with its graphic and revolting descriptions of unsanitary conditions and unscrupulous practices rampant in the meatpacking industry, was an inspirational piece that kept the public's attention on the important issue of unhygienic meat processing plants that later led to food inspection legislation. Sinclair quipped, "I aimed at the public's heart and by accident I hit it in the stomach," as outraged readers demanded and got the pure food law.

Exam Probability: **High**

44. *Answer choices:*
(see index for correct answer)

- a. Pure Food and Drug Act
- b. deep-level diversity
- c. co-culture
- d. corporate values

Guidance: level 1

---

:: Social philosophy ::

The " _____ " is a method of determining the morality of issues. It asks a decision-maker to make a choice about a social or moral issue, and assumes that they have enough information to know the consequences of their possible decisions for everyone but would not know, or would not take into account, which person he or she is. The theory contends that not knowing one's ultimate position in society would lead to the creation of a just system, as the decision-maker would not want to make decisions which benefit a certain group at the expense of another, because the decision-maker could theoretically end up in either group. The idea has been present in moral philosophy at least since the eighteenth century. The _____ is part of a long tradition of thinking in terms of a social contract that includes the writings of Immanuel Kant, Thomas Hobbes, John Locke, Jean Jacques Rousseau, and Thomas Jefferson. Prominent modern names attached to it are John Harsanyi and John Rawls.

Exam Probability: **Low**

45. *Answer choices:*
(see index for correct answer)

- a. Veil of ignorance
- b. Invisible hand
- c. Societal attitudes towards abortion
- d. Freedom to contract

*Guidance:* level 1

---

:: Marketing ::

_____ is the marketing of products that are presumed to be environmentally safe. It incorporates a broad range of activities, including product modification, changes to the production process, sustainable packaging, as well as modifying advertising. Yet defining _____ is not a simple task where several meanings intersect and contradict each other; an example of this will be the existence of varying social, environmental and retail definitions attached to this term. Other similar terms used are environmental marketing and ecological marketing.

Exam Probability: **Medium**

46. *Answer choices:*
(see index for correct answer)

- a. Green marketing
- b. The Cellar
- c. Promise marketing
- d. DirectIndustry

*Guidance:* level 1

---

:: ::

_____ is a region of India consisting of the Indian states of Bihar, Jharkhand, West Bengal, Odisha and also the union territory Andaman and Nicobar Islands. West Bengal's capital Kolkata is the largest city of this region. The Kolkata Metropolitan Area is the country's third largest.

Exam Probability: **Medium**

47. *Answer choices:*
(see index for correct answer)

- a. hierarchical perspective
- b. similarity-attraction theory
- c. East India
- d. corporate values

*Guidance:* level 1

---

:: Management ::

_____ or executive pay is composed of the financial compensation and other non-financial awards received by an executive from their firm for their service to the organization. It is typically a mixture of salary, bonuses, shares of or call options on the company stock, benefits, and perquisites, ideally configured to take into account government regulations, tax law, the desires of the organization and the executive, and rewards for performance.

Exam Probability: **High**

48. *Answer choices:*
(see index for correct answer)

- a. Process capability
- b. Profitable growth
- c. Executive compensation
- d. Crisis plan

:: ::

_____ is a naturally occurring, yellowish-black liquid found in geological formations beneath the Earth's surface. It is commonly refined into various types of fuels. Components of _____ are separated using a technique called fractional distillation, i.e. separation of a liquid mixture into fractions differing in boiling point by means of distillation, typically using a fractionating column.

Exam Probability: **Low**

49. *Answer choices:*
(see index for correct answer)

- a. co-culture
- b. Petroleum
- c. information systems assessment
- d. levels of analysis

:: Electronic waste ::

_____ or e-waste describes discarded electrical or electronic devices. Used electronics which are destined for refurbishment, reuse, resale, salvage, recycling through material recovery, or disposal are also considered e-waste. Informal processing of e-waste in developing countries can lead to adverse human health effects and environmental pollution.

Exam Probability: **High**

50. *Answer choices:*
(see index for correct answer)

- a. Electronic waste
- b. Techreturns
- c. Solving the E-waste Problem
- d. ReGlobe

:: ::

The _____ of 1973 serves as the enacting legislation to carry out the provisions outlined in The Convention on International Trade in Endangered Species of Wild Fauna and Flora . Designed to protect critically imperiled species from extinction as a "consequence of economic growth and development untempered by adequate concern and conservation", the ESA was signed into law by President Richard Nixon on December 28, 1973. The law requires federal agencies to consult with the Fish and Wildlife Service &/or the NOAA Fisheries Service to ensure their actions are not likely to jeopardize the continued existence of any listed species or result in the destruction or adverse modification of designated critical habitat of such species. The U.S. Supreme Court found that "the plain intent of Congress in enacting" the ESA "was to halt and reverse the trend toward species extinction, whatever the cost." The Act is administered by two federal agencies, the United States Fish and Wildlife Service and the National Marine Fisheries Service .

Exam Probability: **Low**

51. *Answer choices:*
(see index for correct answer)

- a. information systems assessment
- b. Endangered Species Act
- c. Character
- d. interpersonal communication

*Guidance:* level 1

:: Social responsibility ::

The United Nations Global Compact is a non-binding United Nations pact to encourage businesses worldwide to adopt sustainable and socially responsible policies, and to report on their implementation. The _____ is a principle-based framework for businesses, stating ten principles in the areas of human rights, labor, the environment and anti-corruption. Under the Global Compact, companies are brought together with UN agencies, labor groups and civil society. Cities can join the Global Compact through the Cities Programme.

Exam Probability: **Medium**

52. *Answer choices:*
(see index for correct answer)

- a. Socially responsible marketing
- b. Collective impact
- c. United Nations Academic Impact
- d. UN Global Compact

*Guidance:* level 1

---

:: Corporate scandals ::

_____ was a bank based in the Caribbean, which operated from 1986 to 2009 when it went into receivership. It was an affiliate of the Stanford Financial Group and failed when the its parent was seized by United States authorities in early 2009 as part of the investigation into Allen Stanford.

Exam Probability: **Low**

53. *Answer choices:*
(see index for correct answer)

- a. Trustor affair
- b. S-Chips Scandals
- c. Stanford International Bank
- d. One.Tel

*Guidance:* level 1

---

:: Leadership ::

_____ is leadership that is directed by respect for ethical beliefs and values and for the dignity and rights of others. It is thus related to concepts such as trust, honesty, consideration, charisma, and fairness.

Exam Probability: **Medium**

54. *Answer choices:*
(see index for correct answer)

- a. The Leadership Council
- b. servant leader
- c. Love leadership
- d. Ethical leadership

*Guidance:* level 1

---

:: Cognitive biases ::

In personality psychology, _____ is the degree to which people believe that they have control over the outcome of events in their lives, as opposed to external forces beyond their control. Understanding of the concept was developed by Julian B. Rotter in 1954, and has since become an aspect of personality studies. A person's "locus" is conceptualized as internal or external .

Exam Probability: **Medium**

55. *Answer choices:*
(see index for correct answer)

- a. Cultural bias
- b. Illusion of transparency
- c. Self-reference effect
- d. Outcome bias

*Guidance:* level 1

---

:: Offshoring ::

A _____ is the temporary suspension or permanent termination of employment of an employee or, more commonly, a group of employees for business reasons, such as personnel management or downsizing an organization. Originally, _____ referred exclusively to a temporary interruption in work, or employment but this has evolved to a permanent elimination of a position in both British and US English, requiring the addition of "temporary" to specify the original meaning of the word. A _____ is not to be confused with wrongful termination. Laid off workers or displaced workers are workers who have lost or left their jobs because their employer has closed or moved, there was insufficient work for them to do, or their position or shift was abolished . Downsizing in a company is defined to involve the reduction of employees in a workforce. Downsizing in companies became a popular practice in the 1980s and early 1990s as it was seen as a way to deliver better shareholder value as it helps to reduce the costs of employers . Indeed, recent research on downsizing in the U.S., UK, and Japan suggests that downsizing is being regarded by management as one of the preferred routes to help declining organizations, cutting unnecessary costs, and improve organizational performance. Usually a _____ occurs as a cost cutting measure.

Exam Probability: **High**

56. *Answer choices:*
(see index for correct answer)

- a. Flag of convenience
- b. Sourcing advisory
- c. American Jobs
- d. Offshore company

*Guidance:* level 1

---

:: Social philosophy ::

> The _____ describes the unintended social benefits of an individual's self-interested actions. Adam Smith first introduced the concept in The Theory of Moral Sentiments, written in 1759, invoking it in reference to income distribution. In this work, however, the idea of the market is not discussed, and the word "capitalism" is never used.

Exam Probability: **High**

57. *Answer choices:*
(see index for correct answer)

- a. vacancy chain
- b. Freedom to contract
- c. Invisible hand
- d. Veil of Ignorance

*Guidance:* level 1

---

:: Patent law ::

> A _____ is generally any statement intended to specify or delimit the scope of rights and obligations that may be exercised and enforced by parties in a legally recognized relationship. In contrast to other terms for legally operative language, the term _____ usually implies situations that involve some level of uncertainty, waiver, or risk.

Exam Probability: **Medium**

58. *Answer choices:*
(see index for correct answer)

- a. Disclaimer
- b. SCRIPDB

- c. Sealed crustless sandwich
- d. Patentability

*Guidance:* level 1

---

:: Culture ::

_____ is a society which is characterized by individualism, which is the prioritization or emphasis, of the individual over the entire group. _____ s are oriented around the self, being independent instead of identifying with a group mentality. They see each other as only loosely linked, and value personal goals over group interests. _____ s tend to have a more diverse population and are characterized with emphasis on personal achievements, and a rational assessment of both the beneficial and detrimental aspects of relationships with others. _____ s have such unique aspects of communication as being a low power-distance culture and having a low-context communication style. The United States, Australia, Great Britain, Canada, the Netherlands, and New Zealand have been identified as highly _____ s.

Exam Probability: **Low**

59. *Answer choices:*
(see index for correct answer)

- a. Individualistic culture
- b. Intracultural
- c. cultural framework
- d. High-context

*Guidance:* level 1

## Accounting

Accounting or accountancy is the measurement, processing, and communication of financial information about economic entities such as businesses and corporations. The modern field was established by the Italian mathematician Luca Pacioli in 1494. Accounting, which has been called the "language of business", measures the results of an organization's economic activities and conveys this information to a variety of users, including investors, creditors, management, and regulators.

:: Business ::

The seller, or the provider of the goods or services, completes a sale in response to an acquisition, appropriation, requisition or a direct interaction with the buyer at the point of sale. There is a passing of title of the item, and the settlement of a price, in which agreement is reached on a price for which transfer of ownership of the item will occur. The seller, not the purchaser typically executes the sale and it may be completed prior to the obligation of payment. In the case of indirect interaction, a person who sells goods or service on behalf of the owner is known as a _____ man or _____ woman or _____ person, but this often refers to someone selling goods in a store/shop, in which case other terms are also common, including _____ clerk, shop assistant, and retail clerk.

Exam Probability: **Medium**

1. *Answer choices:*

(see index for correct answer)

- a. Policy capturing
- b. Vladislav Doronin
- c. Sales
- d. Service recovery

*Guidance:* level 1

In law, _____ is to give an immediately secured right of present or future deployment. One has a vested right to an asset that cannot be taken away by any third party, even though one may not yet possess the asset. When the right, interest, or title to the present or future possession of a legal estate can be transferred to any other party, it is termed a vested interest.

Exam Probability: **Low**

2. *Answer choices:*
(see index for correct answer)

- a. Emanation of the state
- b. Loudermill letter
- c. Matthew W. Finkin
- d. International labour law

*Guidance:* level 1

A _____ is an entity that owes a debt to another entity. The entity may be an individual, a firm, a government, a company or other legal person. The counterparty is called a creditor. When the counterpart of this debt arrangement is a bank, the _____ is more often referred to as a borrower.

Exam Probability: **Medium**

3. *Answer choices:*
(see index for correct answer)

- a. hierarchical
- b. open system
- c. Sarbanes-Oxley act of 2002
- d. similarity-attraction theory

*Guidance:* level 1

_____ is the widespread practice of collecting information and attempting to spot a pattern. In some fields of study, the term " _____ " has more formally defined meanings.

Exam Probability: **Medium**

4. *Answer choices:*
(see index for correct answer)

- a. Organizational project management
- b. Bottleneck
- c. Gregory T. Haugan
- d. Trend analysis

*Guidance:* level 1

---

:: Information systems ::

An accounting as an information system is a system of collecting, storing and processing financial and accounting data that are used by decision makers. An _____ is generally a computer-based method for tracking accounting activity in conjunction with information technology resources. The resulting financial reports can be used internally by management or externally by other interested parties including investors, creditors and tax authorities.

_____ s are designed to support all accounting functions and activities including auditing, financial accounting & reporting, managerial/ management accounting and tax. The most widely adopted accounting information systems are auditing and financial reporting modules.

Exam Probability: **High**

5. *Answer choices:*
(see index for correct answer)

- a. Control flow diagram
- b. Information Processes and Technology
- c. Transport standards organisations
- d. Accounting information system

*Guidance:* level 1

---

:: SEC filings ::

_____ is a prescribed regulation under the US Securities Act of 1933 that lays out reporting requirements for various SEC filings used by public companies. Companies are also often called issuers , filers or registrants .

Exam Probability: **Low**

6. *Answer choices:*

(see index for correct answer)

- a. Form 10-Q
- b. Form 10-K
- c. Form 3
- d. Form 10-K405

*Guidance:* level 1

:: ::

_____ is the field of accounting concerned with the summary, analysis and reporting of financial transactions related to a business. This involves the preparation of financial statements available for public use. Stockholders, suppliers, banks, employees, government agencies, business owners, and other stakeholders are examples of people interested in receiving such information for decision making purposes.

Exam Probability: **High**

7. *Answer choices:*

(see index for correct answer)

- a. imperative
- b. interpersonal communication
- c. Financial accounting
- d. similarity-attraction theory

*Guidance:* level 1

:: Auditing ::

An _____ is a security-relevant chronological record, set of records, and/or destination and source of records that provide documentary evidence of the sequence of activities that have affected at any time a specific operation, procedure, or event. Audit records typically result from activities such as financial transactions, scientific research and health care data transactions, or communications by individual people, systems, accounts, or other entities.

Exam Probability: **Medium**

8. *Answer choices:*
(see index for correct answer)

- a. Audit storm
- b. Auditing Standards Board
- c. Audit trail
- d. Professional Evaluation and Certification Board

*Guidance:* level 1

:: Foreign exchange market ::

A currency , in the most specific sense is money in any form when in use or circulation as a medium of exchange, especially circulating banknotes and coins. A more general definition is that a currency is a system of money in common use, especially for people in a nation. Under this definition, US dollars , pounds sterling , Australian dollars , European euros , Russian rubles and Indian Rupees are examples of currencies. These various currencies are recognized as stores of value and are traded between nations in foreign exchange markets, which determine the relative values of the different currencies. Currencies in this sense are defined by governments, and each type has limited boundaries of acceptance.

Exam Probability: **High**

9. *Answer choices:*
(see index for correct answer)

- a. Monetary unit
- b. Eurocurrency
- c. Spot market
- d. Foreign exchange spot

*Guidance:* level 1

_____ is a managerial accounting cost concept. Under this method, manufacturing overhead is incurred in the period that a product is produced. This addresses the issue of absorption costing that allows income to rise as production rises. Under an absorption cost method, management can push forward costs to the next period when products are sold. This artificially inflates profits in the period of production by incurring less cost than would be incurred under a _____ system. _____ is generally not used for external reporting purposes. Under the Tax Reform Act of 1986, income statements must use absorption costing to comply with GAAP.

Exam Probability: **High**

10. *Answer choices:*
(see index for correct answer)

- a. Management accounting
- b. Corporate travel management
- c. Variable Costing
- d. Semi-variable cost

*Guidance:* level 1

---

:: ::

A _____ is the period used by governments for accounting and budget purposes, which varies between countries. It is also used for financial reporting by business and other organizations. Laws in many jurisdictions require company financial reports to be prepared and published on an annual basis, but generally do not require the reporting period to align with the calendar year . Taxation laws generally require accounting records to be maintained and taxes calculated on an annual basis, which usually corresponds to the _____ used for government purposes. The calculation of tax on an annual basis is especially relevant for direct taxation, such as income tax. Many annual government fees—such as Council rates, licence fees, etc.—are also levied on a _____ basis, while others are charged on an anniversary basis.

Exam Probability: **High**

11. *Answer choices:*

- a. interpersonal communication
- b. corporate values
- c. Fiscal year
- d. information systems assessment

*Guidance:* level 1

---

:: ::

_____ is a means of protection from financial loss. It is a form of risk management, primarily used to hedge against the risk of a contingent or uncertain loss

Exam Probability: **High**

12. *Answer choices:*

- a. information systems assessment
- b. open system
- c. personal values
- d. Insurance

*Guidance:* level 1

---

:: Bonds (finance) ::

A _____ is a fund established by an economic entity by setting aside revenue over a period of time to fund a future capital expense, or repayment of a long-term debt.

Exam Probability: **Low**

13. *Answer choices:*

- a. Panda bonds
- b. Bond Tender Offer
- c. Redemption value
- d. Auction rate security

*Guidance:* level 1

---

:: Management ::

Business _____ is a discipline in operations management in which people use various methods to discover, model, analyze, measure, improve, optimize, and automate business processes. BPM focuses on improving corporate performance by managing business processes. Any combination of methods used to manage a company's business processes is BPM. Processes can be structured and repeatable or unstructured and variable. Though not required, enabling technologies are often used with BPM.

Exam Probability: **Low**

14. *Answer choices:*
(see index for correct answer)

- a. Project team builder
- b. Process Management
- c. Project management
- d. manager's right to manage

*Guidance:* level 1

---

:: Financial ratios ::

The _____ shows the percentage of how profitable a company's assets are in generating revenue.

Exam Probability: **High**

15. *Answer choices:*
(see index for correct answer)

- a. Quick ratio
- b. Incremental capital-output ratio
- c. Return on assets
- d. Accounting rate of return

*Guidance:* level 1

---

:: Business law ::

The expression " _____ " is somewhat confusing as it has a different meaning based on the context that is under consideration.From a product characteristic stand point, this type of a lease, as distinguished from a finance lease, is one where the lessor takes residual risk. As such, the lease is non full payout. From an accounting stand point, this type of lease results in off balance sheet financing.

Exam Probability: **High**

16. *Answer choices:*
(see index for correct answer)

- a. Operating lease
- b. Vehicle leasing
- c. Business license
- d. Ladenschlussgesetz

*Guidance:* level 1

---

:: Management accounting ::

_____ accounting is a traditional cost accounting method introduced in the 1920s, as an alternative for the traditional cost accounting method based on historical costs.

Exam Probability: **Low**

17. *Answer choices:*
(see index for correct answer)

- a. Standard cost
- b. Owner earnings
- c. Factory overhead
- d. Institute of Cost and Management Accountants of Bangladesh

*Guidance:* level 1

---

:: Financial ratios ::

The _____ is a financial ratio indicating the relative proportion of shareholders' equity and debt used to finance a company's assets. Closely related to leveraging, the ratio is also known as risk, gearing or leverage. The two components are often taken from the firm's balance sheet or statement of financial position , but the ratio may also be calculated using market values for both, if the company's debt and equity are publicly traded, or using a combination of book value for debt and market value for equity financially.

Exam Probability: **Low**

18. *Answer choices:*
(see index for correct answer)

- a. Current ratio
- b. PEG ratio
- c. Return on capital
- d. Debt-to-equity ratio

*Guidance:* level 1

---

:: Accounting ::

_____ examines how accounting is used by individuals, organizations and government as well as the consequences that these practices have. Starting from the assumption that accounting both measures and makes visible certain economic events, _____ has studied the roles of accounting in organizations and society and the consequences that these practices have for individuals, organizations, governments and capital markets. It encompasses a broad range of topics including financial _____ , management _____ , auditing research, capital market research, accountability research, social responsibility research and taxation research.

Exam Probability: **High**

19. *Answer choices:*
(see index for correct answer)

- a. Russian GAAP
- b. Accounting research
- c. Special journals
- d. Accounting records

*Guidance:* level 1

:: ::

The _____ of 1938 29 U.S.C. § 203 is a United States labor law that creates the right to a minimum wage, and "time-and-a-half" overtime pay when people work over forty hours a week. It also prohibits most employment of minors in "oppressive child labor". It applies to employees engaged in interstate commerce or employed by an enterprise engaged in commerce or in the production of goods for commerce, unless the employer can claim an exemption from coverage.

Exam Probability: **Medium**

20. *Answer choices:*
(see index for correct answer)

- a. empathy
- b. Fair Labor Standards Act
- c. open system
- d. similarity-attraction theory

*Guidance:* level 1

---

:: ::

In production, research, retail, and accounting, a _____ is the value of money that has been used up to produce something or deliver a service, and hence is not available for use anymore. In business, the _____ may be one of acquisition, in which case the amount of money expended to acquire it is counted as _____ . In this case, money is the input that is gone in order to acquire the thing. This acquisition _____ may be the sum of the _____ of production as incurred by the original producer, and further _____ s of transaction as incurred by the acquirer over and above the price paid to the producer. Usually, the price also includes a mark-up for profit over the _____ of production.

Exam Probability: **High**

21. *Answer choices:*
(see index for correct answer)

- a. personal values
- b. Cost
- c. Character
- d. Sarbanes-Oxley act of 2002

:: Management accounting ::

An _____ is a classification used for business units within an enterprise. The essential element of an _____ is that it is treated as a unit which is measured against its use of capital, as opposed to a cost or profit center, which are measured against raw costs or profits.

Exam Probability: **Medium**

22. *Answer choices:*
(see index for correct answer)

- a. Invested capital
- b. Revenue center
- c. Inventory valuation
- d. Chartered Cost Accountant

:: ::

Generally speaking, a _____ begins on the New Year's Day of the given calendar system and ends on the day before the following New Year's Day, and thus consists of a whole number of days. A year can also be measured by starting on any other named day of the calendar, and ending on the day before this named day in the following year. This may be termed a "year's time", but not a " _____ ". To reconcile the _____ with the astronomical cycle certain years contain extra days .

Exam Probability: **Medium**

23. *Answer choices:*
(see index for correct answer)

- a. Character
- b. hierarchical perspective
- c. open system
- d. Calendar year

:: Generally Accepted Accounting Principles ::

_____ is the accounting classification of an account. It is part of double-entry book-keeping technique.

Exam Probability: **High**

24. *Answer choices:*
(see index for correct answer)

- a. Matching principle
- b. Engagement letter
- c. Normal balance
- d. Management accounting principles

*Guidance:* level 1

:: Accounting systems ::

In bookkeeping, a _____ statement is a process that explains the difference on a specified date between the bank balance shown in an organization's bank statement, as supplied by the bank and the corresponding amount shown in the organization's own accounting records.

Exam Probability: **High**

25. *Answer choices:*
(see index for correct answer)

- a. Entity concept
- b. Bank reconciliation
- c. Open-book accounting
- d. Controlling account

*Guidance:* level 1

:: Management accounting ::

_____ is an approach to determine a product's life-cycle cost which should be sufficient to develop specified functionality and quality, while ensuring its desired profit. It involves setting a target cost by subtracting a desired profit margin from a competitive market price. A target cost is the maximum amount of cost that can be incurred on a product, however, the firm can still earn the required profit margin from that product at a particular selling price. _____ decomposes the target cost from product level to component level. Through this decomposition, _____ spreads the competitive pressure faced by the company to product's designers and suppliers. _____ consists of cost planning in the design phase of production as well as cost control throughout the resulting product life cycle. The cardinal rule of _____ is to never exceed the target cost. However, the focus of _____ is not to minimize costs, but to achieve a desired level of cost reduction determined by the _____ process.

Exam Probability: **Medium**

26. *Answer choices:*
(see index for correct answer)

- a. Management control system
- b. Investment center
- c. Management accounting in supply chains
- d. Spend management

*Guidance:* level 1

---

:: Credit card terminology ::

A _____ is the transfer of the balance in an account to another account, often held at another institution. It is most commonly used when describing a credit card _____ .

Exam Probability: **Low**

27. *Answer choices:*
(see index for correct answer)

- a. Merchant category code
- b. Bank card number
- c. Credit card interest
- d. Balance transfer

*Guidance:* level 1

A _____ is a plastic payment card that can be used instead of cash when making purchases. It is similar to a credit card, but unlike a credit card, the money is immediately transferred directly from the cardholder's bank account when performing a transaction.

Exam Probability: **Medium**

28. *Answer choices:*
(see index for correct answer)

- a. Global Product Classification
- b. Debit card
- c. Digital certificate
- d. Private electronic market

*Guidance:* level 1

:: Business models ::

A _____ is a company that owns enough voting stock in another firm to control management and operation by influencing or electing its board of directors. The  company is deemed a subsidiary of the _____ .

Exam Probability: **Low**

29. *Answer choices:*
(see index for correct answer)

- a. Fractional ownership
- b. Cooperative
- c. Component business model
- d. Legacy carrier

*Guidance:* level 1

:: ::

An _____ is a comprehensive report on a company's activities throughout the preceding year. _____s are intended to give shareholders and other interested people information about the company's activities and financial performance. They may be considered as grey literature. Most jurisdictions require companies to prepare and disclose _____s, and many require the _____ to be filed at the company's registry. Companies listed on a stock exchange are also required to report at more frequent intervals .

Exam Probability: **Low**

30. *Answer choices:*
(see index for correct answer)

- a. Sarbanes-Oxley act of 2002
- b. empathy
- c. Annual report
- d. interpersonal communication

*Guidance:* level 1

---

:: Accounting source documents ::

A _____ or account statement is a summary of financial transactions which have occurred over a given period on a bank account held by a person or business with a financial institution.

Exam Probability: **High**

31. *Answer choices:*
(see index for correct answer)

- a. Air waybill
- b. Bank statement
- c. Remittance advice
- d. Banknote

*Guidance:* level 1

---

:: Inventory ::

_____ is a system of inventory in which updates are made on a periodic basis. This differs from perpetual inventory systems, where updates are made as seen fit.

Exam Probability: **Medium**

32. *Answer choices:*
(see index for correct answer)

- a. Phantom inventory
- b. Periodic inventory
- c. GMROII
- d. Ending inventory

*Guidance:* level 1

:: Accounting in the United States ::

The _____ was formed by the American Institute of Certified Public Accountants in 1972, and developed the Objective of Financial Statements. The committee's goal was to create financial statements that helped external users make decisions about the economics of companies. In 1978, the Financial Accounting Standards Board , whose purpose is to develop generally accepted accounting principles, adopted the key objectives established by the _____

Exam Probability: **High**

33. *Answer choices:*
(see index for correct answer)

- a. Certified Public Accountant
- b. Institute of Internal Auditors
- c. Accounting Today
- d. Trueblood Committee

*Guidance:* level 1

:: Accounting terminology ::

In accounting/accountancy, _____ are journal entries usually made at the end of an accounting period to allocate income and expenditure to the period in which they actually occurred. The revenue recognition principle is the basis of making _____ that pertain to unearned and accrued revenues under accrual-basis accounting. They are sometimes called Balance Day adjustments because they are made on balance day.

Exam Probability: **Low**

34. *Answer choices:*
(see index for correct answer)

- a. managerial accounting
- b. Fair value accounting
- c. Accounts payable
- d. Adjusting entries

*Guidance:* level 1

:: United States federal income tax ::

Under United States tax law, the _____ is a dollar amount that non-itemizers may subtract from their income before income tax is applied. Taxpayers may choose either itemized deductions or the _____ , but usually choose whichever results in the lesser amount of tax payable. The _____ is available to US citizens and aliens who are resident for tax purposes and who are individuals, married persons, and heads of household. The _____ is based on filing status and typically increases each year. It is not available to nonresident aliens residing in the United States . Additional amounts are available for persons who are blind and/or are at least 65 years of age.

Exam Probability: **High**

35. *Answer choices:*
(see index for correct answer)

- a. Rabbi trust
- b. Standard deduction
- c. Foreign housing exclusion
- d. Presidential election campaign fund checkoff

*Guidance:* level 1

:: Financial ratios ::

In finance, the _____ , also known as the acid-test ratio  is a type
of liquidity ratio  which measures the ability of a company to use its near
cash or quick assets to extinguish or retire its current liabilities
immediately. Quick assets include those current assets that presumably can be
quickly converted to cash at close to their book values. It is the ratio
between quickly available or liquid assets and current liabilities.

Exam Probability: **Medium**

36. *Answer choices:*
(see index for correct answer)

- a. Quick ratio
- b. Capital recovery factor
- c. Return on equity
- d. Infection ratio

*Guidance:* level 1

---

:: Banking ::

A _____ is a financial account maintained by a bank for a customer. A
_____ can be a deposit account, a credit card account, a current account,
or any other type of account offered by a financial institution, and represents
the  funds that a customer has entrusted to the financial institution and from
which the customer can make withdrawals. Alternatively, accounts may be loan
accounts in which case the customer owes money to the financial institution.

Exam Probability: **Low**

37. *Answer choices:*
(see index for correct answer)

- a. Banking software
- b. Giro
- c. Numbered bank account
- d. Money market account

*Guidance:* level 1

---

:: Accounting software ::

_____ is a freely available and global framework for exchanging business information. _____ allows the expression of semantic meaning commonly required in business reporting. The language is XML-based and uses the XML syntax and related XML technologies such as XML Schema, XLink, XPath, and Namespaces. One use of _____ is to define and exchange financial information, such as a financial statement. The _____ Specification is developed and published by _____ International, Inc. .

Exam Probability: **Medium**

38. *Answer choices:*
(see index for correct answer)

- a. Money
- b. Comparison of accounting software
- c. Time tracking software
- d. Billback

*Guidance:* level 1

---

:: Television terminology ::

A nonprofit organization , also known as a non-business entity, _____ organization, or nonprofit institution, is dedicated to furthering a particular social cause or advocating for a shared point of view. In economic terms, it is an organization that uses its surplus of the revenues to further achieve its ultimate objective, rather than distributing its income to the organization's shareholders, leaders, or members. Nonprofits are tax exempt or charitable, meaning they do not pay income tax on the money that they receive for their organization. They can operate in religious, scientific, research, or educational settings.

Exam Probability: **Medium**

39. *Answer choices:*
(see index for correct answer)

- a. Satellite television
- b. nonprofit
- c. multiplexing
- d. Not-for-profit

*Guidance:* level 1

A _____ is a person or organization subject to pay a tax. _____ s have an Identification Number, a reference number issued by a government to its citizens.

Exam Probability: **Medium**

40. *Answer choices:*

- a. Max Planck Institute for Tax Law and Public Finance
- b. Taxpayer
- c. Tolerance tax
- d. Taxpayer receipt

*Guidance:* level 1

:: Management accounting ::

_____ is accounting which tracks the costs and revenues by "job" and enables standardized reporting of profitability by job. For an accounting system to support _____ , it must allow job numbers to be assigned to individual items of expenses and revenues. A job can be defined to be a specific project done for one customer, or a single unit of product manufactured, or a batch of units of the same type that are produced together.

Exam Probability: **Medium**

41. *Answer choices:*

- a. Environmental full-cost accounting
- b. Job costing
- c. Bridge life-cycle cost analysis
- d. Inventory valuation

*Guidance:* level 1

:: ::

An _____ is an asset that lacks physical substance. It is defined in opposition to physical assets such as machinery and buildings. An _____ is usually very hard to evaluate. Patents, copyrights, franchises, goodwill, trademarks, and trade names. The general interpretation also includes software and other intangible computer based assets are all examples of _____ s. _____ s generally—though not necessarily—suffer from typical market failures of non-rivalry and non-excludability.

Exam Probability: **High**

42. *Answer choices:*

(see index for correct answer)

- a. cultural
- b. imperative
- c. Intangible asset
- d. interpersonal communication

*Guidance:* level 1

---

:: Quality control tools ::

A _____ is a type of diagram that represents an algorithm, workflow or process. _____ can also be defined as a diagramatic representation of an algorithm .

Exam Probability: **Low**

43. *Answer choices:*

(see index for correct answer)

- a. U-chart
- b. X-bar chart
- c. Regression control chart
- d. Multi-vari chart

*Guidance:* level 1

---

:: International taxation ::

_____ is the levying of tax by two or more jurisdictions on the same declared income , asset , or financial transaction . Double liability is mitigated in a number of ways, for example.

44. *Answer choices:*
(see index for correct answer)

- a. Tax information exchange agreement
- b. Tax harmonization
- c. Double taxation
- d. Variable import levy

*Guidance:* level 1

---

:: Accounting systems ::

In accounting, the controlling account is an account in the general ledger for which a corresponding subsidiary ledger has been created. The subsidiary ledger allows for tracking transactions within the controlling account in more detail. Individual transactions are posted both to the controlling account and the corresponding subsidiary ledger, and the totals for both are compared when preparing a trial balance to ensure accuracy.

45. *Answer choices:*
(see index for correct answer)

- a. Control account
- b. Standard accounting practice
- c. Single-entry bookkeeping system
- d. Invoice processing

*Guidance:* level 1

---

:: Taxation ::

_____ is an estimate of the market value of a property, based on what a knowledgeable, willing, and unpressured buyer would probably pay to a knowledgeable, willing, and unpressured seller in the market. An estimate of _____ may be founded either on precedent or extrapolation. _____ differs from the intrinsic value that an individual may place on the same asset based on their own preferences and circumstances.

46. *Answer choices:*
(see index for correct answer)

- a. Energy tax
- b. East African School of Taxation
- c. Fair market value
- d. Tax audit representation

*Guidance:* level 1

---

:: Mathematical finance ::

In economics and finance, _____ , also known as present discounted value, is the value of an expected income stream determined as of the date of valuation. The _____ is always less than or equal to the future value because money has interest-earning potential, a characteristic referred to as the time value of money, except during times of negative interest rates, when the _____ will be more than the future value. Time value can be described with the simplified phrase, "A dollar today is worth more than a dollar tomorrow". Here, `worth more` means that its value is greater. A dollar today is worth more than a dollar tomorrow because the dollar can be invested and earn a day's worth of interest, making the total accumulate to a value more than a dollar by tomorrow. Interest can be compared to rent. Just as rent is paid to a landlord by a tenant without the ownership of the asset being transferred, interest is paid to a lender by a borrower who gains access to the money for a time before paying it back. By letting the borrower have access to the money, the lender has sacrificed the exchange value of this money, and is compensated for it in the form of interest. The initial amount of the borrowed funds is less than the total amount of money paid to the lender.

47. *Answer choices:*
(see index for correct answer)

- a. Present value
- b. No free lunch with vanishing risk
- c. Snell envelope
- d. Earnings response coefficient

*Guidance:* level 1

---

:: Management accounting ::

_____ is a professional certification credential in the management accounting and financial management fields. The certification signifies that the person possesses knowledge in the areas of financial planning, analysis, control, decision support, and professional ethics. The CMA is a U.S.-based, globally recognized certification offered by the Institute of Management Accountants.

Exam Probability: **Low**

48. *Answer choices:*
(see index for correct answer)

- a. Relevant cost
- b. Fixed assets management
- c. Management control system
- d. Environmental full-cost accounting

*Guidance:* level 1

---

:: Accounting terminology ::

_____ is an independent, objective assurance and consulting activity designed to add value to and improve an organization's operations. It helps an organization accomplish its objectives by bringing a systematic, disciplined approach to evaluate and improve the effectiveness of risk management, control and governance processes. _____ achieves this by providing insight and recommendations based on analyses and assessments of data and business processes. With commitment to integrity and accountability, _____ provides value to governing bodies and senior management as an objective source of independent advice. Professionals called internal auditors are employed by organizations to perform the _____ activity.

**49.** *Answer choices:*

(see index for correct answer)

- a. Basis of accounting
- b. managerial accounting
- c. Share premium
- d. Internal auditing

*Guidance:* level 1

---

:: ::

A work order is usually a task or a job for a customer, that can be scheduled or assigned to someone. Such an order may be from a customer request or created internally within the organization. Work orders may also be created as follow ups to Inspections or Audits. A work order may be for products or services.

**50.** *Answer choices:*

(see index for correct answer)

- a. Job order
- b. co-culture
- c. open system
- d. cultural

*Guidance:* level 1

---

:: Bank regulation ::

_____ is a measure implemented in many countries to protect bank depositors, in full or in part, from losses caused by a bank`s inability to pay its debts when due. _____ systems are one component of a financial system safety net that promotes financial stability.

**51.** *Answer choices:*

(see index for correct answer)

- a. Basel III
- b. Deposit insurance
- c. Committee of European Banking Supervisors

- d. Financial Consumer Agency of Canada

*Guidance:* level 1

---

:: Management ::

The _____ is a strategy performance management tool – a semi-standard structured report, that can be used by managers to keep track of the execution of activities by the staff within their control and to monitor the consequences arising from these actions.

Exam Probability: **Medium**

52. *Answer choices:*
(see index for correct answer)

- a. Balanced scorecard
- b. PhD in management
- c. Sales outsourcing
- d. Product Development and Systems Engineering Consortium

*Guidance:* level 1

---

:: Accounting terminology ::

A _____ contains all the accounts for recording transactions relating to a company's assets, liabilities, owners' equity, revenue, and expenses. In modern accounting software or ERP, the _____ works as a central repository for accounting data transferred from all subledgers or modules like accounts payable, accounts receivable, cash management, fixed assets, purchasing and projects. The _____ is the backbone of any accounting system which holds financial and non-financial data for an organization. The collection of all accounts is known as the _____ . Each account is known as a ledger account. In a manual or non-computerized system this may be a large book. The statement of financial position and the statement of income and comprehensive income are both derived from the _____ . Each account in the _____ consists of one or more pages. The _____ is where posting to the accounts occurs. Posting is the process of recording amounts as credits , and amounts as debits , in the pages of the _____ . Additional columns to the right hold a running activity total .

Exam Probability: **Low**

53. *Answer choices:*

- a. Total absorption costing
- b. Accounts payable
- c. double-entry bookkeeping
- d. Enterprise liquidity

*Guidance:* level 1

---

:: Payment systems ::

An _____ is an electronic telecommunications device that enables customers of financial institutions to perform financial transactions, such as cash withdrawals, deposits, transfer funds, or obtaining account information, at any time and without the need for direct interaction with bank staff.

Exam Probability: **Low**

54. *Answer choices:*

- a. FreshBooks
- b. Voucher privatization
- c. Automated teller machine
- d. CNG Processing A/S

*Guidance:* level 1

---

:: Management ::

_____ is the identification, evaluation, and prioritization of risks followed by coordinated and economical application of resources to minimize, monitor, and control the probability or impact of unfortunate events or to maximize the realization of opportunities.

Exam Probability: **Low**

55. *Answer choices:*

- a. Project management information system
- b. PhD in management
- c. Management styles
- d. Top development

:: Generally Accepted Accounting Principles ::

In business and accounting, _____ is an entity's income minus cost of goods sold, expenses and taxes for an accounting period. It is computed as the residual of all revenues and gains over all expenses and losses for the period, and has also been defined as the net increase in shareholders' equity that results from a company's operations. In the context of the presentation of financial statements, the IFRS Foundation defines _____ as synonymous with profit and loss. The difference between revenue and the cost of making a product or providing a service, before deducting overheads, payroll, taxation, and interest payments. This is different from operating income .

Exam Probability: **Low**

56. *Answer choices:*
(see index for correct answer)

- a. Revenue recognition
- b. Gross income
- c. Net income
- d. Gross profit

:: Investment ::

In finance, the benefit from an _____ is called a return. The return may consist of a gain realised from the sale of property or an _____ , unrealised capital appreciation , or _____ income such as dividends, interest, rental income etc., or a combination of capital gain and income. The return may also include currency gains or losses due to changes in foreign currency exchange rates.

Exam Probability: **High**

57. *Answer choices:*
(see index for correct answer)

- a. Juniperus Capital
- b. Market timing
- c. Investment Securities

- d. Investment

*Guidance:* level 1

---

:: ::

_____ is the process of making predictions of the future based on past and present data and most commonly by analysis of trends. A commonplace example might be estimation of some variable of interest at some specified future date. Prediction is a similar, but more general term. Both might refer to formal statistical methods employing time series, cross-sectional or longitudinal data, or alternatively to less formal judgmental methods. Usage can differ between areas of application: for example, in hydrology the terms "forecast" and "_____" are sometimes reserved for estimates of values at certain specific future times, while the term "prediction" is used for more general estimates, such as the number of times floods will occur over a long period.

Exam Probability: **Medium**

58. *Answer choices:*
(see index for correct answer)

- a. surface-level diversity
- b. cultural
- c. levels of analysis
- d. Forecasting

*Guidance:* level 1

---

:: Management accounting ::

In _____ or managerial accounting, managers use the provisions of accounting information in order to better inform themselves before they decide matters within their organizations, which aids their management and performance of control functions.

Exam Probability: **High**

59. *Answer choices:*
(see index for correct answer)

- a. Inventory valuation
- b. Notional profit
- c. Management accounting

- d. Cost driver

## INDEX: Correct Answers

### Foundations of Business

1. b: Energies

2. b: Project management

3. c: Risk management

4. d: Risk

5. b: INDEX

6. c: Incentive

7. d: Size

8. a: Federal Trade Commission

9. d: Small business

10. d: Board of directors

11. a: Advertising

12. : Information technology

13. : Cooperation

14. b: Life

15. : Schedule

16. b: Sony

17. a: Business

18. a: Venture capital

19. : Balance sheet

20. c: Comparative advantage

21. c: Bias

22. d: Capital market

23. a: Availability

24. b: Cash

25. b: Utility

26. b: Raw material

27. b: Efficiency

28. d: Commerce

29. c: SWOT analysis

30. : Decision-making

31. : Tool

32. d: Interview

33. b: Good

34. c: Percentage

35. a: Ownership

36. c: Return on investment

37. d: Dividend

38. b: Limited liability

39. d: Trade

40. d: Capitalism

41. a: Stock

42. c: Stock market

43. b: Initiative

44. : Creativity

45. d: Privacy

46. c: Direct investment

47. a: Selling

48. d: E-commerce

49. c: Globalization

50. c: Balanced scorecard

51. : Pattern

52. c: Interest

53. b: Sustainability

54. a: Law

55. a: Human resources

56. c: Audience

57. a: Empowerment

58. d: Publicity

59. a: Money

# Management

1. : Problem solving

2. c: Bounded rationality

3. a: Span of control

4. a: Learning organization

5. d: Market research

6. c: Insurance

7. d: Budget

8. : Halo effect

9. a: Good

10. b: Situational leadership

11. a: Human resource management

12. a: Profit sharing

13. a: Referent power

14. b: Project

15. a: Intellectual property

16. d: Centralization

17. c: Knowledge management

18. d: Interaction

19. d: Leadership style

20. d: Free trade

21. b: Sharing

22. a: Balanced scorecard

23. : Consultant

24. a: Quality control

25. d: 360-degree feedback

26. a: Income

27. c: Workforce

28. b: Product design

29. d: Change management

30. b: Job satisfaction

31. d: Trade agreement

32. c: Chief executive

33. c: Assembly line

34. d: Individualism

35. d: Crisis

36. a: Strategic alliance

37. b: Justice

38. b: Social capital

39. a: Offshoring

40. b: Property

41. c: Dilemma

42. b: Employment

43. a: Environmental scanning

44. d: Forecasting

45. b: Motivation

46. d: Management system

47. a: Outsourcing

48. b: Incentive

49. c: Questionnaire

50. c: Arbitration

51. a: Project team

52. c: Mediation

53. a: Recession

54. c: Efficiency

55. b: Authority

56. a: Expert

57. : Organizational culture

58. b: Review

59. : Perception

# Business law

1. c: Exclusionary rule

2. : Beneficiary

3. : Corruption

4. a: Assignee

5. : Petition

6. b: Sexual harassment

7. : Mediation

8. : Criminal law

9. a: Consumer protection

10. c: Option contract

11. c: Competitor

12. b: Punitive damages

13. c: Antitrust

14. c: Indictment

15. d: Economic Espionage Act

16. d: Jury Trial

17. a: Credit

18. : Licensee

19. a: Litigation

20. b: Employment law

21. : Warranty

22. b: Foreign Corrupt Practices Act

23. : Insurable interest

24. a: Corporation

25. c: White-collar crime

26. d: Cause of action

27. : Internal Revenue Service

28. b: Rescind

29. b: Industry

30. d: Policy

31. d: Utility

32. : Argument

33. a: Forgery

34. a: Uniform Commercial Code

35. c: Free trade

36. d: Respondeat superior

37. d: Issuer

38. b: Comparative negligence

39. d: Fraud

40. a: Consideration

41. c: Fee simple

42. a: Private law

43. d: Restraint of trade

44. d: Bad faith

45. d: Property

46. b: Adoption

47. : Presentment

48. a: Joint venture

49. d: Computer fraud

50. d: Breach of contract

51. : Damages

52. d: Tort

53. b: Prima facie

54. d: Consumer credit

55. d: Real property

56. : Lease

57. d: Arbitration

58. d: Cooperative

59. c: Perfect tender

---

# Finance

1. b: Certified Public Accountant

2. : Accrual

3. a: Financial ratio

4. a: Financial accounting

5. a: Cash equivalent

6. a: Choice

7. b: Accelerated depreciation

8. b: Pricing

9. : Ending inventory

10. d: Mutual fund

11. b: Net income

12. d: Annuity

13. c: Firm

14. c: Income

15. b: Receipt

16. b: Current asset

17. c: Selling

18. a: Shareholder

19. b: Net profit

20. a: Absorption costing

21. a: Retirement

22. c: Intangible asset

23. a: Conservatism

24. c: Asset turnover

25. d: Board of directors

26. b: Strategy

27. d: Payroll

28. c: Return on investment

29. : Discounting

30. d: Break-even

31. d: Inventory turnover

32. d: Trial balance

33. : Capital budgeting

34. d: Debt-to-equity ratio

35. d: Buyer

36. : Operating expense

37. a: Operating lease

38. d: Cost object

39. a: Inventory

40. c: Convertible bond

41. d: Historical cost

42. a: Trade

43. : Operating leverage

44. : Balance sheet

45. a: Capital lease

46. d: Management

47. : Variable Costing

48. b: Market price

49. a: Primary market

50. : Future value

51. : Financial Accounting Standards Board

52. a: Internal control

53. : Coupon

54. b: Schedule

55. a: Currency

56. : Issuer

57. c: Commercial bank

58. c: Perpetual inventory

59. d: Yield to maturity

---

# Human resource management

1. b: Organizational learning

2. c: Foreign worker

3. a: Skill

4. : Glass ceiling

5. b: Job evaluation

6. a: Job sharing

7. c: Unemployment insurance

8. a: Bargaining unit

9. a: Whistleblower

10. b: Online assessment

11. b: Job design

12. d: Picketing

13. c: National Institute for Occupational Safety and Health

14. : Social media

15. a: Severance package

16. c: Cost leadership

17. b: Resource management

18. c: New Deal

19. d: Best practice

20. : Free Trade

21. d: National Labor Relations Act

22. a: Work ethic

23. b: Brainstorming

24. a: Profession

25. d: Job performance

26. c: Living wage

27. c: Job description

28. b: Externship

29. c: Fair Labor Standards Act

30. a: Human resource management

31. d: Minnesota Multiphasic Personality Inventory

32. a: Selection ratio

33. c: Impression management

34. d: Deferred compensation

35. d: Social networking

36. a: Lilly Ledbetter

37. c: Restructuring

38. c: Organizational justice

39. b: Material safety data sheet

40. b: Nepotism

41. b: Employee stock

42. d: Emotional intelligence

43. c: Rating scale

44. d: Public administration

45. b: Functional job analysis

46. : Grievance

47. a: Recruitment advertising

48. a: Outplacement

49. d: Affirmative action

50. b: Behavior modification

51. d: Information overload

52. : Just cause

53. c: Globalization

54. c: Distance learning

55. c: Proactive

56. c: Bureau of Labor Statistics

57. : Conformity

58. a: Efficiency wage

59. : Arbitration

# Information systems

1. b: Phishing

2. d: Information management

3. a: Common Criteria

4. : Cookie

5. : Accessibility

6. c: Pop-up ad

7. b: Information literacy

8. a: Vertical integration

9. b: Botnet

10. : Backbone network

11. d: Total cost of ownership

12. : Vulnerability

13. d: Operating system

14. d: Clickstream

15. c: Output device

16. : Business intelligence

17. : Throughput

18. : Business model

19. b: Business rule

20. c: Data link

21. c: Drill down

22. c: Online advertising

23. a: COBIT

24. c: Information overload

25. d: Crowdsourcing

26. c: Information governance

27. d: Software as a service

28. : Data model

29. : Radio-frequency identification

30. a: Application software

31. d: System software

32. c: Domain name

33. b: Interactivity

34. : Affiliate marketing

35. : Usability

36. a: Privacy policy

37. c: Structured query language

38. b: Business process management

39. : Social media

40. c: Identity theft

41. b: Search engine

42. a: Supply chain

43. d: Census

44. b: Groupware

45. c: World Wide Web

46. : Debit card

47. c: Viral marketing

48. b: Virtual world

49. c: Data visualization

50. c: Input device

51. a: Content management system

52. c: Enterprise resource planning

53. b: Carnivore

54. a: Information flow

55. d: Downtime

56. c: Worm

57. d: Enterprise search

58. a: Health Insurance Portability and Accountability Act

59. : Chart

# Marketing

1. c: Social network

2. c: Commercialization

3. : Commodity

4. c: Expense

5. : Situation analysis

6. c: Database

7. : Customer value

8. d: Cost

9. c: Manufacturing

10. : INDEX

11. d: Exploratory research

12. c: Marketing management

13. c: Revenue

14. b: Business Week

15. b: Entrepreneur

16. a: Survey research

17. : Customer service

18. : Data analysis

19. : Economies of scale

20. c: Logistics

21. a: Sherman Antitrust Act

22. : Perception

23. d: Department store

24. a: Publicity

25. d: Billboard

26. b: Supply chain management

27. d: Economy

28. c: Communication

29. d: Retail

30. : Testimonial

31. c: Microsoft

32. a: Information system

33. c: Auction

34. c: Public

35. d: Marketing research

36. : Organizational culture

37. b: Social marketing

38. c: Trademark

39. d: Shares

40. a: Mission statement

41. d: Commerce

42. a: Competitive advantage

43. : Subsidiary

44. d: Mass marketing

45. a: Household

46. a: Integrated marketing

47. a: Wall Street Journal

48. a: Attention

49. a: Marketing

50. b: Cognitive dissonance

51. a: Marketing mix

52. c: Clayton Act

53. b: Interactive marketing

54. c: Consumerism

55. a: Product concept

56. a: Value proposition

57. a: Intangibility

58. c: Personnel

59. d: Data warehouse

---

# Manufacturing

1. : Cost

2. c: Estimation

3. d: Natural resource

4. : Acceptance sampling

5. c: Performance

6. d: Original equipment manufacturer

7. b: Value engineering

8. c: Stakeholder management

9. d: Sunk costs

10. b: Supply chain

11. a: Toshiba

12. a: Quality audit

13. : Steel

14. b: Workflow

15. : Total cost of ownership

16. d: Steering committee

17. : Paper

18. b: Supplier relationship management

19. a: Pareto analysis

20. c: Quality function deployment

21. c: Risk management

22. : Certification

23. : Vendor relationship management

24. d: Supply chain network

25. d: Sony

26. b: Change control

27. c: Accreditation

28. : Tool

29. : Good

30. b: Scheduling

31. c: Production schedule

32. : Interaction

33. c: Synergy

34. b: Check sheet

35. a: Customer

36. : Resource

37. : Request for proposal

38. c: Third-party logistics

39. a: Poka-yoke

40. c: Forecasting

41. c: Mary Kay

42. a: Sputnik

43. a: Process control

44. c: Joint Commission

45. : METRIC

46. c: Management process

47. a: Kaizen

48. : Business process

49. d: Remanufacturing

50. c: Heat transfer

51. : Indirect costs

52. d: Waste

53. d: Manufacturing

54. d: Histogram

55. : Purchase order

56. d: American Society for Quality

57. b: Glass

58. c: PDCA

59. d: Pattern

---

# Commerce

1. : Argument

2. c: Loyalty

3. d: E-procurement

4. c: Drawback

5. b: Economics

6. b: Dutch auction

7. c: Trade

8. b: Cost structure

9. a: Organization chart

10. c: Customs

11. : Bankruptcy

12. d: Compromise

13. c: Variable cost

14. c: Security

15. d: Staff position

16. : Automated Clearing House

17. c: Budget

18. a: Entrepreneur

19. d: Electronic data interchange

20. c: Manufacturing

21. b: Interest

22. : Economy

23. c: Production line

24. c: Excite

25. d: Organizational structure

26. c: Payment system

27. a: Building

28. c: Information system

29. d: Joint venture

30. b: Purchasing manager

31. b: Freight forwarder

32. c: Supervisor

33. c: Invoice

34. c: Household

35. : Basket

36. : Federal government

37. d: Marketing strategy

38. c: Asset

39. b: Authorize.Net

40. a: Case study

41. b: Uniform Commercial Code

42. b: Public relations

43. b: Fraud

44. b: Product mix

45. : Common carrier

46. : Marketing

47. c: Bottom line

48. c: Complaint

49. b: Online advertising

50. : Shareholder

51. b: Initiative

52. c: Credit

53. c: Confirmed

54. : Aid

55. a: Wholesale

56. c: Management

57. b: Graduation

58. d: GeoCities

59. b: English auction

# Business ethics

1. : Global Fund

2. b: Madoff

3. a: Dual relationship

4. d: Referent power

5. b: Nonprofit

6. b: Statutory law

7. c: Pollution

8. b: Better Business Bureau

9. : Marijuana

10. d: Transformational leadership

11. : Medicare fraud

12. b: Antitrust

13. : Hedonism

14. b: Authoritarian

15. a: Biofuel

16. d: Cause-related marketing

17. : ExxonMobil

18. : Marketing ethics

19. b: Greenpeace

20. : Copyright

21. a: Ethics Resource Center

22. d: Right to work

23. a: Clayton Act

24. b: Coal

25. : Supply Chain

26. a: Wall Street

27. b: Lead

28. c: Cultural relativism

29. d: Trade

30. d: Planned obsolescence

31. c: Oil spill

32. a: Tobacco

33. a: Skill

34. : Real estate

35. d: Sustainability

36. a: Sherman Antitrust Act

37. a: Social responsibility

38. : Natural gas

39. d: Habitat

40. b: Consumer Financial Protection Bureau

41. b: Fannie Mae

42. c: Greenwashing

43. a: Martin Luther

44. a: Pure Food and Drug Act

45. a: Veil of ignorance

46. a: Green marketing

47. c: East India

48. c: Executive compensation

49. b: Petroleum

50. a: Electronic waste

51. b: Endangered Species Act

52. d: UN Global Compact

53. c: Stanford International Bank

54. d: Ethical leadership

55. : Locus of control

56. : Layoff

57. c: Invisible hand

58. a: Disclaimer

59. a: Individualistic culture

---

# Accounting

1. c: Sales

2. : Vesting

3. : Debtor

4. d: Trend analysis

5. d: Accounting information system

6. : Regulation S-K

7. c: Financial accounting

8. c: Audit trail

9. a: Monetary unit

10. c: Variable Costing

11. c: Fiscal year

12. d: Insurance

13. : Sinking fund

14. b: Process Management

15. c: Return on assets

16. a: Operating lease

17. a: Standard cost

18. d: Debt-to-equity ratio

19. b: Accounting research

20. b: Fair Labor Standards Act

21. b: Cost

22. : Investment center

23. d: Calendar year

24. c: Normal balance

25. b: Bank reconciliation

26. : Target costing

27. d: Balance transfer

28. b: Debit card

29. : Parent company

30. c: Annual report

31. b: Bank statement

32. b: Periodic inventory

33. d: Trueblood Committee

34. d: Adjusting entries

35. b: Standard deduction

36. a: Quick ratio

37. : Bank account

38. : XBRL

39. d: Not-for-profit

40. b: Taxpayer

41. b: Job costing

42. c: Intangible asset

43. : Flowchart

44. c: Double taxation

45. a: Control account

46. c: Fair market value

47. a: Present value

48. : Certified Management Accountant

49. d: Internal auditing

50. a: Job order

51. b: Deposit insurance

52. a: Balanced scorecard

53. : General ledger

54. c: Automated teller machine

55. : Risk management

56. c: Net income

57. d: Investment

58. d: Forecasting

59. c: Management accounting

CPSIA information can be obtained
at www.ICGtesting.com
Printed in the USA
LVHW051626301019
635718LV00005B/673/P

9 781538 862254